PSYCHOPHYSICS AND HUMAN INTERACTIONS

Art and Science of Integrating Body, Mind and Soul

Shraddhāvān labhate jnānam tatparah samyatendriyah,

Jnānam labdhvā parām s'āntim acirenādhi gacchati.

—Shimad Bhagvad-Gita, 4.39

"He, who has fully controlled his senses, is exclusively devoted to spiritual practice and is full of faith, attains knowledge; having gained knowledge he immediately attains (Supreme) peace."

RADHEY SHYAM KAUSHAL

PSYCHOPHYSICS AND HUMAN INTERACTIONS

Art and Science of Integrating Body, Mind and Soul

New Age Books

New Delhi (India)

PSYCHOPHYSICS AND HUMAN INTERACTIONS:
Art and Science of Integrating Body, Mind and Soul

Published by
NEW AGE BOOKS
A-44, Naraina Industrial Area, Phase-I
New Delhi–110 028 (INDIA)
E-mail: nab@newagebooksindia.com
Website: www.newagebooksindia.com

ISBN: 978-81-7822-475-6

First Edition: Delhi, **2015**

NAB Cataloging-in-Publication Data
PSYCHOPHYSICS AND HUMAN INTERACTIONS
ISBN 978-81-7822-475-6
(Acknowledgements, Preface, Foreword, Abbreviations, Notations and Symbols, Glossary of Words, Terms and Phrases used in the Text, References and Bibliography, Index)

Printed and published by
RP Jain for New Age Books
A-44, Naraina Industrial Area
Phase-1, New Delhi 110 028. India

To my wife

Shashi

And

Grand Children

Sanchit, Aditya, Shruti, Pragya, Shubham and Shreya

Who made it all worthwhile and joyful

"The scientist does not study Nature because it is useful; he studies it because he delights in it, and he delights in it because it is beautiful. If Nature were not beautiful, it would not be worth knowing, and if Nature were not worth knowing, life would not be worth living."

-Henri Poincare'

"Put your heart, mind, intellect and soul even to your smallest acts. This is the secret of success."

- Swami Shivanand

"It is difficult to find happiness in one-self, but it is impossible to find it anywhere else."

- Schopenhauer

Foreword

Every organized society has a set of myths or beliefs which in the form of narratives and mythological stories gives rise to customs, traditions and rituals. These together are called 'Culture'. When two different cultures meet and clash in space and time domains, the dominant culture wins but the vanquished culture also survives in original or modified form. Indian culture is based on the inwardly looking 'Spirituality' *(Rajiv K. Saxena 'Spiritual Tradition and Scientific Innovation in India': In Science and Spirituality in Modern India, (Editor, Makarand Paranjape), Samvad India Foundation, New Delhi. Pp 76-95, 2006)).*

When we received science, in the modern sense, through colonial rule, there was an apparent clash between outward looking materialistic science based culture and inward looking spirituality based culture. This conflict exists in every practicing scientist in our country. It exists even in the educated common man who knows about science. Over decades if not centuries, when 'Pursuits of Science' has become a national policy and when national development is Science & Technology driven, a new divide appeared within each individual. This is the divide between 'Faith & Spirituality' and 'Science & Rationality'.

A consequence of this which is perceivable at the general society level is 'Valueless Science' coexisting with 'Ethics based Life'. Violence in society has increased in general and in science in particular (*Ashish Nandy (Ed) Science, Hegemony & Violence: A Requiem for Modernity, Oxford University Press, 1988*). A partial solution to this is to incorporate 'value education' in our curricular content, especially in science related courses. One such relevant course worth delivering to students could be to teach them the "Art and Science of Integrating Body, Mind and Soul", which in fact forms the basis of all successes in the life of an individual. This book by Dr. Kaushal is an attempt to provide the study material in capsular form to teachers and students in this regard. The author has succeeded in this endeavor. He proves that if we have unity of purpose in thought, word and deed, Peace and Harmony will prevail in our society.

Being a thorough bred Physicist, the author has analyzed the social problem through tools of Physics and Mathematics, thus bringing rigor to his thesis. Most people may think that a sociologist should write this kind of book. Dr. Kaushal has demonstrated in this book, that the divide between 'Science & Religion' can be bridged only when a Natural Scientist analyzes the different dimensions of the problem with the help of scientific method, scientific literature and also religious literature together. Then only, he believes, the conflict can be resolved and PEACE may reign on this earth for Man. Further most of the social sciences including Humanities represent a construct based on Ontology while most of the Natural Science represents Research methodology based analysis and thereby derives Knowledge.

The text is difficult to read in some places and may not be understood by average students. The level of intellect required to understand the author's thesis is high. Moreover it may not be comprehended easily by metro students, totally disconnected from matters of religion and spirituality. It will also be not understood by non-Hindu students as the author quotes extensively from Vedic literature. Students come from different social, cultural, economic and religious and intellectual backgrounds. There lies the role of the true teacher. The institutions have to take steps to appoint inspired and inspiring teachers to teach such a course at the foundation level. However many parts of the book are written very eloquently. It stirs you at places. The readers would be forced to think. I also feel that if the author can do away with the word 'GOD', this book will represent the best secular philosophy with highest content of spirituality! It would be compatible with pure natural science and pure religion. The author has done yeoman service to all by bringing out this new philosophy which explains human experiences in its entirety but in a sublime conceptual framework. Whoever reads this book will feel the ennobling experience just like Schopenhauer when he read the Bhagavat Gita. This book is also of much use to many, other than students. Those who seek a modern non-religious psycho-philosophical understanding of human life, activities and their cosmic significance will immensely benefit from studying this book.

A new Science based value system taking the best from both Science & Religion is the need of the hour. If we explain the scientific basis of our 'Composite Culture', it would bring understanding. Only superstitions and blind beliefs in rituals have to be demolished and discarded. The spirituality should be left intact. The conflict can be resolved not by replacing one value system by another but by understanding the limitations of both. Sir Arthur Eddington has stated to the effect that Science itself is a faith! We have to guard against both.

Delhi
25th February, 2015

Prof. Kambadur Muralidhar
J.C. Bose National Fellow (DST)

Abbreviations, Notations and Symbols

AAD = action-at-a-distance
AADT = action-at-a-distance time
AAT = action-at-a time
b = Being (or *Jiva* or life principle)
B = biological body
$\mathcal{B}$ = non-Self body (a composite of gross and micro bodies)
$\mathcal{C}$ = causal (body) existence
SE = senses of perception and action
E = ego or self-conscience
EFLs = essentials for life
EOLs = essences of life
EP = epi-physical (matter/particle)
FOA = fruits of action
FOUs = faculties of understanding
$\mathcal{G}$ = gross (body) existence
G = A part of gross body (B+SE)
GMW = God-made world
I = intellect, faculty of decision
IF = intuitive feelers
ISO = 'inside out'
IT = intuitive thinkers
M = mind, faculty of emotions/ feelings
$\mathcal{M}$ = micro-body, mindset function
μ = meditation variable/ parameter
MMW = Man-made world
$\mathcal{N}$ = natural existence
OSO = 'outside out'
P = physical (matter/particle)
P = personality matrix
PCM = personality creation mechanism
PM = *panca mahābhūtās* (five cosmic elements)
r = *rajas*
RAM = random access memory
ROM = read only memory
S = *sankalpa* matrix
S = societal existence
s = *sātvik*
SEA = senses of action (motor organs)
SEK = senses of knowledge
SEP = special epi-physical (matter/particle)
SF = sensation feelers
SMBG = *Srimad Bhagvad-Gita*
SNP = systematic of negative pursuits
SO = soul, the inner-most existence
SOA = seed of action
SPP = systematic of positive pursuits
σ = circumstances/environment
t = *tamas*
ST = sensation thinkers
STC = space-time-consciousness
τ = *tanmātrā*
WO = worldly objects or outer world of objects

CONTENTS

Preface

In view of the increasing deterioration of values in a society and, more than that, in the character and personality of an individual, several educational institutions, universities and management schools in India and outside, have felt the necessity of introducing a course in the curriculum which can help in inculcating such values in the younger generation. On the other hand, the younger generation, born and bought up in the age of modern science and technology, has its own attitude towards the world order in general and the family, friends, work place and society in particular. At times they not only question the belief-system whatsoever but also lack in ethical, moral and spiritual values in their behavior and personality. It seems that purely religion-based traditional ways of imparting these values do not work in the present times. However, if a scientific dimension is added to these existing methods of imparting and infusing these values with an appropriate reasoning at their foundation level, then the exercise can yield better results. The present book is planned with this objective in mind. A modest attempt is made to explore the subject of psychophysics by way of developing the Science of the Self and subsequently studying its applications in the real-life day-to-day phenomena in a framcwork that has roots in the Vedic Science. In developing the subject, a variety of concepts, theories and models of physical sciences are freely used in an analogous manner to justify the working principles of subjective Science of the Self.

In fact, the subject of psychophysics (developed long ago by G. T. Fechner of Leipzig in 1860 and considered as good as dead in recent times), has appeared in this book in its new incarnation. Although the book is written in a text book style, but in the absence of availability of a precise and stable syllabus of such an interdisciplinary course, it will definitely serve the purpose of a reference book. Besides students with science background, the book will hopefully appeal equally to philosophers, scientists and psychologists in addition to a common reader. At present only a few institutions plan to have such a course at graduate level. It is my sincere hope that easy availability of an introductory book like this, would accelerate the process of inclusion of psychophysics or an allied discipline on value education in the undergraduate syllabi by more and more institutions. Further, the emphasis on such an education is also given while training the teachers at various levels, training the man power for human management or towards the reformation of criminals in jails, etc.

It may be mentioned that love is an important attribute of the soul (or the Self). As will be argued in Chapters 8, 13 and 15, it is also an important prerequisite for the spiritual life. A demonstration of the universality of this phenomenon of love happens to be one possible end-product of this package. Unfortunately there is a great confusion about the existence of soul among Western thinkers (cf. Chapter 4). In the Indian context, however, the concept of soul or its derivatives (like consciousness) and manifestations (like 'idol' worship) have been an essential part of several traditions, customs and *sanskâras* in many families. Persons are well aware of it right from their childhood. The only question is to bring the word and its meaning into a logical perspective and the same has been the purpose of this book. Further, the three words 'body', 'mind' and 'soul', when they appear in this order in the sub-title of the book, respectively characterize the human existences or personalities at physical, mental and spiritual levels. It is this last level of human-existence that makes a person capable of seeing the entire world order in a unified way (i.e., unity in diversity) with reference to human-human and human-environment relations (cf. Chapter 15).

According to some saints the word 'soul' is defined as the 'inner-most existence' of the body in whose presence the entire 'body-system' works in a self-consistent manner. It may be noted that every human action, originating basically out of an interplay of parameters responsible for the above three existences of human Being, when performed in the outer world, leaves an impact thereof. Thus, the theme of this book, at a deeper level, definitely has roots in the philosophy of an individual. Now there are two ways to impart the rudiments of this philosophy to students: either by limiting the discussions only to a few role models (which are available in all cultures of the world) or by teaching the Art itself of integrating the body, mind and soul, of course in simple philosophical terms, preferably through examples. Obviously, once a student is exposed to this Art or to the science of the Self-management, then he will not only be able to digest the lessons from a variety of role models but will also know as to how to 'create' his own personality. Keeping this second approach in mind, the present book is planned.

It is good to inculcate human and spiritual values in younger generation through role models and the biography of great persons. But at times this leaves only a temporary impact on them, particularly when the student comes to know of the weaknesses or drawbacks of their role model or the great person. The faith of the student in them breaks down. In the modern age of fast researches, the post-mortem of every character is possible for vested interests and the media takes the advantage of that. Thus, this method of imparting the values should be one of the ways and not the only way. Students should rather learn the Science of the Self at certain stage of their career, so that they themselves know the ways and means of creating the personality at their own while also getting lessons from the life of great persons and role models.

With these motives in mind the present book is planned and the abc... of the Sovereign Science of the Self as inherent in Vedic literature, is emphasized.

Using the concepts and frameworks of Vedic science the author in his recent book entitled, "*The Science of Philosophy: Theory of Fundamental Processes in Human Behaviour and Experiences*", published by D. K. Print World, New Delhi, 2011 (pp. 541), has propounded a theory of fundamental processes that take place inside the human Being prior to his performance of any action in the outer world. The presentation of the subject matter in this book has somehow become a wee bit technical and somewhat more advanced from the point of view of students and a common reader. Therefore, the present book is planned at an introductory level amenable to all categories of persons including students. Efforts are made here to follow example-based presentation of somewhat deeper philosophical concepts and that through reasonably small chapters appended with some high skill exercises and a reference to further reading. A glossary of technical words/ terms used in the Text is provided at the end of the book.

Besides offering a general introduction to the subject in Chapter 1, a basis to the subject matter is presented in Chapter 2, in an introductory style. As the title of the book has roots in a philosophy, our efforts in these chapters are to advocate an absolute approach to the subject matter which results from the combination of both modern and Vedic sciences, rather than resorting to any comparative studies at this stage. The subject matter is divided into three parts. Part A (Chapters 3-7) presents the back-bone of the book in the sense that here under the heading of psychophysics we develop a framework for the working of the essences of life through the so-called 'patomic' (philosophical atom-type) model of the human Being in general. As a matter of fact the Science of the Self discussed here and as described in Vedic literature has yet to find a parallel among other philosophies of the world. The author may appear to be biased in this respect but the fact is that the Vedanta philosophy is one of the richest ways of thinking and analyzing the world order. It is also capable of accommodating in itself other philosophies of the world. Any way we shall not go into finer intricacies of this philosophy but confine ourselves to its use only at the rudimentary level and that too in a scientific spirit. Part B (Chapters 8-11), in real sense, describes the integration of body, mind and soul towards the performance of actions by an individual and these actions in turn create his personality. For this purpose, the dynamics of essences of life developed in Part A is freely used here. An analysis of ways and means as to how this 'created' personality interacts with a few or many other human Beings in a society or with Nature or environment is the theme of Part C (Chapters 12-15). In fact Chapters 7 and 12 have become somewhat technical but are necessary for an enlightened reader, others however can use them as glossary of definitions and concepts.

The book is written in a non-sermon-delivering style to a person but truly in an objective style. Efforts are made to present the concepts, phenomena, processes or the experiences, through which each of us goes or can go at one point of time or the other, in a quantifiable and scientific spirit. With due apology to our female readers, all throughout the book the English pronouns corresponding to masculine gender are used for the human Being, of course without any prejudice on the part of the author. Moreover, except for a little difference in the body domain, these are the same essences of life which prevail equally in both man and woman in the philosophical domain.

March 5 (Holika Dahan), 2015 **Radhey Shyam Kaushal**

Acknowledgements

It may be mentioned that the class-room teaching and the conference presentation of work offer very fine examples of human interactions and the same I have been enjoying for more than four decades now. I wish to thank the Head, Department of Physics & Astrophysics, University of Delhi, for extending the facilities of teaching and research in the Department along with other facilities to work, particularly after my superannuation.

The idea of writing such a book on character building came to my mind after attending a *Sanskāram* Meeting in Delhi. During the course of compiling this book, I have been encouraged by and benefitted from the discussions with many of my friends and colleagues in the University and outside. In particular, I am grateful to Prof. K. Muralidhar (Department of Zoology), Prof. Girishwar Mishra (Department of Psychology), Prof. (Mrs.) Sunita Singh Sengupta (Management Studies), Prof. Bhudeo Sharma (Jaypee Inst. of Inf. Tech., Noida), Prof. Dharma Pal Arya (Ex-VC, GKU, Hardwar) and Dr. R.C. Pradhan (Ex-Faculty, Ramjas College) for encouraging me in this endeavor. Words are not enough to express my gratitude to Prof. Muralidhar (DU) and Prof. H. P. Stapp (LBNL, USA) for sparing their valuable time in going through the draft version of the book and putting their honest observations on the package in words. Other friends and colleagues to whom I wish to express my gratitude and who have also been helpful in preparing the draft of the manuscript at various stages are: Dr. D. Parashar, Dr. Ashutosh Bharadwaj, Dr. S. Murugavel, Dr. Awadhesh Prasad and Dr. R. Ramanathan.

I also enjoyed many discussions with some of my like-minded neighbors and friends during our morning and evening walks and the same has enriched my understanding of some concepts of Vedic wisdom. Some of these ideas in fact have appeared as Examples and Exercises in the book. In particular, I wish to thank Late Shri Balram Krishan Arora, Mr. V. S. Agrawal, Mr. Ved Ram Gupta, Dr. Chand K. Bharadwaj and Mr. R. K. Kamara. Further, I do not have words to express my gratitude to my neighbor Mr. A. C. Sogani (Ex-Director, C. S. O., Govt. of India) and my friend, colleague and collaborator, Dr. D. Parashar (Ex-Associate Professor, ARSD College) for their untiring and always available help towards the preparation of the manuscript and for various useful suggestions from time to time. Lectures by Swami A. Parthasarathy and Mr. Shivendra Nagar on Shrimad Bhagavad-Gita have also been helpful.

Lastly, the invaluable co-operation extended and deep sense of patience shown by my wife, Shashi, and children Shraddha, Medha, Mukta and Govind and my sons-in-law Ch. Kunal, Vijay and Manoj during this course of work cannot be ignored and the same is acknowledged from the core of my heart. I also thank Mr. J. S. Patwal for the excellent typing of the manuscript, oftentimes in extra hours.

Radhey Shyam Kaushal

GENERAL INTRODUCTION

Chapter 1

MOTIVATION AND INTRODUCTORY SURVEY

1.1 WORLD-ORDER AND THE HUMAN BEING

In the present age of ever progressing technology and scientific advancements, the new generation is coming up with better and better intelligent quotient but with a poor emotional quotient in the same proportion. While there is enough awareness of civic sense, civic values or of polluting environment among the growing children, a deterioration of ethical and human values in them can be seen world wide. Unless a child is taught these values at its tender/formative age or at the school level, may not be in philosophical terms but through moral stories, the deterioration is bound to exist. No doubt such a moral education has become a part of curriculum and also of several cultural/religious forums but there is a scarcity of role models to follow or of a scientific logical basis in these moral-providing explanations, particularly from the point of view of teenagers or adolescents. Some possible factors responsible for the deterioration of human values are (i) the growing concept of nuclear families, (ii) working parents, (iii) business-oriented school and college systems, (iv) increasing expenses on a child and hence the desire for more perks, particularly for never-ending luxurious life; at times twenty four hours of the day become insufficient in fulfilling such desires. The last but not the least important factor is that an individual does not have time for introspection or for the subjective thinking which in fact also creates the objective world outside for that individual.

As a rule, the new generation is supposed to start from where the old generation has left the creative release. The magnitude and quality of this creative release is well accepted and received by the younger generation on the front of man-made world but it is not equally received and/or perceived on the front of God-made or spiritual world in spite of the fact that the latter has been in the background of the former. While a child is bewildered by the glittering of both the man-made and God-made worlds, he somehow decides to enter the former world as the routes to the latter are neither trivial nor easy to follow. This is how our modern children are growing with the half truth about the world-order. They live with and accept this half-truth for most of the time assuming the same as the whole truth unless they are told about the latter in appealing terms and at an appropriate time.

For example, a teenager or common man very well knows the functioning of his mobile phone or at least the abc ... of its working principles but not the dynamics that works behind his actions and behaviour vis-à-vis his kin, relatives, friends or the society as a whole with whom he has to live through out his life. As a matter of fact, he is least aware of his Self and its working with respect to the external world consisting of both animate (living) and inanimate (non living/dead) stimulants. Not only the knowledge but also a spirit to follow the human values in practice, is only the first step in learning the subjective science of the Self.

The literature is one subject which inculcates maximum human values but mostly in a figurative style and an enlightened student generally does not opt for it for his specialization. Majority has a temptation for the man-made world which dwells on and aims at luxurious life by way of contracting the space and time in terms of every-day progressing means of transport and communication. At times, this way of life ends-up with worries, depression, frustration and the like. On the other hand, an understanding of the God-made (spirited) world that dwells on the dynamics of the essences of life and their role in the outer world, definitely aims at pleasure, peace and possibly eternal joy. The Mother Nature in fact offers an open book in this regard. Scientists, philosophers, common man or spiritual persons all read it in their own way and exploit it to their own-ends and thereby contribute to the creation of these man-made and God-made worlds. At physical level some examples of these concepts are: rivers and forests are God-made whereas canals and parks are man-made. Note that for a human Being the Nature, consisting of both animate and inanimate entities, start right from the external (outer) world continues then to his inner world. The latter includes mind, intellect and the Self-conscience, ego. They all work in the background of his consciousness; otherwise for an unconscious or dead person, the existence of physical world itself is questionable. In fact it is the element of consciousness—a characteristic of the inner-most existence, called soul or spirit that justifies the Being as being a living entity.

1.2 THE BEWILDERING NATURE AND ITS PERCEPTION

Since the time human race came into existence both the 'material' and the 'spiritual ideologies have been evolving in the society more in a parallel manner. Often, there has been (and there still is) the tug of war between these ideologies with regard to their dominance and survival in the society. In fact the materialistic or spiritual concepts originate in one's mind from the fact that as to how he perceives and exploits the objects and stimulants of the outer world. Most of us are convinced or feel satisfied from the physical (objective) reality in Nature as perceived and explored by the objective scientists. Yet some try to explore another aspect of Nature— formless or subjective reality hidden behind the physical reality and whose existence as well cannot be denied by the experts. As a matter of fact only a reasonable understanding of both objective and subjective realities, related respectively to extrovert and introvert personalities in society, is expected to provide the complete truth regarding the functioning of Nature.

As early as in 1860, Gustav Theodor Fechner of Leipzig introduced the subject of psychophysics which, according to him, is an exact science of functional relations or the relations of dependency between body and mind or more generally between physical and psychic worlds. As it will be clear in Part A, psychophysics is the branch of psychology that deals with the relations between physical stimuli and sensory response. An understanding of modern physical theories and their use in developing the subject of mental world in an analogous manner seems to be the need of the day so that a framework for integrating body, mind and soul can be developed in a scientific spirit. Unfortunately, in the Western way of thinking, while the sensory world is well understood through the subject of physics, the psychic or mental world is not explored to the same extent. Contrarily, Indian philosophy for this purpose offers an elegant framework to study and analyze the psychophysical processes in the finest possible manner in terms of the so called essences of life (EOLs).

Note that the same stimulant of physical world can leave different imprints on the minds of different persons depending upon the level of development of their faculties of understanding (FOUs). It is the role of FOUs of an individual in the perception process that has to be understood prior to relying on any conclusion drawn from the observations on the stimulant. While we relegate the details of this mechanism to Part A (cf. Chapter 7), we elaborate here only this process with the help of certain examples. In fact the parameters which contribute to one's FOU and its development, basically are the attributes of his inner EOLs, namely mind for the 'emotion quotient', intellect for the analyzing power or 'intelligence quotient' and self-sense or ego for the correlating capacity of events or 'memory quotient'. A certain proportion of these parameters at a given place and time constitute the level of development of one's FOU. Over and above them all is the 'spiritual quotient' which can be derived from the quality of the overall outcome of the functions of these three EOLs.

Example 1.2.1 : How the same flower is perceived differently by different personalities: Say, there is a flower and it is watched by different categories of persons. For a common man it is just an object of beauty or to smell if it does so; for a poet it however could be an object of metaphor or simile to compare mouth, cheeks or eyes of a beloved; for a botanist it is an item for taxonomy or research as to how it originates from a bud or plant; for an agricultural scientist the species of flower can help to search an appropriate location and climate for its mass scale production, if the crop of flower is useful like that of rose flower; for a lover it is a nice item to offer as a gift; for a physicist or mathematician it might be an object of looking for group symmetries under rotation if the distribution of petals is studied. For an introvert person (philosopher) the same flower can inspire for a realization of an un-manifest (formless) reality in Nature as to how the five cosmic elements (like earth, water, air, fire in the form of sun rays, and ether justifying its own existence in cosmos) have helped in its growth in the present form.

Example 1.2.2: How the same phenomenon is perceived differently by different personalities: In a puppet-show a person sits behind the curtain and manipulates with his fingers a number of fine wires/ strings. The wires are connected to the bodies of the puppets. The audience is thrilled at the movements and gestures of the puppets. The perception of the program will be different for different category of persons. While a common man enjoys the entire program for the period he is present there, an extrovert (scientist) category of person looks at these puppets as free agents, as independent doers. An introvert (philosopher) category person attributes the movements of puppets to fine wires. They make much of the fine threads. There intelligence cannot penetrate beyond that limit to recognize the hand that manipulates them all. These people are right so far as they go. They see a cause and effect. They see the fine wires and their effect on the gross bodies of puppets. But they clearly miss the person behind the curtain. There is however another spiritual or yogi category of persons who can see (perceive) the important role of the un-manifest reality (i.e. the role of the person behind the curtain), which somehow is missed by above three categories of persons.

Thus, the introvert and extrovert personalities perceive the same object of the outer world differently. The following examples will further demonstrate as to how the formless reality in Nature manifests differently in physical world.

Example 1.2.3: How the formless (un-manifest) reality in Nature manifest differently: Initially the electricity is produced on a mass scale at a power house or dam, then it goes to a local power station where a transformer transforms it to a desired wattage, from the local power station it goes to the mains of the house, and from there it passes through different appliances to make the life comfortable. (cf. Fig.1). It is the same formless electricity which flows through a wire and produces (i) the heat, if passed through a heater, (ii) the cold, if passed through a fridge/cooler or air-conditioner, (iii) the light, if passed through a bulb/tube light, (iv) the air, if passed through a fan, (v) the music, if passed through a CD player/gramophone, etc. Note that these features of heat, cold, light, air or music etc. are neither present in electricity nor in the respective appliances, but they are produced as a result of coordination of both electricity and the corresponding appliance. In spite of the fact that the electricity is formless (un-manifest) its existence cannot be denied. Once the electricity is switched off from the power station, none of the appliances would work despite its unit remaining intact. Further, the flow of electricity in terms of its wattage and nature (whether it is A.C. or D.C.) depends on the designing of the local power station at the time of its installation. No doubt all appliances work on different principles but it is the same electricity that produces different effects like heat and cold. Transformers can also help to step up or step down the power but only in a limited range. A flowchart of the above applications is shown in Fig.1.1.

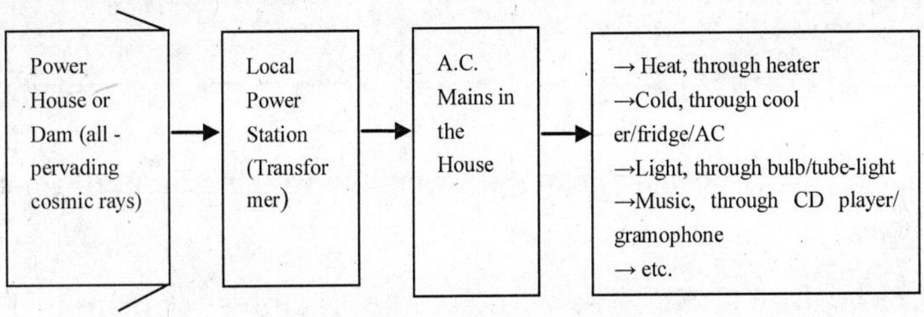

Fig. 1.1: A schematic picture showing as how the formless (un-manifest) reality, i.e. the electric current manifests in a variety of ways.

Example 1.2.4: How the several formless (un-manifest) realities manifest through the same cell phone: Another popular example as to how the several formless (un-manifest) realities become manifest is that of the working of a cell (mobile) phone (cf. Fig. 1.2). The net work signal of electromagnetic (EM) nature initially starts from the (global) network station. Then it proceeds to the local station for the necessary further relay. At the next stage the signal is received by a handset of the mobile phone which is already operative with the help of a battery installed in it, at the time of its making operative. The handset also consists of a SIM card and a memory card possibly with RAM (random access memory) and ROM (read only memory). With regard to its applications, this multipurpose device is used in almost all cases to which our senses of perception are sensitive, but only in one way (and that too in a limited domain). What a wonderful invention of modern science it is ! Some applications of this device are as a phone for communication, to listen to music , as a camera for photography, as a torch for light, as a pocket watch, etc.

After having a feel for the formless reality in Nature through the above undisputable and undeniable examples, we now list a grand and evergreen example of the working of a human Being with regard to the perception mechanism.

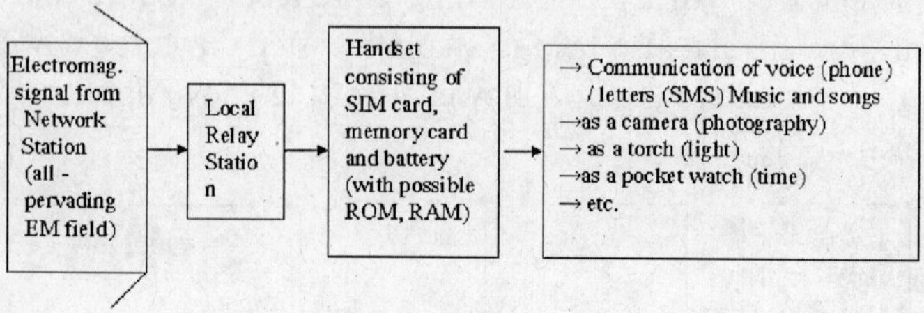

Fig. 1.2: A schematic picture showing the working of a cell (mobile) phone.

Example 1.2.5: How the same formless (un-manifest) consciousness works through different senses of perception and action: As shown in Fig.1.3, there could be a cosmic source of consciousness from where the consciousness proceeds to its localized version, termed as 'soul' (SO) or 'spirit'. The consciousness from this local station with its peculiar properties (in the sense that they are completely different from the attributes of space-time creations or from those of the space time mediated physical interactions) proceeds to be so-called 'micro-body' ($\mathcal{M}$) consisting of mind (M), intellect (I) and ego (E). At the next stage this consciousness manifests through the 'gross body' ($\mathcal{G}$) consisting of biological body (B) and the senses of knowledge and action (SE). It is through these five sensors, namely skin for touch, tongue for taste, nose for smell, eyes for light and ears for sound, that our body works as a perceiver on the one hand and as a responder on the other. While these five sensors (SEK) are instrumental in the processes of perception and response, another five motor organs (SEA), namely hand, foot, power of speech, copulatory organ and anus are instrumental in performing a (physical) action. The details of these processes are postponed to Part A (cf. Chapter 7). In fact, in between the processes of perception and response another process, termed as 'realization' also takes place inside the human

Being. Note that the gross body ($\mathcal{G}$) alone can not do anything without the guidance of micro body ($\mathcal{M}$) and that too in the presence of consciousness - a characteristic of soul (SO) which constitute the so-called 'causal body'($\mathcal{C}$). Further, the mind and intellect play an important role in the perception and response processes whereas ego (faculty of memory) and soul play important roles in the realization process. This is the common parameter of consciousness which originates basically from soul (like the electricity in example 1.2.2). The consciousness actually helps in coordinating and integrating the actions of body, mind and soul and the latter respectively are the representatives of gross, micro and causal bodies.

Example 1.2.3 accounts only for the one-way process, i.e., it is the same electricity, while flowing forward, that makes all appliances operative. Nothing comes in return except for stimulating the outer world. In Example 1.2.4, the communication is, however, both-way but only partially in the sense that two human Beings of matching frequencies have to be available for an effective result. In this case the local battery, a source of producing electric and/or magnetic field which again are part of the incoming signal of electromagnetic nature, acts the role of soul as in Example 1.2.5. Although there is some similarity, but the case in Example 1.2.5 is altogether different. In addition to the perception and response processes here a realization process also appears which in turn helps in the development of FOUs of an individual. The type of formless reality highlighted in this example no doubt could be disputable but cannot be denied from any standard and forms the back-bone in integrating the body, mind and soul of an individual.

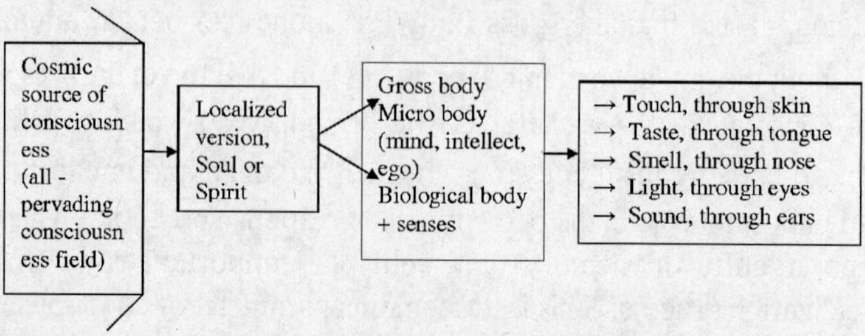

Fig. 1.3: A schematic picture showing as to how the formless consciousness manifests and accordingly perceives the physical reality through different senses of perception.

In philosophical terms, Karl Popper and John Eccles offer the concept of three worlds — the one which we perceive, the second which we study in scientific terms using models and the third which really exists. In view of the fact that there are limitations on the working of both our senses of perception and action as also on scientific theories and the derived laws, the extracted truth about the first two worlds remains incomplete. Therefore, for a common man at least the search of the absolute truth in Nature remains a far cry.

1.3 SUBJECTIVE AND OBJECTIVE SCIENCES AND THEIR DOMAINS OF WORKING

Whether it is the subjective science (experience-based Science of the Self) or the ob-jective science (instrument-based science of the external world) in either case the role of un-manifest (formless) reality in Nature can not be denied. In physical theories, no doubt, all the four fundamental interactions, namely gravitation, weak, electromagnetic and strong are the examples of the formless reality in terms of their action-at-a-distance type property, but the fact is that they are space-time mediated interactions and hence are detectible by physical instruments. On the other hand, human interactions (whether inside the same human Being or with other humans or nonhumans or even with inanimate objects) are beyond the concepts of space and time, i.e. they could very well be action-at-a-time or action-at-a-distance-time type in addition to the action-at-a-distance type. As a result, the viability of physical laws in the domain of subjective science is not sure as it is clear from the following examples:

Example 1.3.1: One can easily predict the (parabolic) path for the inanimate object (i.e. for a piece of stone) thrown in earth's gravity field, but not for an alive bird thrown also in the same field. The free-will of the bird plays some role in this regard.

Example 1.3.2: A person crossing the road at a place has to balance himself with respect to all the three space, time and his consciousness in a considerable proportion, even if the route is familiar to him yet it is not an easy task to define the path precisely in view of traffic.

Example 1.3.3: When you meet a person after a long time and shake hand, note the difference between the two situations :(i) first shake hands and then recognize him, and (ii) first recognize him and then shake hands. Even a little memory conscience about him will allow you to say hello to him from a distance but for details about him the inner dynamics of M, I and E starts working with evolving consciousness. In addition to action-at-a-distance, action-at-a-time type force also comes into existence.

Example 1.3.4: When you drag your friend after holding his arm, note that it is not just the contact force, in conformity with Newton's laws of motion, working here between you and your friend to describe your movement, but many other self-organizing forces of subjective nature (not describable by physics) come into existence.

Dead bodies are as good as the inanimate objects and on them physical laws can be applied. For the dynamics of animate objects, however, an exclusive parameter responsible for the phenomenon of consciousness — an attribute of soul, appears and the same also makes mind, intellect and ego and subsequently the senses and body of an individual operative.

In some sense it is the consciousness which creates space, time and geometry with reference to an individual. While the role of space and time exists and necessary in the domain of $\mathcal{G}$ for the perception and description of the external (physical) world (denoted by WO), it however decreases as one meditates inwardly. A directed or channelized version of consciousness inwardly is termed as 'meditation' and the same in the domain of outer EOLs is called 'concentration'. Both of them can be described by the same variable. In fact, as the consciousness (meditation) variable increases, the stimulant/object unfolds its finer and finer details to the individual depending on the development of his FOUs.

From the point of view of complete understanding of Nature, physical laws suffer from several limitations. Yet physics remains a fundamental science in the sense that the discoveries made in other branches like in chemical and/or biosciences do involve the use of physics-based instruments. In fact many problems in modern research are of interdisciplinary nature and their solutions have become possible only with a non-compartmentalized knowledge.

1.4 PROGRESSING MODERN SCIENCE AND ITS IMPACT

After the advent of advanced computers and scientific technology, almost all branches of knowledge are flourishing these days with newer and newer discoveries. Such an exponentially growing creative release has not only added to a better understanding of Nature but also to the improvement of life style of a common man. For example, modern man has been able to command over all the five cosmic elements of Vedic science. As far as the means of transport are concerned, i.e. car, bus, train etc. on the land; boat, ship, steamer etc. on water; helicopter, airplane, jet, etc. in air; fire proof jackets in forest fire, etc., and rockets in ether (space) etc. With regard to communication, space and time in modern times have been contracted like never before. Besides the research progress in basic sciences like physics, chemistry and biology, there has been considerable progress in the understanding of earth, water, air, fire and ether through subjects like geology, oceanography, climatology, and space technology.

In summary, the boons of progressive modern science have made life full of sensual pleasures and luxuries. With the result the change in society is natural. Even values in society are changing in view of the growing concept of nuclear family or of one parent family. Children and youth in spite of having 'class one' facilities at their home, school or office with regard to their physical survival, at the mental level, however, they often feel themselves hollow and carry a lot of worries and often go in depression. It is only about 6-7 decades ago when the experience-based knowledge was transferred from one generation to another in a more or less unchanged environment. In present times, however the things are different. The technical and instrument-based knowledge is transferred from one generation to another in a fast changing environment. In order to cope-up with this change and partly to fulfill their never ending desires and high ambitions, children and youth undergo pressing agonies in their competitive life, either physically, mentally or emotionally. Their sharing of these sufferings with others like friends and relatives has also become restricted in view of the deteriorating quality of values among human interactions.

Starting from the class room to various cultural and religious forums there is a stress on advocating the human, ethical and social values. However, in the absence of self-observation by an individual, these sermons do not have much impact on him. One possible reason for such a situation is that the art of self-observation is not properly imparted to these modern scientific minds. If a logical basis to this art of self-observation becomes available then naturally the child or youth will imbibe these techniques better and there is every hope of upliftment of his mental level. As a matter of fact both ethical and social values do have their roots in the spiritual or human values and the latter in turn will also be an asset in integrating the body, mind and soul towards the success of an action.

1.5 THE QUESTION OF INTEGRATING BODY, MIND AND SOUL: THE ROLE OF SPIRITUAL THINKING

What a wonderful coordination of gross and micro bodies of a human Being towards the performance of an action the Nature has provided! While all this happens in the presence of consciousness, the coordination becomes an asset in the success of an action. This natural coordination, however, becomes more efficient and effective when it takes place in the light of a *Sankalpa* — a high level determination. In fact the body, mind and soul, in this case, are in unison and this in turn yields maximum success in the action performed by an individual. No doubt the dynamics of constituents of gross and micro-bodies remains the same but the quality (good or bad) of *Sankalpa* docs reflect in the fruit of actions. The nature of *Sankalpa* of a saint or of a drunkard is obviously different. Clearly, the awareness and also the follow-up of spiritual values play an important role in shaping the *sankalpas*.

Example 1.5.1 : Irrespective of the type of grain you put in, the flour-mill or grinder has to grind the grain. The nature of the flour (the fruit of action) that one collects as the end-product, however, could be different yellowish for the corn or whitish for the wheat. Note that this all works when electric current flows in the grinder (i.e. when the consciousness is present in the body).

In the next example we present a case in which the spiritual thinking of one person reflects in his actions at the world level and the same, when realized by the other person at the level of his inner-most existence, also starts manifesting in the actions of the latter rather instantly.

Example 1.5.2: Some policemen are chasing a thief who all of a sudden finds an opportunity to enter in the house of a saintly person. The person asks thief as who is he and why has he come to his house. The thief honestly tells him that he is a thief and the police is chasing him. The thief requests for a shelter, in the house. The person asks him to come in the house and hides him in the room in which his daughter is sleeping. After a while when police reach the house and enquires the person about the thief, the person tells the police that he has not seen the thief but his son-in-law is sleeping in the room. Hearing this, the police men disappear and at the same time thief appears before the person with a changed mind and folded hands. The thief not only expressed gratitude to the person but also he promised to leave the habit of stealing in future and to become a good man.

By giving the status of son-in-law to the thief, the person not only won the confidence of police but also these of his words changed the heart of the thief to the extent that he decided to quit all his ill-habits. The daughter however remained unaware of all these proceedings. This is how the spirituality in one person induces the spirituality in others, may not be in the same proportion. In the next classic analogy (example) we demonstrate as to how the beautiful coordination of various EOLs, leads to a successful performance of an action.

Example 1.5.3: The human body in action is like a moving chariot: Consider the human body as a chariot which is driven by ten horses (five senses of knowledge and five motor organs). The master (soul) is sitting in the chariot and the driver (intellect) is driving the chariot using the rein of mind. To run the chariot rightly (i.e. towards the successful performance of an action) according to the wishes (ego) of the master (soul), charioteer (intellect) has to pull or release the rein appropriately (i.e. to control the mind) so that the movement of horses (senses and motor organs) remains under control.

It is not an easy task to have perfect coordination of body, mind and soul always and everywhere. Instances come when one fails to manage it. In fact the Art of integrating the body, mind and soul belongs to the domain of subjective science or spirituality for which the meditation, self-observation and an understanding of the dynamics of EOLs in addition to an appropriate development of one's FOUs are the pre-requisites.

1.6 MOTIVATION FOR THE BOOK AND THE ARRANGEMENT OF CHAPTERS

From the above survey it can be noticed that even a little knowledge and practice of this Art of integrating the body, mind and soul is capable of changing the behaviour, actions and subsequently the personality of an individual and that too without actually affecting the life style. Generally, it is seen that when a person gets older he develops natural tendency to become spiritual and learns this Art, perhaps after realizing the limitations of the working of this 'man-made' world, but earlier the person learns this Art in life, better it is. Now the question is as to how one can learn this Art. For an open mind seeker there is no problem, as every incidence of day-to-day life becomes the source of inspiration for him. Among other sources for this wisdom, one is the study of religious scriptures which are normally full of spiritual content and the second is by sitting with experienced elders in spiritual terms. Since religion is only the outer garment of spirituality, one is lost in the search of the latter. Similarly, finding an experienced elder in whom one can repose his faith is not an easy task in modern times. While one can keep on looking for these facilities, he can as well start with a self-styled analytical study of this Art. The present compilation is an effort of the author in this direction.

As a matter of fact the Art of integrating the body, mind and soul is based on some fundamental processes which take place inside the human Being prior to the performance of an action. In analogy with physical and chemical sciences these processes in human behavior and experiences have been investigated earlier by the author (Kaushal, 2011) in a technical and quantitative manner. Here, however, the efforts will be to present these concepts in a rudimentary style, mainly from the point of view of the beginners in the field.

We continue this introductory discussion in the next chapter. As a matter of fact, since the subject matter of this book has roots in philosophy, a brief survey of various philosophies will be carried out in the forthcoming chapters. The subject matter in the book is presented in three parts. Part A (Chapters 3-7) forms the back-bone of the book in the sense that here, under the heading of psychophysics, we develop a framework for the working of essences of life through the so-called patomic model of the human Being. A grand analogy to this effect with physical sciences is emphasized in this part. It is the Part B (Chapters 8-11) that is devoted to describe the Art of integrating the body, mind and soul within the framework outlined in Part A. As to how the changed personality of a person appears after learning and practicing this Art is the theme of this Part. As the human Being is a social element, he is bound to interact with other persons. Therefore, in Part C (Chapters 12-15) the human interactions either inside the same person or with other persons are discussed, essentially in a technical and philosophical spirit. Applications to some group activities of a person are also discussed in this part. Glossary of words, terms and phrases used in the text is given in the end to provide their respective details for ready reference.

Chapter 2

THE SUBJECT MATTER AND ITS MEANING FOR THE PURPOSE

2.1. THE SUBJECT REFERS TO THE PHILOSOPHY OF AN INDIVIDUAL

Geographical boundaries of a country keep changing either according to the whims of rulers through wars or of God through natural calamities (like earthquakes etc.), but its character is remembered at least for some time in the pages of history. The character of a country, whether good or bad, ultimately originates from that of individual citizen or their groups and subgroups. It has been found that a person in general has a natural affinity to the place where he is born and to the culture in which he has been brought up. Even modern scientific advancements, although made the boundaries of various cultures porous and contracted the space and time in terms of connectivity, have not affected this affinity. In fact there is no reason as to why this affinity should be affected. After all, an individual in his childhood or in early youth builds up his character or personality in the environment provided by his native place and culture. Moreover, one's childhood remains in the memories through out his life.

As a matter of fact family traditions, culture and religion help an individual in developing an ideology which guides him during the performance of day-to-day activities. Over and above that one also develops his own attitude towards the life and the world-order provided he thinks with an open mind. In view of the fact that the spirituality is the back-bone and a common factor in all religions of the world and the religion is only the outer garment, it is not always and everywhere possible for an individual to depart from the spiritual values, particularly when judging the merit of his actions. No doubt a common man may be impressed just by the outer garment, but a true seeker will never be satisfied with that, he would rather like to explore a deeper and logical basis for the values and their content even in the environment and mundane actions. Once he recognizes the role of spiritual content or spirituality present in them, then his character and subsequently the personality changes and the same manifests through his actions.

At this point it is worthwhile to remark on the spiritual and human values. While human values refer to an individual human Being and human society, the spiritual values, on the other hand, refer to the Nature as a whole including the humans, their society and the environment. Both spiritual and human values, however, originate from the attributes of soul like love, forgiveness, *Karuna*, etc. with respect to an individual and the same attain their cosmic character by way of his interacting with living and nonliving entities. As to how an individual interacts with other animate and inanimate entities in the Universe this becomes part of his way of thinking and constitutes his philosophy towards the world-order. Spirituality essentially means an all-inclusive experience. When there is an all-inclusive experience, human Being feels concerned and caring about everything around him. In fact an introvert person who has learnt the Art of self-realization, also realizes that this existence and the existence outside are not different.

2.2 EVERY CULTURE HAS ROOTS IN PHILOSOPHY: SEARCH FOR A PERFECT PHILOSOPHY

The word 'culture' is normally associated with the traditions, myths and rituals prevalent in a society. It brings the individuals of a society together. These were a few seers or intellectuals who worked on certain philosophy and framed some norms for the performance of rituals. These rituals, over a period of time, became traditions or the so-called 'wisdom of old persons'. Although the farsightedness or the level of development of FOUs of creators of these norms a philosophy through religion did matter, but in general these rituals and traditions are functions of space and time in the sense that they keep on changing from place to place and from time to time.

A religion provides an ordered life style for the common man. Depth and richness of knowledge-component in a religion define its existence and survival over the test of time. Even if the knowledge-component in a religion is rich enough, the question still remains as whether it pertains to Self, non-Self or both with reference to an individual. Naturally, some religions that end-up at the level of Self cannot survive for a long time. On the other hand, those religions which deal with the Science of the Self, non-Self and their coordination can be thought to remain for eternity. Vedic science offers one such religion, called *'Sanātana Dharma'*. The concerned philosophy, in general, can give birth to the so-called the 'science of spirituality', it can also be the candidate for a perfect philosophy. In some sense while religion is the outer garment of spirituality, the culture, on the other hand, is the outer-most garment of the same. Following example will give a feel for the Self and non-Self of an individual.

Example 2.2.1: One should understand that soul (self) is always like a king, distinct from the body, senses, mind and the intellect, all of which in conjunction with five cosmic elements constitute the non-Self (*Prakriti*). The Self is not only the witness of functions of non-Self but also makes them to work.

Example 2.2.2: As one separates the rice from the husk, bran, etc, that are covering it, likewise one should separate the pure Self within from the sheaths of non-Self through discriminative self-analysis and logical thinking.

In the present age of science various cultures of the world are coming closer and there emerges a tendency of their intermixing. Efforts have also been there to find a common philosophical platform for all the cultures with a scientific basis. If such unification of cultures in near future becomes possible at least in the spiritual zone, then the norms for the same have to come from the perfect philosophy. This suggests a need for discipline like 'scientific religion' or 'religious science' for the newly unified culture. It is the ego problem of the followers of the existing religions that will come on the way of this unification, otherwise both science and religion have quite a few commonalities at their foundation and survival level.

What is common in both science and religion is the modeling game. Models are framed on the basis of certain postulates and assumptions and hence set the limits in describing the ultimate reality in Nature. While ultimate truth remains a far cry (a matter of realization only), these are the analogies , similarities, parallelism, metaphor, simile and the like that help in modeling the truth and also in the proliferation of knowledge (Kaushal, 2003, Chaps. 5 and 6). It may be mentioned that founders of various cults and religions in the world are just revivers of this Truth through models or spiritual values with their added experiences and realization, but are not the creators of truth or these values. They are the followers of these cults or religions who fight for their identity or survival, otherwise the human race was very much there prior to the arrival of the respective prophet or saint on this earth. There did exist at least some human values prior to that as well.

Example 2.2.3: Modeling is common to all physical, chemical and biological sciences. For example, for a physicist gases are 'ideal' and 'perfect' (recall the postulates of kinetic theory of gases), surfaces are 'smooth', conductors are 'super' etc. but in reality they are not so. Data clearly shows departure from these idealized pictures. Similar idealization of phenomena does exist in chemistry and biology in view of limitations on both theoretical studies and experimental measurements. In the same spirit, the norms observed by the followers of a religion are also the outcome of certain modeling games with a wide continuous spectrum of social, ethical, moral, human and spiritual values.

Another commonality between science and religion is with regard to their qualitative and quantitative studies. For this purpose, each of them can be considered as consisting of three aspects or components, namely knowledge, methodology and practice. In case of science they can be understood as theory, theory relevant to experiments and experiments, whereas in case of religion they can be identified as knowledge ('*Jñana*'), methods to achieve the knowledge ('*Upāsanā*') and performance of day-to-day rituals ('*Karma*'). Note that the knowledge, as mentioned before, is not the end of story as far as the search of ultimate truth is concerned. It is only necessary but not sufficient. For sufficiency, however, one has to go one step further to learn the process of realization and next to it is the phenomenon of self-realization. It is this last step which brings the individual in tune with the cosmos and makes the individual spiritual in a true sense.

2.3 COMPOSITION OF HUMAN BEING: ESSENTIALS FOR LIFE AND ESSENCES OF LIFE

In biological terms the human body, consisting of inner organs and outer body parts, is a very complicated but perfect creation of God. Again the ways in which various systems like skeletal, respiratory, digestive, (blood) circulatory, reproductive, excretory and over and above them nervous and muscular systems, work in harmony are amazing. Further, in modern times scientists and the experts in the concerned areas have understood considerably the finer details of the working not only of these individual systems but also of their collective harmonious working. Such a wonderful working of the body-machine makes the survival of both humans and nonhumans possible. In order to maintain this body-machine and its working, various essentials are prescribed in different context. However, in sociological context and from the point of view of a common man these essentials are classified as air, water, food and shelter; they are necessary but not sufficient.

Consider a situation in which scientists are able to assemble all these biological systems in their perfectly working condition together as also take care of their mutual coordination and necessary supply of air, water, and food in the laboratory. Then the question arises whether such an assembled structure would work like a human Being even after inserting necessary microchips for emotions, decisions and memory. The answer is No. In fact, the reasons are more than one. The important one is that a battery has to be connected in order that this robot works and that too for limited actions and purpose for which it is designed. It can not depart even one step from what it has been asked to do, in view of RAM (random access memory) and ROM (read only memory) supplied to it in advance. Hence, there is no question of any creative action on the part of computers.

Naturally, in order that a robot works as or becomes a human, something more than that supplied by the objective science is needed and this something additional is definitely beyond the domain of scientists. In nut-shell, beside the biological body one needs some elements like mind for endless emotions, intellect for endless decisions, ego for the endless capacity for memory (in the form of 'my-ism' or 'me-ism'), etc. Over and above them all what one needs is the consciousness and its endless source, i.e. soul, which will make the entire assembly, including the mind, intellect and ego, to work in the same way as a battery becomes necessary for a robot to work. In a broad sense, the essences of life in philosophical terms turn out to be the biological body (B) that includes senses of knowledge and action (SE), mind (M), intellect (I), ego (E) and the soul (SO).

Working of such an assembly of human Being (b) is judged again by human Beings, when placed in the 'field' of worldly objects (WO) consisting of both living and nonliving entities including the relations and worldly desires. These objects act as stimuli for the human Being enabling him to perceive and to react. In inanimate category, the Vedic science classifies such objects as *panca mahabhutas* (PM), namely earth, water, air, fire and ether which in fact are the representative of five cosmic states of matter, namely earth for solids, water for liquids, air for gases, fire for plasmons and ether (firmament) for space in which entire physical world is contained. In some sense, this latter class of worldly objects forms the part of both essentials for life (as there is no question of survival without them) and essences of life (as the human body is believed to be made up of them). We shall return to a detailed discussion of EOLs in Chapter 6.

2.4 BODY, MIND AND SOUL IN ACTION: DOMAINS OF THEIR WORKING

2.4.1 Spectrum of human experiences and actions

For a person, the words body, mind and soul respectively are the synonym of his gross, micro and causal existences of Vedic-science. The human- machine as described above in terms of essences of life (EOLs) is continuously working in a non-stop manner but in the presence of consciousness. The soul, when in action through consciousness, is the 'Being' or 'life principle' in the person. It is the transcendental power which vitalizes the body to act, the mind to feel and the intellect to think. In the absence of soul, they all behave as physical (P)-matter; otherwise they are epi-physical (EP)-matter. A working living Being as a whole is termed as special epi-physical (SEP)-matter, as it also contains the source of consciousness. Except for during the deep sleep or perhaps during the state of coma, the human Being constantly gathering experiences and performing actions accordingly, particularly after interacting with the outer world.

It is not difficult to have an idea as to how the proliferation of experiences and accordingly that of actions takes place. Note that each of our outer organ including five senses of knowledge in the body can interact with the outer world independently. Then mind does have its own many ways to gather the feeling about the object(s). If it is prepared to obey (which is not always possible, however, meditation helps in this respect), then intellect also has infinitely many ways to guide the mind and subsequently the body and the senses. It is this last step in which the lessons learnt from the performance of actions are stored in the faculty of memory as experiences. These experiences if collected for the first time in this or in previous (!) life span(s) at times become standards for further improvements by way of enabling the intellect accordingly.

Example 2.4.1: Seer-Seen Chain: When eyes see an object the object is seen and the eyes are seer. They really see it when the conscious mind is in coordination with eyes, otherwise they do not. Therefore, at the next stage the mind is seer and the eyes are seen. Similarly, the mind feels about the object precisely when the conscious intellect is in tune with the mind to discriminate the finer details of the object, like its nature, qualities, geometry, etc. At this stage the intellect is seer and the mind is seen. Once all this is done, then the information about the object (positive or negative) is stored as experience in the faculty of memory for its future use. Since this all happens with EOLs illuminated with consciousness— a characteristic of soul, therefore, the ultimate seer becomes the soul. To be more specific, while the Being b is the union of $\mathcal{G}$, $\mathcal{M}$ and $\mathcal{C}$ as $b \equiv \mathcal{G} \cup \mathcal{M} \cup \mathcal{C}$, the EOLs for each domain are identified as $\mathcal{G} \equiv \{WO, B, SE\}$, $\mathcal{M} \equiv \{M, I, E\}$, $\mathcal{C} \equiv \{SO\}$. Suppose a person tastes a sweet, he will feel the taste when his mind is coordinating with the tongue; otherwise a person in the deep sleep cannot feel it. Further, it is only the presence of intellect that can discriminate or tell the degree of sweetness. Once the sweetness, say that of a particular cake, is judged by the tongue and finally stored in the faculty of memory E, then it is E which retrieves the taste or the sweetness of the cake to express the same. This expression is possible only through limited words or actions and thereby debars one from expressing completely the reality of taste. The same, in fact, remains a matter of realization only by the soul.

In spite of the fact that there is a proliferation of actions and experiences due to different permutations and combinations of EOLs, there does exist a systematic ordering in them towards their classification. An example to this effect will elaborate the fact.

Example 2.4.2: Recall that the bottom of sea does exist and it is calm, quiet and stable with respect to the water and its waves.

Even the water in contact with the bottom is almost at rest, but as one proceeds from bottom to top disturbances and fluctuations start through variety of waves. Disturbances one can notice maximum at the top (water surface). Similar is the case with the quantity of human actions — apparently large at the body level, somewhat less at the mind level and minimum at the soul level. Since the fluctuations are seen mostly on the surface of water with huge depth, one can as well note the fact that the manifestations are only finite of the infinite un-manifest.

Note that all the experiences stored and the corresponding actions performed, are not of the same category in terms of quality and quantity as the 'human–machine' is working in both inner and outer domains. Depending upon the level of development of one's FOUs, No doubt, these experiences reflect in actions but they can end-up with any of the EOL. In such a situation one searches for the Universality (in terms of space, time and meditation variables) of experiences from the point of view of their survival as values in a society. Broadly speaking the entire gamut of human experiences and actions can be placed in three classes, namely the one's originating from the gross-body ($\mathcal{G}$) domain, the one's originating from the micro-body ($\mathcal{M}$) domain and the one's originating from the causal-body ($\mathcal{C}$) domain. $\mathcal{G}$–domain basically strives for the essentials for life, $\mathcal{M}$-domain for a betterment of $\mathcal{G}$-domain, and $\mathcal{C}$-domain for a betterment of both $\mathcal{M}$- and $\mathcal{G}$-domains. In summary, the life is nothing but a series of experiences. Note that the ultimate experiencer is the soul which in collusion with the sub-conscious part of $\mathcal{M}$ (cf. Sect. 3.1) stores the reminiscences of actions performed. With regard to this storage of reminiscences, the concept of Universality plays an important role and the same helps in filtering out some of them. To understand the Universality concept better, some lessons from physical theories may be helpful.

2.4.2 Lessons from Physical Theories I

It is worthwhile to highlight two important concepts of physics which are related to the dynamics of an object namely the concept of constant of motion or dynamical invariant and that of relativity. With a view to establishing the universality of physical laws, these concepts are explored earlier in the classical physics and in recent times in the context of modern physics. While there are seven constants of motion (energy, three components of each of the linear and angular momentum), relativity is also studied in the classical as well as in modern context with reference to the velocity of light. When we say that the total energy of a closed system is conserved, it means that it does not change with time and it is a constant of motion, i.e., it remains the same forever provided the same physical conditions prevail. In the same vein, one can as well have physical quantities which do depend on both space and time but can still be constant of motion, they are called dynamical invariants.

Similarly, for the relative motion there have been efforts to find a point at absolute rest, but without having one in physical theories, i.e., the search for inertial frames. At one time sun was considered to be at rest for planetary motion but later on this reference point was shifted to the centre of our galaxy for the motion of several solar systems including ours. Now it is considered somewhere else to describe the motion of galaxies and so on. But for laboratory experiments the physical theories are developed by assuming the centre of mass of the whole system of particles at rest. Even in this case one looks for the quantities (called relativistic invariants) which remain the same in all reference frames, i.e., they are not affected by the relative motion.

Whether they are the constants of motion, dynamical invariants or the relativistic invariants, once they exist and become available, they not only help in a better understanding of the natural phenomenon in terms of symmetries but also help in giving a universal character to physical laws. In the same vein, if the norms governing the behavior and actions of an individual or that of a society which, in turn, will define the ethical, moral or spiritual values are set in a space-time invariant or in a relativistic invariant manner, then they will carry the universal character, i.e., they will hold forever and everywhere may be with limited domains of workability. Some of these discussions are continued in Sect. 15.4.2.

Vedic science clearly prescribes such norms for all the three working domains, namely for $\mathcal{G}$- , $\mathcal{M}$- and $\mathcal{C}$-domains of a human Being through the so-called '*Sanātana Dharma*'. As one proceeds from $\mathcal{G}$-domain to $\mathcal{C}$-domain in terms of the gathered experiences and corresponding actions, the universality character in terms of the space-time invariance or the relativistic invariance of the norms increases and thereby makes the spiritual values as Universal. Moreover, the change in values appears more in the $\mathcal{G}$-domain, somewhat less in $\mathcal{M}$-domain and the least in the $\mathcal{C}$-domain and why should it not be so, after all in the $\mathcal{C}$-domain we are close to the point of rest. As a matter of fact, the change is noticeable when there is a changeless factor, i.e. the soul. An example will suffice to elaborate the meaning of these statements.

Example 2.4.3: Life as a rotation of potter wheel: Consider the motion of a potter wheel rotating on a pivot and the potter is preparing clay-vessels of all sizes and shapes. The points just above the pivot are almost at rest whereas those near the circumference of the wheel are in maximum motion and thus the change in the position of points appear faster near the circumference as compared to those at the centre or near the pivot. It could as well ideally be zero at a point just above the pivot.

Note the following points from this example:

(i) If one can visualize the circumference region as the $\mathcal{G}$-domain, then the $\mathcal{M}$-domain towards the centre but in the middle and the $\mathcal{C}$-domain in the central region of the flat wheel.

(ii) Changes are noticeable more in the circumference region than in the central region likewise in the $\mathcal{G}$-domain than in $\mathcal{C}$-domain.

(iii) If one wants to stop or start the wheel, then he has to apply relatively less force in the circumference region and more in the central region, may be ideally infinite force at the centre. Similarly, it requires more focused energy through meditation to enlighten the central soul-region as compared to that of the domain of worldly objects in the circumference region.

(iv) Faster the wheel moves, more is the tendency of $\mathcal{M}$- or $\mathcal{G}$-domains to fly apart from the centre (centrifugal force) for a non-rigid wheel. On the other hand, they remain just idle for slow or no motion. Similarly, spirituality remains a far cry for a fast-life person (or for a person with a turbulent mind) in spite of the fact that he is in the zone of maximum noticeable centrifugal force (consciousness).

2.4.3 Roles of mind and ego in defining the domains

Brain is the most complicated part of our biological body. In recent times there have been considerable efforts by neuroscientists and brain experts to identify the nerve centers or zones in the brain which are responsible for one's emotions, decisions and memory. Indirectly, scientists are in search of philosophical entities like mind, intellect and ego. But the question is whether they will succeed in their efforts or not. In spite of the fact they have succeeded in doing so for a few cases, the answer remains No as far as the understanding of entire gamut of human experiences and actions is concerned. The reason is simple— all such discoveries are based on the data collected using only the space-time mediated electromagnetic signals or such electronic devices. The phenomenon of consciousness or the consciousness in whose presence the brain works, is definitely beyond the space-time structure of Nature. Moreover, for modern scientists of Western thinking it will take some time to understand and digest the concept of consciousness or its plurality in human behavior and experiences.

With reference to psychological studies on mind, intellect and ego, they are also carried out using such physics-based devices to collect the data and analyze them using the statistical methods. Thus, the conclusions drawn from such empirical studies are not fool proof as far as the role of consciousness in human behavior is concerned. Such analytical studies may be successful for a group of persons or a society but not for an individual. In summary, an understanding of the phenomenon of consciousness in totality and its role in human actions is not yet in sight either by scientists or by psychologists in near future. In such a situation, there is no harm in exploring the Vedic wisdom on this aspect, particularly to find a plausible answer to the question of integrating body, mind and soul where one has to rely heavily on the understanding of the phenomenon of consciousness.

An immediate and practical approach to have a feel for the philosophical domain is the one suggested by yoga experts, i.e. by deep breathing or by controlling the breathing. The moment one thinks of taking deep breath or start with deep breathing, he immediately feels like entering a different zone from the physiological one and in no time a state of meditation becomes possible. In fact the meditation is a process which helps in diffusing the worries, negative thinking and takes an individual out of the state of depression. An outline to achieve this state is as follows: Sit calmly and start taking deep breath. Next allow all thoughts to flow in a natural way but keep a watch on their occurrence. A trick to do this is by dividing the micro-body in two parts, namely the gross part as a composition of gross components of each of M, I and E and the sub-conscious part as a composition of subtle components of each of M, I and E. The gross part of micro-body participates actively in the outer world processes through B and SE, while the sub-conscious part has the tendency to connect the being b to the domain of causal body or spirituality. It is the sub-conscious part that remains observer during the flow of thoughts, but stores all experiences from them in E. On the other hand, the gross part acts as a kind of sensor of thoughts during their flow (see, Fig. 3.1).

As it will be argued latter, the mind M offers first threshold to enter from $\mathcal{G}$ -domain to $\mathcal{M}$ -domain, i.e., from worldly values to ethical and moral values, and the ego E (particularly its subtle component) offers the second threshold to enter from $\mathcal{M}$–domain to $\mathcal{C}$-domain, i.e. from moral values to the spiritual values. For many of us it is not difficult to control the mind and enrich the zone of moral or ethical values as the fruit of actions in $\mathcal{M}$-domain but the suppressing of E (with reference to "my-ism" or "me-ism", self-conscience, desire for respect, praise, etc) is not an easy task even for seers and saints to enjoy the life of spiritual zone. Thus, the mind and the ego hold special status in all EOLs with regard to their roles in the performance of actions by an individual. An example will support some of these ideas:

Example 2.4.4: Thinking of the greatness of the ocean, once a well requested the ocean, "Sir, you are so great that you embrace and merge in yourself all big rivers and small drains, then why not me, just a small source?" Then ocean replied, "It is not the question of big or small, but that of boundaries. First you come out of your (rigid) boundaries and learn to flow, only then I can embrace you or merge you in myself". True, it is the boundary of self-conscience or ego that prevents a person from doing many good things. It is the boundary of ego E that keeps the Self separate from the non-Self; otherwise they are one and the same. As a matter of fact, the soul appears to be finite because of ignorance. When ignorance is destroyed, the Self reveals itself by itself.

2.5 BODY, MIND AND SOUL IN SEARCH OF PLEASURE, PEACE AND JOY

The (finite) soul when in tune with the (infinite) cosmic consciousness field, is characterized by its qualities like Eternity, Purity, Reality and Bliss. However, when it manifests in a Being, particularly the human Being some or many of these qualities do not reflect in it because of the limitations of the reflecting devices in the human Being. As a matter of fact it is the interplay between the non-Self and the Self that suppresses these qualities in the latter and brings in the multiplicity of these attributes. To be more specific, it is the intellect which allows such divisions and gives the feeling of pleasure and pain, peace and unrest, joy and sorrow; otherwise for a person in deep sleep or in coma many of these feelings are absent. In fact, it is the same eternal joy (Bliss) – a characteristic of soul, that manifests differently in the three domains, namely as pleasure in the $\mathcal{G}$–domain, as peace in the $\mathcal{M}$-domain and as joy in the $\mathcal{C}$-domain. As to how these manifestations are delusively understood when the nature of the soul becomes clear, it can be seen from the following example:

Example 2.5.1 (Chinmayanand, 1998, Verse 22): Consider the shining of the full moon on a water surface which is undergoing the ripple formation due to wind. If one watches the ripples or waves on the water surface, the reflected moon through them will appear as dancing. In fact the trembling that belong to the water are attributed through ignorance to the reflected moon dancing on it; like wise, the agency of action, of enjoyment and of the other limitations (which really belong to the mind) are delusively understood as the nature of the soul but in reality it is the game of shattered and disturbed mind. When the water calms down and becomes steady, we do not see the shattered moon on the water surface, rather it re-assembles to form one-whole image. Similarly, when one has purified mind and consolidated its strength by reconstructing it to be firm and steady, the glory of the Self gets automatically reflected in all its beauty, unshaken by the dualities around.

There are several individual-based parameters which not only control the quality and intensity of these feelings but also set the limits on their perception. This parametric dependence primarily arises from both internal causes like the level of developments of one's FOUs, or the evolution of his mindset function or the order of dressing of his EOLs with consciousness or his circumstances or the alike and external causes like space, time, environment etc. Although the quality, quantity and the extent to which these feelings take place differ from person to person, but here in what follows we discuss them with reference to a common man. With regard to the quality of these feelings, it appears in three colors namely *tamas*, *rajas* and *sātvik* as per Vedic science and in the spirit of three respective adjective degrees good, better and best. In fact, this trinity of *gunās* represents the three modes of working of *prakriti*. The quantity of their role in a particular process or phenomenon depends on the external stimuli or the sense-objects. The extent of enjoyment again lies in the domain of individual based parameters. Next we elaborate on these feelings at the levels of body , mind and soul.

2.5.1 Body in search of pleasure

Although entire 'body-system' (i.e., the human Being with all EOLs) comes into operation when a person comes in contact or interacts with an external sense-object, but corresponding to each sense of perception a specific type of sense-object is designated. In Vedic science there is one cosmic element associated with each sense of perception; for example, the following sequence is observed: ether-sound-ear; air-touch-skin; fire-shape- eyes; water-taste- tongue and earth-smell-nose. It may be noted that these are the individual-based parameters (as attributes of both inner and outer EOLs) which affect the success or the fruits of the concerned action during the process of interaction with a stimulant, of course at different levels of EOLs. As a result, the evolutes of three *gunās* or modes of *prakriti* in the form of worldly enjoyments as well as the means of attaining such enjoyments, immediately come into existence to decide the quality of the later. In other words, many of us go for pleasure out of these contacts and interactions with stimulant irrespective of their quality, i.e., whether they are of *sātvik-*, *rājasik-* or *tāmasik-*type. For example, ears go for nice words, eyes go for a pleasant view, nose goes for a pleasant smell, tongue for a tasty food and skin prefers a pleasant touch. With regard to the intensity of feeling of the pleasure, the following example will suffice:

Example 2.5.2 (Adi S'ankeracharya, Verse 78): In order to have a feel for the extremes of sensual pleasures certain cases in Nature are well known. For example, a deer becomes mad after the music, a moth becomes mad for the light of a lamp, male-elephant becomes mad for the mating-touch with his counterpart after having flavor of smell from her, a fish running for the taste dies sometimes and bees becomes mad for the smell. These are some peculiar ways for attaining the extreme of pleasure by nonhumans, but only with a single dominating sense of perception. What will really happen to a human Being who has five dominating senses of perception and all of them are capable of working at the same time. Naturally, a control on senses through the mind is necessary.

In this case, not only the senses involve themselves in their sense-objects, but also often both the parts of micro body, namely gross and sub-conscious parts are in tune with them. All this seems to be natural as far the way of life of a common man is concerned. It is just like swimming downstream of a river; otherwise to swim against the stream extra efforts need to be made by an individual by way of uplifting the level of development of his FOUs. Thinking as well as actions of such persons are body-dominated in collusion with the gross part of micro body. There is no question of working of the $\mathcal{C}$-domain.

2.5.2 Mind in search of peace and pleasure

As 'body' is synonym of gross body $\mathcal{G}\equiv$ {WO, B, SE}, the 'mind' here is also synonym of micro-body $\mathcal{M}\equiv$\{M,I,E\}. A common man whose actions are confined mostly to the $\mathcal{G}$–domain, gets satisfied by drawing sensual pleasure at large and peace in terms of emotional joy or rational delights which may be minimum. However, for an intellectual category of person (say philosopher/scientist) peace becomes primary compared to pleasure out of the interactions he had with the external world. For him, emotional joy or rational delights or the alike becomes the priority over sensual pleasure. With regard to the interactions with external world, they are mostly AAD and AAT type to have all pros and cons about the given experience or situation. If such persons are left in a luxurious life-style, then they draw pleasure only to a limit, i.e., only to the satisfaction of the gross part of micro-body. Their sub-conscious part, however, remains always in touch with higher goals, the attainment of which, in due course of time, will provide them peace through the success or fruit of actions thus performed. Such persons, if come to know the fact that even peace is temporal, circumstantial or environment-dependent, then they start looking for higher quality of peace, i.e., happiness or joy, which belongs to the domain of soul.

2.5.3 Soul in search of joy, peace and pleasure

It is an unwritten rule that as the level of development of FOUs of a person increases, his worldly needs and desires decrease. In the limiting case, it has been found that a yogi-category of person can survive almost with negligibly small needs or just by dwelling on five cosmic elements. In other words, as the experiences and actions of a person with regard to the world-order shift from $\mathcal{G}$-domain to $\mathcal{C}$-domain (generally via $\mathcal{M}$-domain), his spiritual tendencies increase and subsequently he starts searching for joy rather than starving for peace or sensual pleasure which basically are the space, time and circumstance dependent. Ideally speaking, one can as well starve for an eternal joy which is Universal, i.e., independent of space, time and also of circumstances. It is termed as Bliss. In this case, as per SMBG (cf. Verse 2.55), one feels satisfied in the Self (soul) through the Self (soul). Only yogi-category of persons can enjoy such a rare gift of God and such a person is born rarely in a society.

It may be mentioned that whether it is the feeling of joy, pleasure or peace, they are all the creations of mind. They, for example, are not perceived by a person in deep sleep when the mind ceases to exist.

Example 2.5.3: When one looks through a pair of green goggles everything looks green. However, when one looks at things with naked eyes, there is no green color. Therefore, the greenness (pleasure, peace or joy) is due to the glasses (mind).

2.6 CONCLUDING DISCUSSION

With a view to developing a formal framework for understanding the processes leading to the integration of body, mind and soul of a human Being an introductory survey of such phenomena and processes is carried out in these two chapters. To prepare a ground for the subject matter, outlines of several rather disconnected topics are presented in Chapter 1. In this chapter, after elaborating the meaning of the subject matter in modern context and tracing its roots in a philosophy, a composition of human Being in terms of essences of life is discussed. Then we identify the terms 'body', 'mind' and 'soul' with the Vedic concepts of gross, micro and causal existences of a human Being which in turn are expressible as sets of certain EOLs. Once we do that, then it becomes rather easier to identify the domains of working of these three existences. This also helps in analyzing the nature of their respective functions towards attaining the pleasure, peace or joy by an individual.

It may be mentioned that for an individual to have the success of the performed actions, the integration or coordination of his body, mind and soul is not only necessary but also sufficient. Further, to understand the mechanism of coordination better there is nothing wrong in using the analogies from physical concepts and theories. Lessons thus obtained from physics sometime offer guiding principle in such studies. In this spirit we have already used the concepts like dynamical invariants and relativity and plan to use some more in the forthcoming chapters. As a matter of fact, we plan to study and analyze the fundamental processes involved in human behavior and in the experiences related to an integrated body, mind and soul of a person in the same way as one studies them in the context of (i) atomic processes in terms of only a few elements of periodic table, (ii) nuclear processes in terms of a few nucleons, and (iii) elementary particle processes in terms of a few building blocks of the Universe, or for that matter the processes in chemistry in terms of only a few selective ions.

Further Reading

For a discussion of the Self and non-Self, see (Kaushal, 2011, p. 406); for a discussion on models in science, see (Kaushal, 2011, Appendices B and C) and (Kaushal, 2003); for some of the examples presented in this chapter, see (Chinmayanand, 1998). For a discussion on dynamical invariants see (Kaushal, 1998) and on relativity, see (Goldstein, 1981, p. 275).

High Skill Exercises and Projects

2.1 Elaborate on the meanings of (i) world-order and its maintenance, (ii) creative release. Discuss the role of integration of body, mind and soul in the success of an action.

2.2 How do the meanings of the term 'psychophysics' as used by Fechner, and the one used in the present book, differ ? For this purpose, prepare a summary of concepts, models and phenomena of theoretical physics (cf. Sects. 2.4.2, 6.2, 12.1, 12.5.1 and 15.4.2) which are used to analyze a variety of psycho-processes at different stages of development of the subject.

2.3 In the series of examples of manifestation of an un-manifest in Sect.1.2 add two more cases — one from sciences and other from humanities or social sciences.

2.4 In the series of Examples 1.3.1-1.3.4, add two more cases (e.g., one is that of car driving) in which the trio of space, time and consciousness works in harmony and with a comparable role of each of its constituents.

2.5 How do the essentials for life and the essences of life differ? List them and describe their role in the existence and survival of a human Being.

2.6 Discuss how the spiritual thinking and the nature of *sankalpâs* affect the integration of body, mind and soul and subsequently the success of an action.

2.7 What morals and lessons does one actually draw from Examples 1.5.2 and 1.5.3?

2.8 Analyze the Example 2.4.1 of seer-seen chain for one case of each of the other four senses of knowledge, namely ear for music, nose for smell, skin for touch and eyes for external beauty, shape and size.

2.9 Having lessons from Example 2.4.4, think of other example(s) from daily life which can elaborate on the mind and the ego as two thresholds (barriers) to attain the (supreme) Self.

2.10 A story based on Example 2.5.3: A woman living in her flat watches every morning through her window on the drying cloths of the neighbor in their balcony and makes comments on the cleanliness of clothes and tells her husband about it every day. This act of wife goes on for several days. Husband got fed-up with these same comments of his wife every day. One day he got up early in the morning and cleaned the glass of their window and later, when wife gets up , she as usual watches the drying clothes of the neighbor through her window and notices the improvement in the cleanness. She felt happy that neighbors have finally become wiser in washing the clothes cleanly. Then her husband explains the role of the glass in describing the nature of cleanness. What moral do you draw from this story in view of Example 2.5.3?

2.11 Define the term 'happiness' in terms of pleasure and joy as per Sect. 2.5. Explain how it is linked with the eternal joy.

2.12 Judging the quality of a person: The quality of a person is ascertained from the response of his senses to sense-objects. If it is negative then his senses are under control; if it is positive, then they are not in control. It is the conscience (force) from inside which decides the nature of the response. Consider this process and analyze the same with reference to three major vices, namely lust, anger and greed in the personality of a person. (Hint: SMBG, Ch.2).

PART A

PSYCHOPHYSICS: THE SCIENCE OF THE SELF

Chapter 3
SUBJECTIVE AND OBJECTIVE SCIENCES

3.1 SUBJECTIVE AND OBJECTIVE ASPECTS OF A CONCEPT

The subjective and objective flavors of a concept can be understood in more than one way. First, in view of Example 2.4.1, the seer-seen chain is nothing but a subject-object chain with ultimate doer as soul. When the consciousness flows outward, i.e., towards WO to understand the world- or cosmic-order with the help of outer world accessories it is the objective flavor of the concept that dominates; otherwise when it flows inward, i.e., towards SO to understand the same but with inner world accessories, then it is the subjective flavor again of the same concept.

Second, in the process of understanding the same world-order, while the philosopher-category of person rely more on the subjective flavor, the scientist-category of person goes with the objective flavor. Naturally, for the latter category person the space-time structure of Nature— a creation of consciousness, becomes an important aspect of study and that too in an objective style, whereas its role is minimum or zero in the studies by the former category person.

Third, as mentioned in Sect. 2.4.3 and displayed in Fig.3.1, the micro-body **M** of a human Being can be considered as consisting of two parts— the gross and subconscious parts. Note that the gross part of **M** is relatively more active in common man and scientist-category of persons and this make them to have an objective view of the world-order, whereas it just appears in a balanced form in philosopher and yogi-category of persons. The subconscious part however dominates in the latter and accordingly moulds them to take a subjective attitude towards the world-order. A rational thinking with subjective attitude gives birth to subjective science in the same way as the rational thinking with objective attitude gives the birth to objective science.

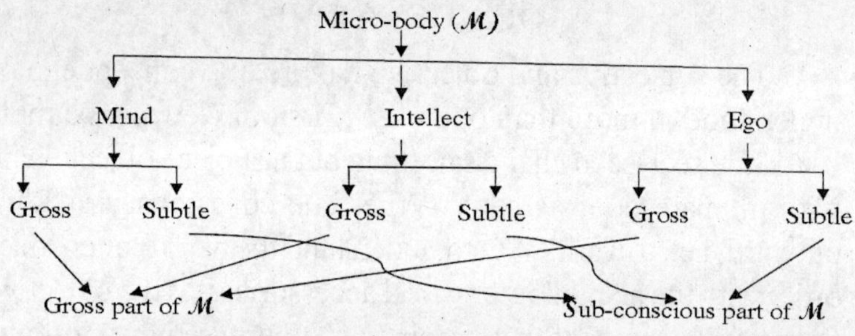

Fig. 3.1: Schematic display of as how the micro-body M splits into gross and sub-conscious parts.

3.2 SOME REMARKS ON THE RESEARCH METHODOLOGY FOLLOWED IN MODERN TIMES

It is the rational thinking that remains in the background of the scientific temper and also gives birth to creativity. In fact, the growth of creativity is the true measure of progress of human race in general. In recent times, this has become a fashion to give scientific flavor to almost every discipline of knowledge and study the same in an objective style often times by using the language of mathematics.

In objective sciences, namely in physics, chemistry and biology, one follows the following research methodology to study a phenomenon in Nature. A scientist first observes a phenomenon, then collects the data on that and tries to look for a possible correlation among the data. Once the correlation among the data is traced then that helps in establishing a law and the same at the next stage is used to make the predictions. These predictions are later on verified by experiments. Once all this goes through smoothly, the scientist feels satisfied from his study of the phenomenon.

This methodology is not only restricted to hard disciplines like the ones mentioned above but in recent times it has also been extended to study the soft disciplines like social science, behavioral science, psychology and economics. To visualize the phenomenon in physical terms certain analogies, which in turn give birth to models, are used at the stage when formulating the law out of the correlations found in the data. These models, at times constrained with so many assumptions and postulates, however, describe only the partial truth in Nature and that too after they become in tune with experiments.

It may be mentioned that in hard disciplines the objects of study basically are the inanimate entities (even in biology while studying the physiology or the dynamics of inner contents of the body, the role of consciousness is tactfully avoided) and the laws so derived work successfully only within experimental limits. On the other hand, in soft disciplines the objects of study are the animate entities like the human Beings or animal kingdom and the laws are derived mostly on the basis of statistical studies. These laws are not as rigorous as in the hard disciplines because the dynamics of an individual, as we have seen in Chapters 1 and 2, in itself is very complicated, then what to say of a collection of individuals. No doubt, the external environment can be maintained to be the same at the time of collecting the data but what is the guarantee that the consciousness or the free-will of each individual will remain the same to the desired degree of accuracy. Moreover, an important question that remains with these studies is that as to what extent one can rely on the statistical laws derived basically using the inanimate dice.

While this methodology still adopted by the experts of soft disciplines and also by the experimentalists of hard disciplines, theoretical workers in hard disciplines somehow are not satisfied with such empirical studies of a phenomenon. They rather look for formal and rigorous approaches in theoretical terms to explain the same set of data but at the most fundamental level and in a unified way. To this effect, the search for unified theories in physics and the subject of genetics in biosciences are a few examples of such developments. In soft disciplines, however, it is going to be a two-step study. In the first part, one should study the human Being in terms of essences of life and then the study of collection of human Beings in terms of essentials for life. Our aim in this part of the book is to present one such a frame work within which the entire gamut of human experiences and actions can be understood at the most fundamental level.

3.3 SEARCH FOR LAWS IN SUBJECTIVE SCIENCE

3.3.1 Formal and empirical laws

In view of the varying spectrum of human understanding in a society, the knowledge component of a culture has been flourishing in two possible ways, namely proliferation and abstraction, at all points of time in the history. While proliferation aspect of knowledge is attributed to the frequent and maximum use of analogies, simile, metaphor, parallelisms, etc. by a common man to elaborate the same fact repeatedly, the abstraction aspect is however linked with the presence of higher strata of seers and saints in the society. The abstraction aspect is like a mathematical formula, which if designed once then the proliferation aspect is nothing but like solving plenty of examples on that basis. To clarify these concepts, we further cite some examples here from hard disciplines (cf. (Kaushal, 2003)) and postpone the cases from soft discipline to the next subsection.

Example 3.3.1: Recall the Pythagoras theorem which states that in a right angled triangle the square of hypotenuse is equal to the sum of the squares of other two sides. The proliferation aspects of this result are its applications to dozens of problems of day-to-day life relating to the height and distance and to millions of problems in geometry itself. The abstraction aspect on the other hand, is that this theorem is a particular case of the well known Diophantine problem.

Example 3.3.2: Recall the Newton's equations of motion. The proliferation side of them are their applications to hundreds of problems in dynamics in different situations. The abstraction aspect, on the other hand, is that these equations can be derived from the same Newton's second law of motion, or for that matter this second law of motion is a particular case of Lagrange's equation of motion which in turn are derivable from the Hamilton's principle of least action— a feature that also exists in human behavior and action.

Example 3.3.3: Recall the four basic laws of electromagnetism, namely Gauss's laws in electrostatics and in magnetism, Faraday's law of electromagnetic induction and Ampere's circuital law. All these four laws have very wide applications in electrodynamics and in electrical engineering. In fact it is the Faraday law of electromagnetic induction that has revolutionized the life style in many different ways by providing a number of house hold appliances. This is their proliferation aspect. On the other hand, these laws have roots in Maxwell's equations which in turn are the particular cases of Lagrange equations derived for the electromagnetic field in general. This is their abstraction aspect.

Thus, we have seen that the empirical version of a law in the beginning is phenomenon dependent, i.e., it may be different for different phenomena. Later, however, the empirical laws pertaining to a particular category of phenomena, turn out to have roots in a generalized concept and thereby giving birth to a formal (generalized) version of the law. Further this formal version keeps on changing with the stage of abstraction. Another example to this effect is as follows:

Example 3.3.4: Boyles and Charles laws basically are empirical laws. They are, however, derivable from the same (formal) kinetic theory of gases, which again has roots in the classical statistics for thermal systems.

These are the examples borrowed from a hard discipline like physics, but note that similar has been the trend with other hard disciplines as well as with all the soft disciplines, may not be in mathematical terms but definitely at the conceptual level. In fact, in soft disciplines, the proliferation aspect is very common which helps in developing many more empirical laws. However, there is a scarcity of formal theories in these disciplines. The abstraction is normally carried out while studying the philosophical foundations of a subject. Since the human Being and the related dynamics are the main objects of study in soft disciplines, such studies, however, remain incomplete in the absence of a clear picture of a functional human Being in terms of his EOLs.

3.3.2 Empirical laws and the facts governing the human behavior and experiences

The wisdom of old persons and thought in terms of their sayings and proverbs offer certain undeniable facts which at times also work as laws governing the dynamics of an individual and of a society as well. We shall return to some of these details in Chapter 8. Vedic science provides many empirical laws, of course some of them originate from the highest degree of abstraction, which are useful for practical living. Swami Parthasarathy (Parthasarathy, 1992), perhaps for the first time, has made an attempt to identify some of these laws and facts in 'Vedanta Treatise', from the point of view of a common man. In what follows we list some of them with plausible elaborations:

1. The spiritual development of a person is inversely proportional to his worldly requirement.
2. The fundamental quality of human mind is that it broods over memories of the past or over expectations of results which can come in future. It hardly remains in the present. Vedanta provides ways and means of controlling the mind.
3. Knowledge proceeds from known to unknown, i.e. the knowledge of anything can be conveyed only in terms of known factors. Numerous factors stuffed into the brain cannot provide with a grain of knowledge, unless they are expressed through known. In some sense this hints and suggests the proliferation of the knowledge that exists possibly in an abstract form well inside the human Being or in cosmos.
4. The fundamental principle of living is evolution towards higher. One should not be static but keep on flowing like river to reach the goal in an insistent and persistent manner. Where there is stagnation, there is decay, disease and death.
5. As are the experiences, so is life. In fact life takes a turn for the better.
6. World is ever changing. Nothing in this world remains static; "change or perish" is the law of Nature.
7. Imperfection is inherent in Nature. One should not complain. That is the nature of the world. Keep on striving and correcting until the state of absolute perfection within the Self is achieved.
8. Environment and circumstances keep changing all the time. As long as the world exists there will be change

and struggle. There can be no static millennium. A person has to meet this problem of life by adaptation and re-adaptation to the recurring changes of the world.

9. One can find peace and harmony only by purifying his inner personality. When one purifies himself, he finds that the world is purified.
10. The characteristic feature of life is motion, activity or energy. The living Being grows, moves about and performs all sorts of activity and not the dead one. The law of evolution impels all living Beings to keep moving. Evolution is marked by striving and struggling in life. Where there is no effort and exertion, there is degradation and death.
11. One has to move with time. Time marches on. If one does not keep pace with time he will devolve. Even a society or nation which does not progress with time, will be ruined.
12. One is attracted by the worldly objects because their pleasures are instantaneous. The happiness that is found within oneself is bitter to start with. But it develops later into enlarging ripples of bliss. It is a strange phenomenon, sorrow appears in a mask of joy and joy appears in a mask of sorrow.
13. True happiness, born out of inner purification, is that which is like poison at first but in the end is like nectar. The false happiness, on the other hand, arising from the union of senses with their objects is that which at first like nectar but in the end like poison.
14. As soon as one comes out from the inactive (*tamas*) phase to the active (*rajas*) phase, he gets involved and entangled in his activities and thereby becomes attached to things and Beings of the world. The fact is that as much as he has possessed anything, he has been possessed and ob-

sessed. The moment he claims possessiveness he is possessed by his own possessions.

These laws and facts give some glimpses of as how a person should live in and interact with this world for a happy and peaceful life. As it can be seen, most of these laws pertain to the role of an individual in a society or nation, however some of them (e.g., law numbers 2,5,9,12 and 13) definitely take one to the dynamics of inner EOLs, i.e., they link with the **M**-domain. Hence, rank-wise they are one order higher as far as the abstraction aspect of knowledge is concerned. They basically offer guidance for the success of higher quality actions than that offered by the rest. In fact, the laws found for the actions of **M**-domain at times are very crucial towards the success of an action in the outer world. Note that the laws of **M**-domain while connect to **G**-domain at one end, they also connect with **C**-domain (i.e. with spirituality) at the other end. However, the abstraction aspect of knowledge for the **C**-domain further becomes of higher order. In summary, as one proceeds from **G**-domain to **C**-domain, the subjectivity in one's attitude increases.

3.4 SEARCH FOR A FORMAL BASIS OF EMPIRICAL LAWS

Note that the viability of these empirical laws in human behavior and experiences cannot be denied. While the intuition and wisdom of old persons may have been possible sources of these laws, it remains doubtful whether one has ever bothered for a formal basis for them or not, as one generally does in physical theories. Naturally, for the formal basis, if the necessity is felt then the same has to come from the Science of the Self. Clearly, the social science dealing with the collection of individuals is out-rightly ruled out. The subject of psychology alone in which the studies are focused around a particular EOL, i.e. mind, cannot provide such a basis. It is true that the studies in these disciplines in recent times have taken a new turn in the sense that the comparative studies and use of models have done a great deal of fine-tuning of the subject matter, but the fact is that the approaches adopted for this purpose are still empirical in nature. It is only the subject of philosophy which is capable of providing such a basis. This philosophy again has to be a perfect one in the spirit of Sect. 2.2 and it should be capable of accommodating the explanations of entire gamut of human experiences and actions. Further, such a philosophy has to originate at the most fundamental level out of the dynamics of EOLs.

It is not that the type of empirical laws presented above or the similar ones exist only in Vedic literature, some of them are rather universal and also exist in other cultures and religions of the world in one form or the other. In other cultures however, their foundation remains weak and the laws remain totally empirical. In Vedic literature, there exists a profound description of actions of each domain in terms of corresponding EOLs. Not only this, there does exist an abstraction of knowledge of highest degree of which these empirical laws turn out to be the proliferation aspect at certain stage. Some possible reasons as to why the Vedic wisdom is not well recognized in modern times, in spite of its richness in quality and quantity, are (i) Vedic seers never bothered for their name and fame, and (ii) in spite of an in-built rationality in the ideas, their quantification through models or through mathematization could not be pursued. For these reasons, the knowledge remained mostly subjective, intuition-based and a matter of realization in spite of its very practical applications in day-to-day life.

3.5 CONCLUDING DISCUSSION

With a view to preparing a ground for the forthcoming chapters a discussion of subjective and objective sciences is carried out in this chapter. As the Science of the Self falls under the subjective category, some of its aspects are highlighted here. For example, while the proliferation aspect of knowledge takes place in the objective domain, the subjective domain mostly deals with its abstraction aspect. In fact, this concept of abstraction and proliferation aspects of knowledge also works with reference to pure and applied aspects of the subjects like physics and mathematics in an analogous manner (see, (Kaushal,2003)).

It is argued that the empirical laws whether belong to subjective science or to objective science represent the proliferation aspect of knowledge. On the other hand, the formal version of these laws seems to have roots in the abstraction aspect of knowledge. While several empirical laws and facts governing the human behavior and experiences are cited here, the Universality of some of them in every culture and religion is highlighted. As far as the search for a formal basis of empirical laws in the domain of subjective science is concerned, it has to be pursued in a perfect philosophy like the one described in Vedic science.

***Further Reading*:**

For further discussion on subjective and objective sciences, see (Kaushal, 2011, Chapter 6); for further discussion on abstraction and proliferation aspects of knowledge, see (Kaushal, 2003, Chapters 5 and 6); for more empirical laws in human behavior and experiences, see (Parthasarathy, 1992) and (Kaushal, 2011, Chapter 5).

High Skill Exercises and Projects

3.1 Compare the seer-seen chain of Example 2.4.1 with the subject-object chain introduced in Sect.3.1.

3.2 Explain how the gross and sub-conscious parts of micro body **M** play roles in identifying objective and subjective aspects of a concept, respectively.

3.3 "Tendency of putting the available knowledge in a nut-shell defines the process of abstraction, whereas variety of its applications in the outer world defines the process of proliferation". In view of this statement analyse the Examples 3.3.1-3.3.4 and seek a justification of the same.

3.4 To justify the statement of Exercise 3.3, find some examples from soft disciplines like humanities and social sciences. [Hint: Pick some capsule verses from SMBG (say, from Ch.2) and discuss their applications in the behavioral domain].

3.5 Attempt to trace some examples from human behavior and experiences, family and society for each of the empirical laws listed in Sect. 3.3.2. [For example, with regard to the happiness discussed in laws 12 and 13, note the following story: Once a person asked the honey bee, "you collect every drop of honey after going to thousands of flowers and putting a lot of labor and efforts. But see that people take it away in no time: Do you not feel unhappy about it?". Honey bee replied, "Well, people just take away the honey only but not the art of extracting the honey. Therefore, there is no question of becoming unhappy". Note the height of satisfaction or happiness of honey bee].

3.6 Write a paragraph on how the subjectivity in one's attitude increases when he proceeds from **G**-domain actions to **M**-domain actions.

3.7 Analyze and explain how the formal basis of the empirical laws pertaining to human behavior and experiences (cf. Sect. 3.3.2) has roots in the science of the 'Self'.

Chapter 4

THE SELF AND ITS UNDERSTANDING: WESTERN PERSPECTIVE

The word 'self' has been used differently in different contexts again as a noun, adjective, prefix or suffix. As per the dictionary meanings 'self' means "person's or thing's own individuality or essence" or "person or thing as an object of introspection or reflexive action" or in general it is used in the sense as "without external agency or assistance". While the last meaning appropriately hints us to the EOL, soul, the other meanings also revolve around the set of inner EOLs including the soul. Recall that it is the Self (soul) or its derivative consciousness that plays an important role in the entire process of integrating the body, mind and soul of an individual towards the performance of an action. Therefore, we plan to devote this and the next chapter in discussing and analyzing briefly the meanings of this word with reference to the Western and Indian ways of thinking, respectively in historical perspective. Note that in Western schools of thought the word spirit is used more frequently than the word 'Self' or 'soul'.

4.1 VIEWS OF PHILOSOPHER-SCIENTISTS OF EARLY DAYS

In historical perspective it appears that the concepts of matter and spirit had been in discussion since the origin of human race. The Western thinkers were however bewildered mostly by the natural phenomena that occur in the outer world.

Their thinking and accordingly the philosophy grew mostly around the 'matter' in terms of its structure and existence in the universe. In general, it was the space time structure of Nature that had been explored to its highest degree in the Western schools of thought by way of developing the tools of geometry, arithmetic, algebra and analysis. As far as the quest for 'spirit' and its characteristics is concerned it remained at low pitch. Its knowledge and discussion confined mostly to the 'second-class' of intellectuals and that too not in a good taste from the point of view of social working. As a matter of fact the concept of 'spirit' was largely explored in the context of occult sciences. In the Eastern context it has been the other way round, i.e., more emphasis on the exploration of 'spirit' or soul and somewhat less or equal emphasis on the exploration of matter but that too in a subjective style.

Another question that puzzled the minds of Western thinkers for quite sometime (and even today it is a matter of research for them) was whether it is the concept of 'mind over matter' (i.e., the power of mind to control and influence the body and the physical world in general) or that of 'matter over mind' which dominates the maintenance of world-order. Clearly in Indian philosophy which falls under the domain of subjective science, the 'mind over matter' has been the subject of exploration, whereas the concept of 'matter over mind' prevailed in Western philosophy. In this philosophy the exploration of Nature was mainly focused around its space-time structure – an aim of objective science. Further, for this case the famous biologist Francis Crick suggests the following hypothesis: 'You, your joys and sorrows, your memories and ambitions, your sense of personal identity and freewill, are in fact no more than the behaviour of a vast assembly of nerve cells and their associated molecules'. In a nut-shell 'you are nothing but a pack of neurons', i.e., the human Being is not more than a matter entity.

For modern science it might take centuries to make these statements viable and that too for a robot, for the human Being however this philosophy does not work in practice by any standard. The following example will further support such observations on this philosophy.

Example 4.1.1: Consider the situation in which a person plans to cross the road at the zebra-mark. Here, in general, all the three parameters space, time and consciousness play a role on equal footing in a successful and safe crossing of the road. According to the Western view, here the Fermat principle of least time and/or the Hamilton principle of least action would suffice to determine the optimal path. However, according to the Eastern or Indian view, in addition to these principles, the consciousness of varying degree manifesting through various body parts or through the mindset function of the person crossing the road will also play an important role. In other words, the person is free to take judicious decision to run or walk on the road by adjusting a convenient speed, depending upon the availability of the remaining time for the crossing. As a matter of fact the optimization now need to be done for a more realistic situation in which a parameter for consciousness also appears in addition to that for space and time (Kaushal, 2011).

Thus, for understanding the complete truth in Nature the Western approach is from the objective domain to the subjective one and that too by using mostly the objective tools and apparatus. Even modern researches are based on this concept of matter over mind. In these studies, the efforts have been to look for the philosophical entities like mind, intellect or ego, if at all they are there inside the human body. This is done by way of just identifying certain centers in the brain responsible for the attributes of these entities like emotions, decisions, etc. In such million dollar projects, not only biochemists, biophysicists, physiologists including brain and neuroscientists but also psychologists and parapsychologists are jointly or independently involved. In fact studying the characteristics of these EOLs in parts makes sense, but if they succeed in identifying these inner EOLs in the body (which in some sense appears to be an impossible task since a living Being is a highly complicated (nonphysical) open system unlike any other open system in physics) then this will correspond to the phrase 'matter over mind' and thereby the behavior of a living Being will become completely controllable by a machine.

4.2 PHILOSOPHY OF IMMANUEL KANT

About 250 years ago German philosopher Immanuel Kant advocated a fine description of objective component of ultimate reality in Nature in terms of its space-time structure and in society in terms of moral values. In fact, similar concepts have formed the basis for the development of modern science in the West. No doubt, such thinking began with Descartes and Galileo, but Kant was the first one to become conscious of these things. This kind of stock taking of knowledge was basically a criticism and Kant himself called his great books as critiques — the "Critique of pure Reason"; the "Critique of Practical Reason", the "Critique of Judgment". He called his philosophy as the "Critical philosophy" or "Critical Idealism". As far as the actions of an individual and their execution in the day-to-day life are concerned, the same appear in the philosophy of Kant through the principle of morality which he has advocated in great detail in his later "Critiques". Kant regarded human actions as "phenomenal" when looked at them from an anthropological point of view. As a result these actions are subject to the law of cause and effect.

According to Kant, we are born and grow with different natures, which in turn lead to different likes and dislikes, inclination and disinclination, temptations, temperaments, abilities to perform an act, etc. These differences, though dealing with matters of fact over which we have no control, are attributed to different external environments to which an individual is subjected and responds differently in accordance with the principle of causality. Human actions, thus, are considered as the result of interaction of character and environment and are not to be praised or blamed but understood.

In view of the fact that there are many inconsistencies and gaps that appear in the philosophy of Kant, it cannot offer a unified theory of human actions. For example, in this philosophy causality appears at different planes and there are several missing links in it, particularly when he considers a sharp separation of moral and phenomenal worlds. On the other hand, as we shall see in the next chapter, Vedanta philosophy offers a complete package for such descriptions.

In summary, Western philosophy emerged and grew under the four heads, namely meta-physics, epistemology, ethics, and aesthetics. In metaphysics knowledge is developed around the search for ultimate reality in Nature; in epistemology one looks for the origin, validity and limits of that knowledge; ethics deals with the question of morality and judgment in a society, and finally a beautiful description of Nature (mostly described in the domain of objective science) forms the part of aesthetics.

4.3 CHANGING TRENDS IN MODERN CHURCHES

Two major cultures flourishing in the West and nourishing the spirituality are those emerging out of Quran and Bible. Both these religions while talk of the ultimate reality (cosmic consciousness) in one form or the other, however, lack from the description of a proper methodology to be followed to achieve or digest that reality. The Quran while emphasizing on a unique un-manifest and formless reality, also reminds an individual about the same very frequently during the daily and multi-times prayer so that a person remains constantly aware of his limitations during the performance of actions in the world. The Bible, on the other hand, talks of love and affection— the characteristics of the ultimate reality and emphasizes on its spreading and propagating through out the man-made and God-made worlds. And why should it not be? After all it is the love — the force of attraction in its universal form that is prevailing all over in cosmos among both the animate and inanimate entities, then what to say of the planet earth. While we shall return to a detailed discussion of this feature of ultimate reality later (cf. Sect. 8.1), the Bible, however, emphasizes on it through (a) a give and take principle, (b) motherhood, and through (c) friendship like that of lover and beloved as it appears on the Valentine day.

As mentioned before, the change is natural and every culture for its existence and survival has to go with this change, like physical theories have to go with improved experiments. In this respect while Islam appears to be static, the Churches are constantly making efforts to adopt the changing mood of the masses and that two after a long period of struggle. From this point of view, certain categories of Churches have not only started accepting the scientific truths but also the evergreen truths of Eastern philosophy about the Self and its manifestations. This will definitely help in bringing the entire world together as a single family in view of the contracted space and time in the present age of science.

4.4 VIEWS OF PHILOSOPHER-SCIENTISTS OF MODERN TIMES

While looking for an explanation of natural phenomenon in theoretical terms, particularly the one in which the human Being or its consciousness is directly involved, modern scientists tactfully avoid the role of consciousness or that of the Self. However, in view of now available advanced technologies (in terms of computers on theoretical front and in terms of fairly accurate data on experimental front), one can how long afford to deny the role of such concepts in the explanation of data. This situation holds for the data collected on both microscopic and macroscopic systems. Note the following well known examples in this regard.

Example 4.4.1: Recall the roles of Schrodinger quantum mechanics and of Heisenberg uncertainty principle in successfully explaining the data on microscopic systems. But note that the former is founded on a probabilistic concept by way of discarding the role of the Self whereas in formulating the latter principle the role of consciousness in defining the uncertainties in the measurement is ignored. For these reasons, it is worth-while to remind here the statement of Einstein as "God never plays dice" or the concept of 'extended apparatus' of von Neumann in which the human Being becomes the part of the measuring device.

Example 4.4.2: A monkey wants to reach the top of a pole of height say 13 feet. In every upward jump he covers 3feet but slides down 1foot because of the smoothness of the pole. Now the question is as in how many jumps the monkey will be able to reach the top? Obviously, the answer is in six jumps. Here we make assumptions and idealize the situation. We ignore the role of free will or of consciousness of the monkey and solve the problem perhaps for a robot and not for a monkey.

With regard to the Self and its understanding modern scientists seem to be confused for more than one reason. Firstly, their philosophical background does not permit them to think beyond mind and subconscious mind. The Self appears to them as black box. Secondly, the knowledge of Self belongs to the domain of subjective science in which the laws of objective science as such do not work. Now there are two possibilities either seek the extension of the existing laws to the subjective domain by way of accounting for the consciousness or else find alternative laws of which the existing laws of objective science turn out as particular cases. Handling either of the situations is not an easy task unless one understands the Self or its attribute like consciousness in totality.

In this regard the ignorance of the Self or of its attributes on the part of a theoretical scientist while remains one aspect, in another aspect scientists in general are divided even on the issue of accommodating these 'Self'-inspired concepts in physical or biological theories. No doubt the difficulties of different types may be there at research level but the difference of opinion is seen even at the school level. Recently, there has been such a controversy in the US society with regard to incorporating the concept of Intelligent Design in the Darwin theory while teaching the later in the class room. For them, both the cases of intelligent Design and the natural selection of Darwin were under scrutiny. Some schools of thought were convinced that the Universe was possibly created not out of random mutation and natural selection but by an Intelligent Design of an unseen power. The latter part was, however, not approved of for the school curriculum. But in reality it is not so. Intelligent Design of an unseen power does play a role. This will become clear from the following example.

Example 4.4.3: Suppose a person wants to reach the top of the highest mountain. There are two possibilities; he can proceed in a specific direction with the highest point in view, or he can as well start walking in a random direction with a finite probability of reaching the top. In both cases the chance of reaching the top is equal if one keeps aside the question of space and time. In fact the difference in the two cases arises when the role of space and time is brought in and that is important in the material world and perhaps not that much important at the higher (spiritual) level. The former choice corresponds to intelligent Design and the latter to natural selection. As a matter of fact the decision to opt for a particular choice depends on the level of development of FOUs of the person and accordingly his actions will emerge.

As far as the consciousness aspect of the Self is concerned it has been investigated recently in several contexts. For example, attempts have been there to understand the age-old problem of mind-body interaction but now in terms of mind –brain complex using the language of quantum neuro-dynamics. British mathematical physicist Roser Penrose advocates his own ways to account for the consciousness in physical theories. In another case, the role of consciousness in a physical phenomenon can possibly be understood through the so-called "top-down bottom-up" approach. In this approach, the hierarchy of cause and effect in a complex system (like human Being) is analyzed and compared at different levels, namely in "bottom-up" (i.e., from materialistic domain to the spiritual one) and "top-down" (i.e., from spiritual domain to the materialistic one) actions. This will become clear from the following example.

Example 4.4.3: An example demonstrating the top-down and bottom-up actions: suppose one plans to find answer to the question as to why an aircraft is flying. In the bottom-up case, it flies because air molecules move at different speed over the top and the bottom wing surfaces to create a pressure difference that lifts the airplane against gravity – Bernoulli's principle. In the same-level terms, the airplane is flying because the pilot is flying it, after a rigorous training or testing process to develop the requisite skills. However, in the top-down picture, an airplane flies because it was designed to fly! A team of engineers at the same point worked within a historical context of the development of metallurgy, combustion, lubrication, aeronautics, machine tools, computer aided design and so on. Further, all this occurred in the economic context of a society and with a need for transportation. On the other hand, a brick can not fly as it is not designed to fly, i.e., the intentions, will-power or desire was very much there to do the job. Here lies the subjective component in the whole discovery which came down to the practical level.

4.5 CONCLUDING DISCUSSION

From the above survey it appears that in the Western schools of thought the understanding of the Self and its role in human actions still remains insufficient from the point of view of projecting it in an objective style. The studies have been carried out mostly in a 'patchwork' or 'piecemeal' manner. As a matter of fact, since the days of Cartesian partition, the development of science in the West took place on the basis of conscious distinction between the 'physique' (objective reality) and 'psyche' (subjective perception). In this duality scenario, the role of God, if any, was supposed to be confined only to the latter while the former developed strictly in a mechanistic manner and the laws governing the world-order were formulated accordingly. There was a kind of over confidence in the techniques of objective science, particularly after the startling successes of Newtonian mechanics and the allied disciplines of optics and thermodynamics which seemed to leave nothing indeterminate.

It may be mentioned that in the West the experts of law and order (and that too of the man-made material world) at times decide the imparting of these realities of life to a common man or school kids rather than a person directly realizes them from Nature, of course with an 'open eye'. In summary, the Western philosophy still remains inadequate as far as the globalization of spiritual concepts in modern times is concerned.

Further Reading:

For further details of the trio of space, time and consciousness see (Kaushal, 2011, p. 240); for the philosophy of Immanuel Kant, see (Kant, 1883) and (Lindsay); for details of Schrodinger quantum mechanics, uncertainty principle, and mind-body problem, see (Goswami, 1990; Goswami, 1992; Stapp, 2009); for more discussion on Intelligent Design and Darwin theory, see (Richards, 1999; Jhunjhunuwala, 2005; Chalmers, 1996; Fisher and Dean, 2006; Townes, 2015); for details on bottom-up top-down concept, see (Laughlin, 2005; Ellis, 2005) and on limits on science, see (Weisskopf, 1977).

High Skill Exercises and Projects

4.1 Is it possible for a robot to have all the three existences, namely $\mathcal{C}$, $\mathcal{M}$ and $\mathcal{G}$, like a human Being? Obviously, the answer is No, comment. Discuss and prepare lists of type of actions (i) which are possible to perform by a robot of today but not by a human Being, (ii) which are not possible to perform by a robot of today but by a human Being, and (iii) which are possible to perform by a robot of today as also by a human Being.

4.2 Can a robot perform actions more than what it has been taught to perform? Compare the actions possible to perform by a best modern robot to those performed even by a small child.

4.3 It is the consciousness of human Being manifesting through M, I and E which creates the space, time and geometry. (Obviously, a dead body cannot do this job). In view of this statement refute the phrase 'matter over mind' over 'mind over matter'.

4.4 With reference to human actions, make a survey of critical philosophy of Kant. Trace the fundamental basis that is advocated in his philosophy towards the performance of human actions. Compare the depth of this fundamentality with the one highlighted in Chapters 5 and 6 with reference to Vedic science.

4.5 Keeping in mind the discussions of Sect. 4.4, write a paragraph on the Vedic concept of '*Vasudheiva kutumbakam*' (i.e., treating the whole planet earth as one family).

Chapter 5

THE SELF AND ITS UNDERSTANDING: INDIAN PERSPECTIVE

Some of the religions followed in the Eastern part of the world (namely, China, Japan, East, South and South-East Asia) have roots in India. In spite of the fact that modern scientific advancements have made the boundaries porous of almost all religions of the world, in India itself there are some religions now with porous boundaries, namely Hindu, Sikh, Buddha and Jain, that are followed by the people. There exists an element of 'Self' or of its derivative(s) in one form or the other in the philosophy of each of these religions followed in this part of the world. Buddhism, while has quite a few similarities with Christianity of the West in practical and ethical terms, Jainism emphasizes the purification of the Self in this birth itself through *tapa*. In some sense, while Sikhism and Buddhism present the progressive component of Hinduism, they do have roots in Vedic Wisdom. However, Jainism goes for different sources of its ancient wisdom. In addition to these religions there are several other cults and sects in Hinduism, apparently different and, at times, rigid too at the surface level, but originate out of the same Vedic culture. Here, in this book, we shall follow the philosophy of the Vedanta, i.e. the Science of the Self, which by and large is common and applicable to entire human race then what to say only of Asian people.

In Indian context the Science of the Self has been considered as supreme. A great deal of Vedic literature focuses on it and the same is developed in a very systematic manner. In fact, there are many systems in Vedic literature itself that are supplementing each other and suggested by different seers at different points of time to impart this supreme knowledge to a common man. Here, we present a brief survey of this science and refrain ourselves from going into the details. Regarding the supremacy of this science, it is worthwhile to quote here from the work of great poet Kālidasa:

Ātma jnānam vidurjnānam jnānānyāni yāni tu,
Tāni jnānāvabhāsāni sārasyānava bodhanāt.

"The knowledge of the Self is the only true knowledge, the rest of knowledge is just mirage that does not lead us to the absolute truth."

The Vedic literature while describing this science, also prescribes the ways and means to achieve the eternal joy by knowing this absolute truth (Kaushal, 2011, Sect. 4.1).

5.1 THE QUESTION OF IDENTIFICATION AND QUANTIFICATION OF THE SELF

Note that the word 'Self' will be used for soul in this book and the word 'self' in the spirit of an instrument meant for the reflexive action or for person or thing as object of introspection. The latter meaning however coincides with the word '*Jiva*' (or 'life principle') of Vedic Science.

It may be mentioned that whether it is the 'Self' or 'self' both are appropriately identified in Vedic science and that too in very distinctive terms. While the 'Self' or soul is one of the EOLs and it is the source of consciousness in the Being, the 'self', on the other hand, is the set of inner EOLs including the soul. Somehow these concepts are not so vivid in the Western perspective but they have been repeatedly emphasized in Vedic science in one context or the other. Any way, we shall discuss the importance of these terms in the light of Vedic literature without actually differentiating them much.

With regard to the quantification of the Self, it is already situated in each individual or in living being as a 'second' quantized version of cosmic consciousness field (see, (Kaushal, 2011; Kaushal, 2013)). However efforts have been made in modern times to quantify the Self in mathematical terms as well (see (Kaushal, 2011; Singh, 2012). In order to have a feel for its quantification or identification in the body, the following examples will suffice.

Example 5.1.1: Take the case of Indian Government. It functions from New Delhi, but it sounds odd when we say that the Government is in New Delhi alone, i.e. not in other parts of India. The Government may have its headquarters in the north but the overall hold and grace of Government falls equally in other parts of India as well. On every inch of the country it has its sway. Its laws are applicable throughout the length and breadth of the Indian land. Yet, to meet the Government one has to go to New Delhi. Exactly the same is the role of the Self (soul) and its attribute consciousness in the functioning of human Being through his EOLs.

In fact peculiar are the ways of addition or multiplication for the quantified version (element) of consciousness and so is the case with its functioning inside the body. The following examples throw some light on these aspects:

Example 5.1.2: Let T_1 be the temperature of one room and T_2 be that of the adjacent room. Now both the rooms are joined by opening the common connecting door, then the question is as what will be the resultant temperature of both the rooms. Will it be (T_1+T_2)? Obviously, the answer is No. Similar is the case with quantified consciousness or souls, in general.

Example 5.1.3: In a train, the steam in the engine supplies the power for the locomotive to pull the train of carriages. It has neither favour nor any prejudice against anybody travelling in the attached compartments. The steam has no particular destination to reach except that it is the part of all pervading water vapor present in the atmosphere. In the same way, the soul, when it expressed itself through EOLs of a Being functions without its actual involvement in terms of say loss or gain to an individual organ.

5.2 DESCRIPTION OF THE SELF IN VEDIC LITERATURE

5.2.1 The concept of the Self in Vedas: Cosmic connections

Out of the four *Vedas*, *Yajurveda* is full of description of rituals, *Atharvaveda* is full of description of Ayurvedic medicine and technology, *Sāmaveda* gives description of various other aspects of life including music and philosophy. As all these aspects are meant for an individual or for human race in general, naturally the description of the Self is bound to be there in these Vedas of later period.

The oldest one, i.e., *Rigveda*, is full of cosmic concepts, like the origin of cosmos, universe, multiverse and the description of Nature. Further there is description of cosmic processes responsible for the origin and existence of animate (Beings) and inanimate (non-Beings) objects and that too in absolute terms out of the five cosmic elements. There is hardly anything for comparison or analogy except for some personifications of cosmic elements. *Rigveda* rather hints to cosmic Self and not much to the Self. From the meaning(s) of verses, if one reads between the lines, a kind of cosmic consciousness field has been postulated (Kaushal, 2013) at the most subtle and fundamental level in which the EOLs of an individual in their cosmic version are embedded, like the cosmic desire, cosmic intelligence and cosmic mind in addition to the five cosmic elements. The functional knowledge of these cosmic entities, in terms of certain principles, constitutes the all-pervading cosmic wisdom. As per se, the knowledge in Vedas is nothing but this cosmic wisdom which had been transcended from cosmos at different space-time points and that through different Grand Seers of the time. Note that this entire wisdom is meant for an individual as his Being is a part of local, global or cosmic society of Beings. If not much in the *Rigveda* as such, but definitely there is a considerable description of the Self and its derivatives in other Vedas. In what follows we cite some *Sūktās* from Vedas mainly to give some glimpses and support some of these observations:

Example 5.2.1: Note the following verses from *Rigveda* as quoted in *Satyārth Prakāsh* (Swami Dayanand):

> *Iyam visrastiryata ā babhuva yadiv ā dadhe yadi vā na;*
> *Yo asyādhya ksah parame vyomantso amgaveda yadi vā na veda.*

(*Rigveda*, *Mandal* 10, *Sūkta* 129, *Mantra* 7)

"O (Anga) man, know only Him and not any other who is creator, sustainer and destroyer and also responsible for enlightening this multifaceted, all-pervading Creation (*'Sristi'* , derived from the word *'Srajan'*) in which the entire Universe (or Universes) also constantly undergo creation, sustenance and destruction".

Tama ā sittamasā gulmagre-apraketan salilam sarvmā itam;
Tucchayenābho vapihitam yadāsittapasastan mahinā jāyateikam .

(*Rigveda*)

"Prior to Creation, this entire Universe in its micro but ether-like form was completely dark, neglected, not even knowable during darkness and was locally embedded in the Creation".

Example 5.2.2: There is another verse from Yajurveda:

> *Purusa-aeveda & sarva yadbhutam yacca bhāvyam;*
> *Utāmratatva syesāno yadannenātirohati.*

(*Yajurveda,* Ch.3)

"O man, One who is present in all in totality, imperishable, Master of all Beings and Who is beyond the concept of animate and inanimate, is the Creator of the past, present and future of this time-bound Universe".

Note that this is one way of translating these verses; otherwise the translation, transliteration and the interpretation of Vedic Verses in modern times has become a topic of research worldwide. As per se, the Beings in general and the human Being in particular is a miniature of the cosmos (micro-cosm), i.e., whatever present in the cosmos, the same manifests in the composition of human Being. Further it is said to be the perfect creation of God (the word 'God' can be considered as the abbreviation of the three basic qualities of the cosmic consciousness field, namely generator, organizer and destroyer) as compared to other species which in fact remain partial creations in relative terms. In Table 1 we present a correspondence of EOLs associated with an individual Being (b) and those present in the cosmos according to certain plausible interpretations of some Vedic verses.

Table 5.1: Some analogies between the micro and the cosmic versions of the Grand Creation.

S.No.	Micro-version Human Being (b)	Cosmic Version
1.	Soul (SO)	Cosmic consciousness field
2.	Ego (E)	Cosmic desire of the Creator
3.	Intellect (I)	Field of cosmic intelligence
4.	Mind (M)	Field of cosmic mind
5.	Biological body B and the senses of knowledge and action (matter inside the body in the form of solid, liquid, gas, plasmon and ether)	Field of cosmic elements or *panca mahābhūtās* (earth, water, air, fire and ether) along with their perception/ reception features with reference to gross and micro existences of a person
6.	Worldly objects (WO) or the external stimulant	Manifest and ever changing cosmic creation (*prakriti*) and the (associated) world-order

As time passed on in the history, this Vedic wisdom in its original form became out of reach to a common man in terms of the development of his FOUs. This knowledge, therefore, was later transcribed successively in simpler and simpler versions over different periods of time and the same was put before the masses in a variety of ways in different scriptures of different cults.

5.2.2 Description of the Self in other Vedic scriptures

As far as the description of Supreme Self (cosmic consciousness field), the Self and its derivatives like consciousness, or of the methodology to realize the Self by a person is concerned, they all are presented in variety of ways in Vedic scriptures of later period, i.e. after the Vedic era. Since it is not possible to present here the views of different saints and seers on this subject (and in fact the author is also not competent enough for this task), therefore, we just make a few passing remarks on this grand knowledge of the East.

After the Vedas, the next stage for the compilation of Vedic wisdom was the period of *Brāhmana Granthās, Brahm Sutra* and *Upanisads*. The description of the Self, its cosmic connections and also of its attributes is although spread all over these scriptures in the question-answer form among different characters and in different contexts, but the maximum of it appears only in some *Upanisads* like *Kathopanisad, S'vetās'vatara Upanisad* and a few more. Then came the period of great Indian epics namely the *Rāmāyana* and later that of *Mahābhārata*. These epics in general also contain a lot of knowledge about the Self through conversations among various characters. However, it is the epic *Mahābhārata* in whose heart the eternal, time-tested knowledge of Sovereign Science of the Self is planted in the form of *Srimad Bhagvad-Gita*, i.e., as the divine song of the Lord. The unparallel conversation between Lord Krishna and Arjuna in SMBG, in fact, presents a systematic development of the science of the Self and that too in a variety of ways. We shall discuss such details from SMBG in the next section. Here, we cite some situations from *Upanisads* where such aspects of the Self are highlighted.

Example 5.2.3: In *Kathopanisad* the death-God, Yama Raj, gives a detailed lesson to Nachiketa, the son of Risi Uddālaka on the Science of the Self (see, for example, Verses 18 and 19, Chapter 1, Valli 2).

Example 5.2.4: In *S'vetās'vatar Upanisad,* Chapters 3 and 4 are exclusively devoted to the description of and the methodology adopted in the science of the Self.

Example 5.2.5: In *Brihadāranyaka Upanisad* the conversations between Risi Yāgyavalakya and his wife, Maitreyi frequently have a discussion on the Self or soul and on its attributes like love, etc.

In more recent years, Adi-Shankaracharya, in his *prakarana* books, namely '*Vevek Chudamani*' and '*Atmabodha*' has compiled a lot of work on the understanding of the Self and that too in an introductory style.

5.3 DESCRIPTION OF THE SELF IN SRIMAD BHAGVAD-GITA

As far as the Sovereign Science of the Self is concerned SMBG presents the essence of all Vedic scriptures. All aspects of this science, namely the existence and the eternity or immortality of soul, its cosmic connections, its role pertaining to rebirth, its role in human experiences and actions through the entire set of EOLs and that too in an unattached manner, its role vis-à-vis that of non-Self in the maintenance of world-order etc. are vividly described in this capsule package. The conversation between Arjuna (the questioner of finest degree) and Lord Krishna (the responder of highest degree) takes place in about 700 verses at different levels of understanding. Starting with friendly level, then teacher-disciple, Master-subordinate levels and finally it takes place at the level of two souls in the cosmos. It is this last level of conversation that convinces the finest questioner like Arjuna about the world-order and its maintenance. At this stage only, Lord Krishna appears as a true transcendent and great seer of cosmic wisdom.

An important word used all through SMBG is 'yoga', derived from the Sanskrit word '*yuja*' which means 'connecting' the two objects. Now the question is as what are those two objects? In fact, they are the Self and the non-Self and connecting them according to certain aspect of human experience is called the corresponding yoga. For example, there is a mention of three types of yoga in SMBG, namely yoga of knowledge, yoga of action, and yoga of devotion. The knowledge pertaining to the Self, the action performed for the sake of action without attachment and expecting fruits, the devotion carried out in a self-less manner are the essences respectively of yoga of knowledge, yoga of action and yoga of devotion. In other words, the necessary condition for the human experiences like knowledge, action and devotion to fall in yoga category is that these aspects should be consciously in tune with the Self or so to say with the super Self; otherwise if they are carried out with reference to the non-Self alone, then they become the cause of worry and depression in the long run. In some sense this philosophy also helps in integrating the body, mind and soul towards the positive pursuits in life. In summary, certain aspects of human experiences need to be pursued ideally in such a way that the Self, although involved in all these pursuits but simultaneously remains unattached from the non-Self. It is not an easy task to command over this Art but the fact is that the practice makes a man perfect. Moreover, the suppression of ego in the form of 'me-ism' or 'my-ism' also makes it possible to some extent.

Example 5.3.1: To be more specific, a very fine description of the Self and its role in human experiences can be found in SMBG in Chapters 2-5 with reference to yoga of knowledge and yoga of action. While Chapter 12 is devoted to a discussion on yoga of devotion, Chapters 7-11 highlight the connections of the Self with its cosmic version '*Brahma*' and again through its manifest and un-manifest versions.

5.4 THE SCIENCE OF THE SELF AND THE INTEGRATION OF BODY, MIND AND SOUL

Keeping in mind the surveys carried out in the previous and this chapter on 'the Self and its understanding' it can be noticed that the West while has been trying to understand the Self, the East has already understood the Self. Any way, after having a feel for the role of this un-manifest reality in human experiences and actions, we are now in a position to proceed in both the directions, namely (i) to develop a general framework for the Science of the Self in which an explanation of entire gamut of human experiences and actions can be sought, in terms of the dynamics of EOLs, and followed by (ii) to understand the Art of integrating the body, mind and soul again using the dynamics of EOLs itself. No doubt, the former science provides a basis for the latter Art and accommodates it as a particular case, but the fact is that the latter is of immediate use for an individual in his day-to-day life. As a matter of fact a perfect coordination or integration of body, mind and soul is a must for the success of an action and it becomes the greatest success of the Science of the Self as well. In the forthcoming chapters we discuss a foundation of this science and later in Parts B and C we shall attempt to understand this Art of integrating body, mind and soul, in a generalized perspective of human existences and more through the practical examples from MMW and GMW.

It may be reminded here that the body and mind when defined as 'body'$\equiv\mathcal{G}\equiv$\{SE,B,WO\} and 'mind'$\equiv\mathcal{M}\equiv$\{E,I,M\} are the inanimate entities at their own, but when illuminated by the consciousness—an attribute of soul, then they become functional. Therefore, No doubt a conscious-body-mind system is a perfect coordination for the success of an action but at times only a 'conscious body' or a 'conscious mind' (i.e. a pair-wise coordination) can also be equally effective depending upon the type and nature of the action performed. As a matter of fact the conscious body or the conscious mind is the dressed versions of the nascent $\mathcal{G}$ or $\mathcal{M}$ with consciousness and in the process of their dressing the roles of other EOLs also creep in (see, Sect. 7.2 and (Kaushal, 2011, Chapter 8)).

5.5 CONCLUDING DISCUSSION

As compared to the West the Self and its related aspects are understood better in the Indian context. Not only this, there are enough hints for its identification and quantification in Vedic literature and the scriptures including *Vedās* which are full of descriptions of the Self in a variety of ways. While some *Upanisads* speak a lot of it, SMBG offers a capsule description of this Sovereign Science of the Self. In particular, some of the aspects of the Self described in SMBG through conversations of Arjuna and Lord Krishna are (i) its existence and eternity, (ii) its connection with cosmic consciousness, (iii) its role pertaining to rebirth, (iv) its role in human experiences and actions, and (v) its role vis-à-vis that of non-Self in understanding the world-order through the 'yoga of knowledge', 'yoga of action' and the 'yoga of devotion'.

As final remarks with regard to understanding the Self by a person, we repeat here the words of Lord Krishna in SMBG (cf. Verse 2.29) as "hardly any one perceives this soul as marvelous, scarce another likewise speaks thereof as marvelous, and scarce another hears of it as marvelous; while there are some who know it not even on hearing of it".

Further Reading:

For the identification and quantification of the Self (soul), see, (Kaushal, 2011; Kaushal, 2013) and the references therein; For the cosmic connections of the Self through cosmic consciousness field, see (Saraswati, Swami Dayanand, Samullāsa 8), and (Kaushal, 2013), in fact Vedic verses are quoted here from '*Satyārtha Prakāsh*'. For further work on the aspects of the Self, see, SMBG and (Goendka, '*Vedanta Darshan*' and '*Isadi Nau Upanisads*').

High Skill Exercises and Projects

5.1 Think of some more examples like Example 5.1.2 where the mathematical law of addition fails. What conclusion do you draw from such examples regarding the nature (or quantum) of consciousness. [Hint: One example is that of pressure in physics].

5.2 Describe in detail how the Vedic wisdom went from the state of abstraction to the state of proliferation over a period of time, i.e. from the Vedic period to the period of *Purānās* (or of *Rāmāyana* and *Mahābhārata*).

5.3 Explain how the process of integrating body, mind and soul towards the success of an action is affected when carried out in full awareness of the Self.

5.4 Analyze the case of bounded energy (consciousness) flow like water flows between the two banks of a river: Imagine the case when the river flow is not confined by banks on either side then water will never reach its destination — the ocean. In the same way the consciousness (energy) flows between the boundaries of good and evil as far as the working of a person in this world is concerned in order to reach the destination—Self or Supreme. Elaborate on this analogy.

5.5 Elaborate on the analogy of Exercise 5.4 to the case when the boundaries are not sharp straight lines but are zigzag in both the cases, namely when water flow in river and consciousness flow in life.

5.6 Write an essay on the description of 'Self' in Vedic literature.

5.7 According to a saint "genius is the ability to receive from the Universe". Justify this statement in the light of discussions in Sect.5.2.1.

5.8 Can you get some clue about the dark energy and dark matter — the concepts discussed in recent times in the context of theories of early Universe — from the Vedic verses highlighted in Sect. 5.2.1? Do a survey of Vedic literature from this point of view.

Chapter 6

THE DYNAMICS OF ESSENCES OF LIFE: MODELING THE INDIVIDUAL

6.1 WHY THE MODELING OF AN INDIVIDUAL IS NECESSARY?

From preceding chapters it becomes clear that if we want to understand the human experiences, behavior and actions in terms of their origin and operative parts then just the concept of human Being as an organic or biological system does not suffice. The dynamics of EOLs does play a role at every moment and everywhere during his existence in an alive form.

It has been argued earlier that the reality in Nature appears in two forms— un-manifest and manifest. The un-manifest is infinite whereas the manifest is finite. While one can realize the un-manifest reality inside to any extent, for the sake of its maximum possible expression outside all methods whether they belong to $\mathcal{M}$-domain (i.e. the domain of psyche) or $\mathcal{G}$-domain (i.e. the domain of physique) studies show the limitations. Therefore, the manifest appears to be finite at all levels. It has also become clear from preceding chapters that the human Being is also a finite manifestation of the infinite and this finiteness in his manifestation enters at two stages, namely (i) when the human Being is considered as a sample (microcosm) of the cosmos at its origin level, and (ii) when this microcosm interacts again with the cosmos at the functional level. While it will take some time for the philosopher-scientists (who accept the limitations of laws of objective science and also think beyond them) to digest the first level truth, for the second level truth, however, they have already started bothering themselves.

As a matter of fact when a human Being interacts with the outer world, the interaction takes place at two apparently different levels, namely via $\mathcal{M}$-domain and $\mathcal{G}$-domain. Scientist conveniently assumes only the $\mathcal{G}$-domain interactions and accordingly frame the models and develop the theories normally by suppressing the role of $\mathcal{M}$-domain at the cost of certain assumptions or postulates. The philosopher-scientist, on the other hand, does bother for the role of $\mathcal{M}$-domain interactions in his studies in addition to that of the $\mathcal{G}$-domain interactions. No doubt, the $\mathcal{M}$-domain interactions are sometimes negligible and are beyond the reach of experiments for some phenomena but there are many other phenomena in which $\mathcal{M}$-domain interactions are significant and the assumptions made in the theory do not appeal and suffice.

Example 6.1.1: In recent years there are attacks from many sides on the foundational aspect of quantum mechanics. In spite of the fact that the probabilistic interpretation of the quantum wave function in the Schrodinger picture successfully works for a variety of microscopic systems, the role of consciousness is once again revisited in this style of working through Schrodinger cat paradox. This will perhaps demand a review of the Einstein statement, namely "God never plays a dice" with reference to the probabilistic interpretation.

Example 6.1.2: The understanding of the dynamics of neurons and that of brain studies perhaps will remain incomplete without bringing in the role of consciousness in them through EOLs (Stapp, 2009; Part IV).

It is true that the $\mathcal{G}$-domain interactions suffice up to a certain level of experimental observations; but when experiments are fine tuned using ever advancing technologies, the role of $\mathcal{M}$-domain interactions cannot be denied indefinitely and accordingly theories need a modification (or alternative routes to approach the data) for the variables/ parameters responsible for the 'human role' in the experimentation. In fact, on this issue of incorporating the role of consciousness in theories, the scientists of the world are divided: Some believe in knowingly denying the role of this reality, perhaps due to non-availability of theoretical tools or lack of understanding of this phenomenon of consciousness, whereas others have accepted this reality and attempting to modify the theories for this purpose (Penrose, 1994; Stapp, 2009).

With a view to accounting for the role of 'human component' in physical, psycho-physical and psychic processes through the $\mathcal{M}$-domain interactions with the outer world, a clear picture of human Being in terms of its EOLs, preferably through a model, is necessary. This will not only help in understanding the fundamental processes taking place inside the human Being prior to and after his performance of an action, but will also suggest a way out to account for consciousness in physical theories, if so required in future.

6.2 LESSONS FROM PHYSICAL THEORIES II

If the Seers of Vedas knew the modern physical theories in terms of their analytic content then, in author's opinion, they would have come out with a perfect science accommodating both of its aspects, namely subjective as well as objective. Even now, the intuitionist approach of finest degree followed in Vedic science, if combined with modern physical concepts, can do wonders as far as a better or perhaps the best understanding of the world-order is concerned. In this regard the author has already explored (Kaushal, 2011) the viability of certain physical concept in giving a firmer footing for Vedic concepts. Here, in order to have some lessons from physics and other sciences, we cite some situations from the history of science when the modeling of a system/phenomenon became the necessity. In fact, the modeling becomes the necessity when one wants to analyze and understand the variety of accumulated properties of certain class of apparently different systems in terms of some minimal constituents of an ideally designed model of the system.

Example 6.2.1: Case of periodic Table of chemical elements: Recall the situation in atomic physics. There was an accumulation of data on the chemistry of atoms which scientists were trying to analyze in terms of some minimal number of atoms and their constituents. Starting with the work of Lavoisier in 1789, who prepared the periodic table with 33 elements only and with some crude rules it took a very long time in the history to have the present arrangement of elements in the Table. Even the present arrangement, suggested by Russian Chemist Mendeleev in 1870, has been the subject of scrutiny in recent times by several specialists.

Example 6.2.2: Case of shell model of nucleus: As for atoms, there was also accumulation of data on nuclear properties, structure and reactions for a quite some time. It was only after the discovery of the shell model of nucleus by M.G. Mayer in 1949 that the data could be explained uniformly in terms of the dynamics of some minimal number of constituents such as neutrons and protons. Even this picture of nucleus has been the subject of scrutiny in recent years for heavy nuclei via Nelson model, etc.

Example 6.2.3: Case of quark model for hadrons: There was accumulation of data on nucleon and meson resonances for a quite some time until a model in terms of three building blocks (called quarks) came into existence at the most fundamental level in 1964. In recent years the same model is now extended to 6 quarks to accommodate a larger set of baryons and mesons.

Example 6.2.4: Case of double-helix model of DNA: In genetics there was also accumulation of data on the origin and functioning of all living organisms and viruses until a helical model for the macro molecule of Deoxyribonucleic acid (DNA) was proposed by Watson and Crick in 1953.

Example 6.2.5: Case of Kekule structure of benzene: In organic chemistry the accumulated data was classified under certain categories only after the discovery of Kekule structure for the benzene by the German organic chemist August Kekule in 1865.

Note the similarities in all the above cases. As a matter of fact with regard to human experiences, behavior, actions and personalities, a similar accumulation of data has been known now for a quite some time. They are mostly derived from psycho-clinical studies. As far as the explanation of these data is concerned, there is no such a model as we have one for each of the above cases. In psychology while data itself is derived from statistical methods, the explanations are also empirical in nature. On the other hand, the intuitionist approach of Vedic science also offers the finest explanation of these data in terms of dynamics of EOLs or through SPP or SNP but in a subjective style. Now the question is can we have a viable model for the human Being, as we have in the above cases of objective science, to explain the data uniformly for all Beings in an analytic manner? The answer is, Yes. Such a model, called patomic model of human Being, has already been in use for a quite some time (see, (Kaushal, 1994; Kaushal, 2000; Kaushal, 2011)). Here, in the next section, we shall revisit the foundation of this model in the present context.

6.3 THE PATOMIC MODEL

6.3.1 An atom-like model of the human Being

While going through the studies of structure of matter in physical sciences one comes across the atomic model. This model, through the inverse square law of forces, not only works at the microscopic level but its validity in the form of the law of gravitation is well known for the motion of heavenly bodies. The validity of this law is also noticed at the level of quarks (smallest possible building blocks of the universe known today) at short distances. According to the atomic model of matter, there is a heavy positively charged mass (called nucleus) localized at the centre in a small spatial region. The light negatively charged particles (called electrons) are revolving around this nucleus in elliptical paths. The laws of force as a result of which the electron can stay in any of these orbits (called states) are rather well known: they are electrostatic force of attraction (given by the inverse square law) and the centripetal force experienced by the revolving electron. Depending on whether the energy is supplied to or extracted from the atom, the electron performs the transitions to higher or to lower energy states, respectively; otherwise it prefers to stay in the lowest energy state. As we go away from the centre, the spacing between successive energy levels decreases. This fact can be attributed to the nature of the law of force on the electron.

On the other hand, every human Being (not restricted by the boundaries of caste, color, creed or country) is considered to have the EOLs as mentioned before, namely, worldly object (WO), biological body (B), senses (SE) of perception or knowledge (SEK) and organs responsible for action (SEA), mind (M), intellect (I), ego (E) and soul (SO). The existence of all these EOLs is necessary for a human Being, no matter how their individual proportion varies. However some of them may be absent in the case of non-human Beings or in physically handicap or mentally challenged persons. For detailed meanings of these EOLs we refer to the Glossary of words or (Kaushal, 2011, Appendix A).

Consider the human Being b (now onward termed as only Being) as revolving around the nucleus of the worldly objects WO placed at the centre. The Being b can stay in any of the finite number of states specified by B, SE, M, I, E, SO as in Fig.6.1. These states are multiply degenerate (as a result of their dressing with consciousness, to be discussed later) and do not have well defined widths/boundaries. In fact every state (except B and SE) may be considered as to have a gross and a subtle component (cf. Fig. 3.1). The gross component along with a fraction of subtle components of each of the states M, I, and E constitutes a working B or SE. In other words the working B is a very complicated and composite structure. At any instant the Being b is subjected to experience two types of force—one is attraction towards the centre WO while the other is repulsion which is away from the centre. In Vedic science these two forces respectively are termed as '*pravratti*' (attachment to WO, which leads to the outward action) and '*nivratti*' (detachment from WO, which leads to the inward (subjective) action). Of course, the attractive force always dominates as long as b is in the lower (excited) states. Note that the state B which is very close to the centre WO is the ground state of b.

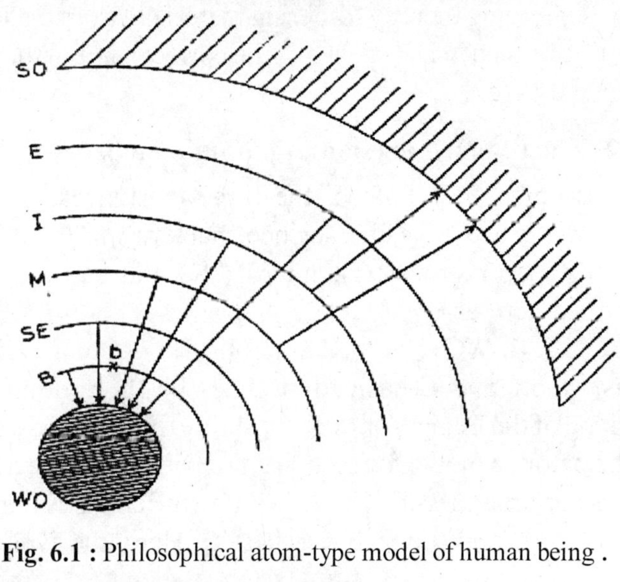

Fig. 6.1 : Philosophical atom-type model of human being .

The Being b, can perform the transitions. The downward transitions (i.e. towards WO) from any of the states (except SO) are more likely and favorable than the upward transitions (i.e. towards SO). In general, the upward transitions to the state SO are possible only from the states M and I and that too after overcoming the subtle (micro) component of E (cf. Fig.6.1).

As we go from the state B to the state SO both the level-spacing and the level-width increase in such a way that in the region of SO onward there is all continuum (the shaded area in the figure). Furthermore, the pervading property also increases as we go from state B to SO. The importance of space-time concept is maximum at the level of B and decreases to zero at the level of SO. Even at the level of M it has a negligible importance. Such a picture of human Being based on Vedic science (cf. Sect. 6.5) is termed as 'patomic' (philosophical atom-type) model. Also, the dictionary meaning of this latter word can be derived from the word 'patois' meaning thereby 'differing materially from the literary language' which in fact speaks of the correct spirit of the model discussed here.

6.3.2 The reduced version of patomic model

As mentioned before, the three existences of human Being described in Vedic science, namely *sthūla*, *sūkshma* and *kārana* or gross ($\mathcal{G}$), micro ($\mathcal{M}$) and causal ($\mathcal{C}$) are identified here as

$$\mathcal{G} \equiv \{SE, B, WO\}; \qquad \mathcal{M} \equiv \{E, I, M\}, \qquad \mathcal{C} \equiv \{SO\}.$$

Thus, $\mathcal{G}$, $\mathcal{M}$ and $\mathcal{C}$ basically define the three domains of working of the Being b or they constitute the 'reduced version' of the patomic model for studying the behavior and actions at a gross or broad level. Thus, the human Being b is the union of sets $\mathcal{G}$, $\mathcal{M}$ and $\mathcal{C}$, viz. b $\equiv \mathcal{C} U \mathcal{M} U \mathcal{G}$. Here, the symbol 'U' stands for the union of sets. Symbolically, b ≡ {SO, E, I, M, SEK, SEA, B, WO}.

Note that in a functional Being, though SO manifests through all the EOLs or through the three existences of b in terms of relative and absolute consciousness, yet it constitute a separate subset $\mathcal{C}$ of unique element. In fact it is a sort of super or universal set. Further for the working of $\mathcal{M}$ and/or $\mathcal{G}$ the presence of $\mathcal{C}$ in the background is a must.

This is the picture of the perfect creation of God i.e. of the human Being. With regard to the existences of other non-human Beings according to this theory, one can consider the possibilities of other subclasses, like $\beta_1 \equiv \mathcal{C} \cup \mathcal{M}$ and $\beta_2 \equiv \mathcal{C} \cup \mathcal{G}$. For further details we refer to (Kaushal, 2011).

6.3.3 Fractured patomic model

There exist a large number of species in Nature which deviate from this above discussed structure of the human Being in terms of some missing, undeveloped or underdeveloped EOLs in them. While there are cases of physically and/or mentally challenged individuals even among the human Beings, varieties of non-humans do exist in Nature with these characteristics. As a result, not only their actions and subsequently the behavior in the field of WO become different but they also undergo different types of exchanges when interacting with a perfect human Being (cf. Fig.6.1). For this purpose, the concept of 'fractured' patomic model is proposed by the author to analyze the interactions of such Beings with the external world and also with other Beings. For details we refer to (Kaushal, 2011, Chapter 10).

6.3.4 Dressing rules for EOLs and multiplicity of states

The dressing of an entity (it could be an EOL or a *mahābhūta*) with consciousness basically describes its evolution with consciousness in a discrete way. The successive dressing of an entity with consciousness reveals finer and finer of its details and the same, in turn, enhances its understanding. On the other hand, this improves the functional efficiency of inner EOLs as far as the understanding of WO/PMs is concerned. Further, this concept of dressing was prevailing in Vedic science in the form of *panci karan* rule for *paòca mahābhūtās* in a crude-form to generate a perceived *mahābhūta* from the nascent one. In analogy with this *panci karan* rule for *panca mahābhūtās* of Vedic science, a *trikaran* rule for the trio of M, I and E and a *dvi-karan* rule for B and SE have been suggested earlier by the author (Kaushal, 2011). These are the *tri-karan* and *dvi-karan* rules which give the multiplicity of states M, I, E, SE and B. Not only this, it has been argued that the infinitely dressed versions of M, I and E and that of *panca mahābhūtās* E_a, W, A, f, E_t with consciousness become the part of cosmic consciousness field (Kaushal, 2013). For a discussion on dressing of inner EOLs, see Sect. 7.2.

6.4 SOME REMARKS ON THE ARRANGEMENT OF EOLs IN PATOMIC MODEL

1. Force law: Like the inverse square law of force for the electron-nucleus system, the force law for the Being-WO system is not yet known. However, there are some attempts to find the quantum of consciousness through certain phenomena but no success so far. In such a situation, the explanation of consciousness manifesting phenomena arising out of the interactions of the human Being either with the physical world, with another human Being or with many other human Beings, while becomes possible through patomic model, the predictive power of the latter however remained poor.
2. Level-spacing: Spacing between successive-energy

states is basically the feature of the force law. While for the inverse square law in atomic systems the spacing between successive levels decreases, leading to a continuum for the infinite value of the principle quantum number, for the patomic model it is postulated to increase with increasing subtlety of ingredients as per common experience. Again note that for the atomic system this happens in the space-time domain whereas in the patomic model it is in the domain of meditation variable. Clearly, larger and larger practice of meditation is needed to proceed successively from a lower state to higher. One mathematical frame work proposed (Kaushal, 2003) for these features of level spacing in patomic model is that of quantum mechanical rigid rotator in which the level spacing increases with quantum number. However, in the absence of having a mass-type character for the Being b, these explanations though justifiable in qualitative terms but the prediction of the model remains poor. Moreover, in the human experience zone a rigid binding between the Being and the worldly objects (WO) is well known at least for a common man.

3. Level Width: Dressing of EOLs E, I, M, SE and B with consciousness according to *trikaran* and *dvi-karan* rules, as argued earlier, suggest the possibility of level width of desired degree and the same in turn becomes the measure of development of FOU of an individual (cf. Sect. 7.2).
4. Transitions: The frequent downward transitions of the Being b give rise to transient pleasure or very often pain to an individual whereas the rare upward transitions of Being b lead to peace and later joy and after that eternal joy as well.
5. 'Outside out' and 'inside out' pictures: It may be recalled that in case of atoms the electrons in the outermost or

next to the outermost orbits participate in chemical reactions or in describing the properties of metals. This is 'outside out' picture that works for atoms. However, in the case of patomic model, the 'inside out' picture works, i.e., when b dwelling in B interacts first with WO or in general it is the $\mathcal{G}$-domain that interacts initially with the outer world, then comes the number of $\mathcal{M}$-domain through M, I and E and finally that of $\mathcal{C}$-domain. We shall use such prescriptions in future chapters to explain the human behavior in certain situations. Parts B and C of the book are devoted to apply such a dynamics of EOLs.

6. Excitations and de-excitations: Note that there is 'electromagnetism' inside the atom (electrostatic forces are present due to charges and the revolving charges produce magnetism) and it is excited when electromagnetic energy is supplied to it which results into upward transitions of the electron. The atom is de-excited when the electron performs downward transitions and thus the energy is released. Note two facts from here: (i) the nature of the exciting energy or the one released is the same as the interactions present inside the atom, and (ii) the atom is considered as a closed system i.e. it does not interact with the surroundings except for with the electromagnetic radiation. In case of patomic model both these features differ. The system of a conscious (alive) human Being is not closed. It is always prone to interactions not only inside the human Being itself but also with the external world via consciousness. It is the consciousness (through meditation/ concentration variable) present in the Being and his faculty of memory that make the situation different. Also note that this system is prone to AAT and AADT type forces in addition to the contact

and/or AAD type forces known for a physical system. With regard to the excitation or de-excitation of a patomic system, for a conscious person it is possible in both the situations, namely (i) when the system interacts with WO or the external stimulant, and (ii) when the system does not interact with WO or stimulant but the interactions inside the human Being are predominant (see, Chapter 7). For example, anger, depression, sensual pleasure, etc. initially are the result of excitations. Once they are in the process of cooling down then they are the result of de-excitation of the Being b. Further, it also matters whether the human Being is interacting with an animate or inanimate object of the outer world. As a whole this is a very complicated mechanism and we therefore restrict ourselves from going into further details here. However, for more details we refer to (Kaushal, 2011).

6.5 A BASIS FOR THE PATOMIC MODEL IN VEDIC SCIENCE

There is a support for the above picture of human Being in terms of EOLs from different corners of Vedic science. Only difference is that the author has tried to put them in the present form analogous to atomic model for the structure of matter. In some Vedic scriptures the EOL, E is replaced by the so-called '*Vāsanās*' or '*Samskārās*'. If we go into the deeper meaning of ego or the faculty of memory or the Self-conscience, then all these words are synonym to each other.

If one goes with the standard phrase (saying) of Vedic science, namely '*yathā pinde tathā brahmānde*', i.e., 'whatever is in the human body, the same is there in the cosmos or vice-versa', then the spirit of the phrase in some sense is justified in view of discussions in Sect.5.2.1. Coincidently, the viability of this phrase can also be noticed in physical science where the same inverse square law in structural form works not only for heavenly bodies but also at the level of atoms and quarks, i.e., at the cosmic as well as at the micro level. In another case, a phrase similar in spirit can be traced in '*Satpatha Brāhmana*' (cf. Verses 5.2.5.4 and 1.2.5.5) where it is expressed as '*hivaisnavoyad vāmanāh; vāmno ha visnurāsa*".

As far as the ordering of EOLs in patomic model is concerned, there exists a clear description of this picture in SMBG (cf. Verse 3.42) through the verse,

Indriyāni parānyāhurindriabhyah param manah,
Manasastu parā buddhiryo buddheh paratastu sah.

"The senses are said to be greater (in terms of fineness or subtlety) than the body; but greater than the senses is mind. Greater than the mind is the intellect; and what is greater than the intellect is He (the Self or soul)".

This verse of SMBG beautifully introduces the arrangement of EOLs and they, in the same order, play roles in day-to-day life and behavior of an individual. Lord Krishna in SMBG while describing the Science of the Self to Arjuna, clearly maintains this ordering of EOLs and that too in different contexts.

6.6 CONCLUDING DISCUSSION

Having lessons from the history of several branches of science, the necessity of a model for the human Being is emphasized. Accordingly, a formal model is designed in terms of the EOLs of a Being with a view to explaining the accumulated data on human behavior and experiences. This model of human Being though has a basis in Vedic science however its scope and viability is there for the entire human race in general, as its foundations are scientific and logical.

Meanings of several concepts and terms known for the atomic model such as the force law, level width, level-spacing, transitions and the processes of excitation and de-excitation are analogously traced here for the patomic model.

With regard to applications of the patomic model all remaining chapters in Part B and Part C of this book are devoted to this effect. In the next chapter, however, we employ this model to the fundamental processes and interactions that take place inside the human Being prior to his performance of an action.

Further Reading

For further details on patomic model, see (Kaushal, 1994; Kaushal, 2000) and (Kaushal, 2011, Chapter 2 and Appendix A). For the concept of rigid rotator in the present context, see (Kaushal, 2003, Chapter 1).

High Skill Exercises and Projects

6.1 Keeping the discussions of Sects. 2.2, and 6.2 in mind, comment on the concepts of a perfect philosophy and a perfect science.

6.2 In the spirit of Examples 6.2.1-6.2.5, elaborate on the phrase, "models can only describe the partial truth and guide to the reality in nature but they cannot be the reality itself".

6.3 The level separation between successive levels in the assumed patomic model has some resemblance to that of rigid rotator in quantum mechanics. In view of this, comment on the nature of (rigid) binding of the Being b with the worldly objects WO in the patomic model.

6.4 What is the fractured patomic model? After accounting for the presence or absence of any or some of the EOLs out of M, I, E, eyes, ears, nose, tongue and skin, list the possible varieties of non-humans. [Hint: See, (Kaushal, 2011, Table 10.1)].

6.5 Classify the physically and/or mentally challenged persons on the basis of 'fractured' patomic model. On this basis, discuss their behavior and experiences with reference to each missing

EOL in them. At the next stage compare the roles of these missing features in a human and a nonhuman. [Hint: see, (Kaushal, 2011, Chapter 10)].

6.6 Differentiate between 'inside out' and 'outside out' pictures of interactions of a human Being with external stimulant. Analyse their roles in the following two situations arising when you meet one of your old friends: (i) you first shake hands and then recognize the friend, and (ii) you first recognize your friend from a distance and then shake hands. [Hint: Note that action–at-a-time type forces play a role].

6.7 As an example of the phrase, '*yathā pinde tathā brahmānde*', note the analogy and viability of the inverse square law of force in physics at both cosmic level (Newton's law of gravitation) and at micro level (Coulomb law inside the atom). Write the two structures mathematically and compare them at the levels of (i) symbols and their meanings, (ii) mathematical content in the structures, and (iii) the scales at which these structures work. Extend these studies to the cases of (a) quark-antiquark forces at short distances, and (b) law of intensities for two light sources.

Chapter 7

FUNDAMENTAL PROCESSES AND INTERACTIONS INSIDE THE HUMAN BEING

In the preceding chapter, a formal model for the human Being in terms of his EOLs is described. This model, in analogy with the atomic model, no doubt, is highly appealing but the predictive power of the dynamics involved remains poor, mainly because the force law among EOLs is not known in analytical terms. The intuitionist approach of Vedic science regarding the dynamics of EOLs provides a lot of wisdom for this purpose and works in practice as well. In this and the forthcoming chapters we use this frame work to analyze and study certain fundamental processes and the associated interactions that take place when the human Being b (a) interacts with himself during meditation, intro-inspection or self-observation, and (b) interacts with the surroundings. Note that the surroundings consist of both animate and inanimate objects. Within animate category again there are two possibilities, namely the interactions with humans and with nonhumans. For humans, one uses the patomic model however for nonhumans, a fractured patomic model need to be used. For the details of these processes and interactions we refer to our earlier work (see, (Kaushal, 2011, Chapters 8-10)). Here we shall concentrate mainly on the study of the case (a) above which, as we shall see in later chapters, plays an important role in the development of vertical component of the personality (cf. Chapter 14) of a person.

7.1 FIVE SENSES OF KNOWLEDGE AS SENSORS AND WINDOWS FOR OUTSIDE INTERACTIONS

While talking about the transient nature of human (biological) body, saints and poets have counted ten doors/ gateways to the closed structure, which are: two eyes, two ears, two nostrils, one mouth, skin cover as a whole, copulatory organ and anus. Nature has supplied to all these gateways some primary sensors in the form of thin hairs or soft sensitive skin mainly to protect the corresponding organ from the external agents like the dust or unwanted contacts. Some selective categories of these gateways or their parts are however sensitive to the fine character of the external agents. They are affected even by the attribute of the agent which sometimes create the medium of propagation for the attribute of the stimulant or the agent. Such selective categories of gateways are identified five in numbers, namely eyes, ears, nose, tongue and skin and they are termed as the senses of knowledge (SEK). In fact they act as sensors of a higher degree and are partly responsible for providing the perception of the outer world through various interactions depending on the external stimuli.

7.1.1 Five senses of knowledge in action in biophysical terms

Note that the senses when illuminated with the consciousness of an individual (or are in tune with the conscious brain) supply information about or the knowledge of the outer world. The process of perception varies from sense to sense in bio-physical terms. For example, eyes are responsible to perceive the shape or geometry of the object, they work in the presence of light and their working is based on the same principle as that of a camera; ears are responsible to perceive the sound of the object, if it is there; they work on the same principle as that of a gramophone. Similarly, the working of other senses, i.e. of nose, tongue and skin with reference to their perception of the outer world has been understood by scientists to a very fine degree. One is amazed by the physiology, the construction and the working of these senses of knowledge in human body. Over and above that is the wonderful working of the nervous system the Nature has provided to a person and the same plays an important role in the perception process. In fact there is a system by which a nerve (e.g. optical nerve in case of an eye) or nerves attached with each sense organ that carries the information, received at the level of sense organ and transmits the same to the brain. Finally, it is the brain that stores the message and accordingly gives command to the sense organ to act outside. There are certain nerve centres in the brain working through neurons and are responsible for storing the memory about and discriminating the features of the external objects.

There may be some exceptions, otherwise for an average person the sense organs responsible for knowledge work within certain limits. For example, our eyes are sensitive only to VIBGYOR part of the huge electromagnetic spectrum, ears are sensitive to sound of the frequency range 20 Hz – 20000 Hz and the alike. Some animals are found to have extraordinary sense perception with reference to one or a few sense organs but not for all the five at the same time. Further, it may be mentioned that in general the sense-objects are received and registered in the brain when the conscious thoughts are attached to them; otherwise they go un-noticed. It is worthwhile to list some amazing facts found about the sensitivity of these sense organs. For example, the human nose is so sensitive that it can tell the difference between 10,000 different scents. A patch of skin, the size of a finger nail, may contain more than 1000 touch sensors and 1.5 feet of nerve fibers. Further, the most touch sensitive areas of skin include the lips and fingertips and have more than 3000 touch sensors per square 0.5 inch. In general, sense organs of children are found more sensitive than those of old persons.

In addition to these five external sense organs, namely eyes, ears, nose, tongue and skin, the human body has many more inner senses. In fact inside the body there are some microscopic sensors that detect, for example, the blood content, temperature, the position of the joints and many other things as and when the body put such requirements. Further, there are senses in the brain itself that also act as sensors. The part of the brain that deals with the nerve signals coming from different parts of the body, also acts as a sensor and accordingly sends the command. Among them all, the most sensitive part corresponds to skin and is responsible for the external touch. Next, we analyze these biophysical studies in philosophical terms. Today these two types of studies appear like two disjoint sets but one never knows tomorrow the former may be accommodated in the later one as a particular case or the vice versa.

7.1.2 Five Senses of knowledge in action in philosophical terms

As far as the sensing feature of the senses of knowledge is concerned the biophysical processes end-up at the level of brain. For this purpose, not only the brain but also the sense organs for that matter have to be conscious. An unconscious brain or sense organ however can neither perceive nor respond. It is the understanding of consciousness that makes the hell of difference between the two styles of perception of an object of the outer world, namely biophysical and philosophical. Before proceeding further the reader is reminded of discussions on the perception process (cf. Sect. 1.2) and on the seer-seen chain (cf. Example 2.4.1). In both the cases the hint is that the soul is the ultimate perceiver, realizer or seer of an object.

It may be mentioned that for a biophysicist, the reaching of information at the level of brain and then its subsequent analysis in the spirit of 'matter over mind' (cf. Sect. 4.1) is more important than knowing the conscious aspect of brain. Similarly, for a sense organ to work, note that it has to be conscious in addition to its connection with the brain through a nerve. For a biophysicist, the consciousness itself or its roles, in the form of memory storage in the brain or in the form of discriminatory power of the brain, remains a black box. No doubt, a biophysicist can understand the perception and response aspects of the brain but who is the final realizer of the phenomenon; it is not clear to him.

On the other hand, a philosopher may not go into the finer details of the construction of senses of knowledge but is capable enough to analyze not only the perception and response processes in the spirit of 'mind over matter' (cf. Sect. 4.1) but also to explain as to how the phenomenon is realized at the end-point by the Self. For this purpose, in addition to gross-body, the micro-body of the human Being also plays an important role. Further, it is the dressing of inner EOLs with consciousness in the first stage that later enhances the level of development of one's FOU. All this in fact matters in enriching the faculties of memory and decision of a human Being. Some of these concepts will be discussed in the forthcoming sections.

What is important in the philosophical version of the perception process is the attachment and detachment of mind with sense-objects rather remotely, i.e. without actually coming into contact with them through the senses. (This happens due to AAD and AAT type forces together which are beyond the domain of biophysics). This attachment or detachment of mind of a person with sense-objects respectively depends on his liking or disliking for the latter and accordingly the person makes effort to achieve them and subsequently draws pleasure or pain out of them. It is this aspect of mind that keeps it busy all the time as long as it is conscious. Sometimes this aspect of mind poses greatest hurdle in the process of integration of body, mind and soul towards the success of an action. Note that the pleasure or pain so obtained is transient in nature and a man of wisdom does not dwell in them for long and further thinks of the success of higher goals which in turn will lead to the peace of his mind.

7.2 MIND-INTELLECT DUO WORKS AS A FILTER OF THOUGHTS

Recall the concepts of abstraction/proliferation of knowledge discussed earlier in Sect.3.3.1 and that of as how the human experiences and actions multiply as a result of permutation and combination of functions of EOLs (cf. Sect. 2.4.1), of course in the presence of consciousness. While a common man keeps himself indulge in this kind of plurality and multiplicity of thoughts, speech and actions, the man of wisdom, on the other hand, always thinks of filtering or compartmentalizing them according to certain criteria. For this purpose the conscious version of the mind-intellect duo comes into action and works effectively to supply an essence of the same to the faculty of memory for its storage and future use. The following example will further clarify this aspect of the duo.

Example 7.2.1: Normally, the truth is hidden and covered by the mesh of words in the same way as fruits on a tree are covered by the cluster of leaves. The mind-intellect duo acts as a winower. It retains the truth or essence and sweep out the rest of junk in the same way as the rice are separated from the husk, bran etc using the winnower.

In order to understand the filtering aspect of the duo, it is necessary to have a feel for the dressing mechanism for inner EOLs with consciousness and in what follows we discuss the same in brief.

7.2.1 Dressing of inner EOLs with consciousness

As mentioned before, the EOLs of a person work when they are illuminated by or enlightened with the consciousness, i.e. in the presence of soul. Not only this, an external object is perceived when only conscious EOLs participate in the process of perception. This in fact is the basis for the *panci-karan* rule for creating perceived *mahābhūtās* from the physical (nascent) ones in Vedic science. Now the question is as to how the EOLs, particularly the inner ones, M, I and E get dressed with the consciousness emanating from the soul (cf. Fig.6.1). To this effect, the author has proposed earlier (Kaushal, 2011) a *'trikaraṇ'* rule (in analogy with the *panci-karan* rule for PMs) which takes care of dressings of inner EOLs M, I and E.

Note that the increasing consciousness means more and more intense meditation, characterized by the variable μ. Further, note that the dressing of an EOL or of an external object with consciousness tantamount as to how these entities evolve with the variation of meditation variable μ. In mathematical terms, there are two ways to study this aspect, namely as discrete evolution and as continuous evolution with respect to μ. While the author has studied both these ways earlier, however, here, we restrict ourselves only to discrete evolution and that too of inner EOLs through a '*tri-karan*' rule. According to this rule, a dressed EOL is the sum of 50% of its undressed version and 25% of undressed version of each of the other two EOLs. Thus, for example, the first-order dressed versions $\widetilde{M}^{(1)}$, $\widetilde{I}^{(1)}$ $\widetilde{E}^{(1)}$ respectively of M, I and E can be expressed in terms of the undressed (nascent) ones by simple algebraic relations of the form,

$$\begin{aligned}
\widetilde{M}^{(1)} &= \frac{1}{2}\mathrm{M} + \frac{1}{4}\mathrm{I} + \frac{1}{4}\mathrm{E}, \\
\widetilde{I}^{(1)} &= \frac{1}{2}\mathrm{I} + \frac{1}{4}\mathrm{E} + \frac{1}{4}\mathrm{M}, \qquad (7.1) \\
\widetilde{E}^{(1)} &= \frac{1}{2}\mathrm{E} + \frac{1}{4}\mathrm{M} + \frac{1}{4}\mathrm{I}.
\end{aligned}$$

Similarly, for the second-order dressing one writes

$$\begin{aligned}
\widetilde{M}^{(2)} &= \frac{1}{2}\widetilde{M}^{(1)} + \frac{1}{4}\widetilde{I}^{(1)} + \frac{1}{4}\widetilde{E}^{(1)}, \\
\widetilde{I}^{(2)} &= \frac{1}{2}\widetilde{I}^{(1)} + \frac{1}{4}\widetilde{E}^{(1)} + \frac{1}{4}\widetilde{M}^{(1)}, \qquad (7.2) \\
\widetilde{E}^{(2)} &= \frac{1}{2}\widetilde{E}^{(1)} + \frac{1}{4}\widetilde{M}^{(1)} + \frac{1}{4}\widetilde{I}^{(1)},
\end{aligned}$$

and in general for the nth order dressing one writes in terms of $(n\text{-}1)^{th}$ order dressed EOLs as

$$\begin{aligned}
\widetilde{M}^{(n)} &= \frac{1}{2}\widetilde{M}^{(n-1)} + \frac{1}{4}\widetilde{I}^{(n-1)} + \frac{1}{4}\widetilde{E}^{(n-1)}, \\
\widetilde{I}^{(n)} &= \frac{1}{2}\widetilde{I}^{(n-1)} + \frac{1}{4}\widetilde{E}^{(n-1)} + \frac{1}{4}\widetilde{M}^{(n-1)}, \qquad (7.3) \\
\widetilde{E}^{(n)} &= \frac{1}{2}\widetilde{E}^{(n-1)} + \frac{1}{4}\widetilde{M}^{(n-1)} + \frac{1}{4}\widetilde{I}^{(n-1)}.
\end{aligned}$$

It is not difficult to check that at every order of dressing , one has

$$\begin{aligned}
\widetilde{M}^{(n)} + \widetilde{I}^{(n)} + \widetilde{E}^{(n)} &= \widetilde{M}^{(n-1)} + \widetilde{I}^{(n-1)} + \widetilde{E}^{(n-1)} \\
&= \mathrm{M} + \mathrm{I} + \mathrm{E}, \qquad (7.4)
\end{aligned}$$

which implies that the entire process of dressing of EOLs goes in a self-consistent manner, i.e. without affecting their nascent versions.

Several deductions from these simple relations have been analyzed by the author earlier (see, (Kaushal, 2011)). Interestingly, the conclusions drawn there from conform to many Vedic concepts. Here and in future sections we highlight only a few of them. Note that now one can immediately define a nth order dressed micro-body as $\widetilde{\mathcal{M}}^{(n)} = \{\widetilde{M}^{(n)}, \widetilde{I}^{(n)}, \widetilde{E}^{(n)}\}$. For the infinitely dressed case, n=∞ , and one obtains the infinitely dressed versions of M, I and E as $\widetilde{M}^{(\infty)}$, $\widetilde{I}^{(\infty)}$, $\widetilde{E}^{(\infty)}$. These latter versions correspond to the cosmic mind, cosmic intelligence and cosmic desire as discussed in Sect. 5.2. Thus as and when the meditation becomes more and more intense then, either one, two or all the three EOLs M, I and E tend to achieve the supreme (cosmic consciousness) in accordance with the yoga of devotion, yoga of action and yoga of knowledge of Vedic science.

7.2.2 Levels of development of faculty of understanding of an individual

In order that an EOL should work, it has to be dressed with consciousness at least in the lowest order. However, higher orders of its dressing will make it more efficient and sharp towards its functioning. Within this framework one can as well understand the meaning of the commonly used phrase in this book, namely "the level of development of the faculty of understanding". In fact the faculty of understanding is nothing but a composite of the trio M, I and E with the same or differently dressed versions of them. For example, if $\widetilde{M}^{(m)}$, $\widetilde{I}^{(n)}$ and $\widetilde{E}^{(r)}$ be the dressed versions of M, I and E, respectively with m[th], n[th], and r[th] –order dressing obtained from eqs. (7.1) - (7.3), then a composite dressed version of the micro-body $\mathcal{M}$ of the form, $\widetilde{M}^{(m,n,r)} \equiv \{\widetilde{M}^{(m)}, \widetilde{I}^{(n)}, \widetilde{E}^{(r)}\}$, defines the faculty of understanding of an individual. The set of values of m, n and r, viz. (m, n, r) accordingly defines the level of development of this faculty. Clearly, m=n=r=0 does not make sense for a conscious human Being and m=n=r=1 is the must for all three EOLs of a person to work. For mentally challenged persons or for nonhumans (fractured patomic model), however, any one, two or all the three m, n and r could be zero. While the extreme (∞, ∞, ∞) defines a yogi of the highest degree, other higher values of m, n and r in the set (m, n, r) define persons of varying personalities with different specialization and super specialization, it could as well be of philosopher or scientist category. We shall return to some of these discussions in Chapter 9.

7.2.3 Filtering of thoughts

As mentioned before, there is a very wide spectrum of experiences and actions through which the mind of a human Being passes over a period of time. A great deal of them is out of attraction and repulsion rooted in the sense-objects. Knowing fully well that the most of them are of no use, the person does not know as to how to discard some over the rest. In fact, the EOL, M is very turbulent by nature and has the tendency to remain involved in these multiple and multifaceted experiences and actions. This generally happens with a common man. A man of wisdom, however, applies his highly dressed intellect to sort out the desirable over the unwanted ones. The degree of such filtering of thoughts by a person depends on as to which order he has dressed his intellect with consciousness by a process, the so-called 'meditation'. Once such a filtering is done, then the essence of all experiences and actions is stored in the faculty of memory E. Naturally highly dressed version of E will correspond to a large storing capacity of the faculty of memory.

This, in turn, will make a scope of better *sankālpās* towards future experiences and actions.

In summary, the dressing of EOLs with consciousness is tantamount to (i) an increase in the meditation parameter (μ), (ii) development of FOUs, (iii) enhancement of knowledge (in both quality and quantity) over ignorance, and thereby providing finer and finer experiences, which in turn will lead to a refined behavior. Note that the absence of knowledge is ignorance and the quality of knowledge matters in the success of an action. An example will suffice to clarify these aspects of inner EOLs.

Example 7.2.2: Knowledge can overcome ignorance like peeling of covers of onion: The knowledge of the Self has been considered as supreme and the Self appears like the inner-most part of the onion. The different layers of onion can be considered as different layers of ignorance and the peeling of them one by one, as one proceeds from outside to inside, is equivalent to saying that the knowledge of Self becomes finer and finer. While the outer layers may correspond to the knowledge of worldly objects, the inner layers correspond to the domain of spirituality.

One can as well compare this example with that of a potter wheel of Example 2.4.3. In fact the meditation and its role in filtering the experiences and actions with the help of a dressed intellect are the examples of self-interactions inside the human Being. Now in what follows, we concentrate on these aspects of human interactions.

7.3 MEDITATION: AN EXAMPLE OF SELF INTERACTION

7.3.1 Meditation as an Art of diffusing the mind-body interaction

In the process of meditation one concentrates himself on watching the dynamics of EOLs, particularly that of mind and tries to control or channelize these dynamic (but non-physical) forces. In some sense there is a kind of interaction between the micro-body $\mathcal{M}$ and the gross-body $\mathcal{G}$ of a Being that persists. Note that the SEs have a natural tendency to interact with external sense-objects in the field of WO, but only in the presence of conscious mind. During meditation, this tendency of SEs needs to be checked and the same is possible only after consistent efforts of mind, particularly by engaging the latter in the objects higher than that of sensual nature. This may not be a difficult task to achieve such a state of concentration by a common man for a short while. The difficulty, however, arises in attaining such a state forever and everywhere while living in this world. This requires a lot of practice by an individual. The task may be difficult but not the impossible one, particularly by those who know the 'art of living' in this world or in general the 'Art of integrating the body, mind and the soul'.

In meditation (which is an example of Self-interaction) while mind keeps on making such efforts in the guidance of intellect (or in the presence of *sankālpās*), SEs, on the other hand, look for a chance to involve in the sense objects, since the human Being has to eat, to see, to smell, to hear and to touch in the domain of WO for his survival. This continues for the nourishment of his gross body and till the time the person is alive. However, he can keep on diffusing this kind of mind-body interaction via meditation every day provided he has determined to do so and understands the limits not only of SEs but also of enjoying the sense objects. A stage comes when the mind is silenced and there are no thoughts or desires, whatsoever. Only at this stage one realizes as to who and what really he is – the vast, eternal consciousness.

With regard to definition and method of meditation note the following points: (i) As mentioned in Sect.1.3, a directed or channelized version of consciousness inwardly is termed as 'meditation' and the same outwardly in the domain of outer EOLs is called 'concentration'. (ii) Although the meditation is possible in any position, but it is convenient to attain it in the sitting position. Sit straight with straight neck calmly and with closed eyes, concentrate on his Self, and consider as if mind is divided into two parts – one acts as an observer and the other remains as an actor. While the second part wanders here and there, the first one will continuously check the activities of the second. In the beginning, the second part will dominate the scene but slowly as one progresses in practice, the first part will start dominating the second. This is a tip for meditation to start with.

Meditation itself has a big spectrum – starting with concentration in the domain of outer EOLs it continues upto *Samādhi* in the domain of $\mathcal{C}$, i.e., beyond $\mathcal{M}$, as per Vedic science. In this spectrum, there comes another stage when the 'meditation' is focused on viewing the non-Self as separate from Self in all the experiences and actions performed.

7.3.2 Meditation as an act of separating non-Self from the Self

In Vedic science the role of '*Ahamkāra*' (a version of ego E) is discussed at great length. It is this EOL which plays an important role in all fundamental processes that take place inside the human Being (see, (Kaushal, 2011, Sect.13.1)). This Sanskrit word when broken as, *Ahamkāra* = *Aham+kara*, implies the meaning that 'I am the doer', i.e. an action which is rich with the feeling of *aham* or 'I-ism'. This 'I-ism' starts right at the level of WO and continues through B, SEA, SEK, M, I and finally upto SO. This 'I-ism' intricately so interwoven in the expression of all experiences and actions performed by an individual that he starts forgetting the role of SO and considers himself as the ultimate doer, whereas in reality it is not so. In fact 'I-ism' or 'me-ism' is a kind of wrong belief carried by the person by identifying the Self (SO) with the non-Self ($\mathcal{B}$), where $\mathcal{B}$ is defined as $\mathcal{B}=\mathcal{G}\cup\mathcal{M}$, i.e., as the union of $\mathcal{G}$ and $\mathcal{M}$.

This wrong belief has to be replaced by the right belief, i.e., by realizing SO and $\mathcal{B}$ as two distinct entities, which apparently are bound by the 'false' ego E. Here comes the role of meditation rather in an intense form. While wrong belief goes unnoticed to an individual, its replacement by the right belief becomes rather impossible for a majority of persons as the bondage between $\mathcal{B}$ and SO is unexpectedly subtle. Even the enlightened souls do make a mistake very often on this front. No doubt the expression of ego E through actions at times appears natural for the survival of an individual in this world but for a person of spiritual taste the suppression of E is necessary. Of course, this is an art to suppress E but that comes through persistent meditation only. In what follows, we present an example to demonstrate as how much difficult it is to suppress the ego E even by the intellectuals:

Example 7.3.1: According to a story, a scientist had perfected himself in the art of reproducing his own replica. One day he realized that the death-god was searching for him as the end of his life had arrived. With a view to deluding the death-god, since the scientist wanted to remain immortal, he reproduced seven replicas of himself. The replicas were so perfect that the death-god could not identify the original scientist out of the lot and was confused. But not for a long time. Death-god came with a clever idea. Addressing all eight of them, he said, "you have reproduced so perfectly that it is difficult to find out the original scientist but you have left a tiny flaw". Hearing this, the scientist immediately reacted and shouted, "Impossible ! where is the flaw", "Right here", said the death-god. Thus, death-god recognized the original scientist from among the replicas and carried him of.

Thus the suppression of ego is a difficult task. In the next section we try to discuss this subtle mechanism in more analytical manner.

7.4 INTERACTIONS INSIDE THE HUMAN BEING: THE TRIO OF M, I AND E IN ACTION

In Vedic science the interaction of a human Being with *panca mahābhūtās* is described through the so-called '*tanmātrās*'. (In the language of modern physics these *tanmātrās* basically are the quanta of interactions, for example, for electromagnetic field we have photon, or for gravitational field we have graviton, and so on). This concept of *tanmātrās* was further generalized by the author (see, (Kaushal, 2011, Chapter 8)) for several other human interactions including for the ones appearing here for the constituents of the micro-body $\mathcal{M}$. For further details we refer to our earlier work. Schematic picture of these subtle interactions is shown in Fig.7.1.

As mentioned before, the outward actions of a human Being are the result of a large number of processes taking place inside the human Being at the level of conscious (or dressed) micro- and gross-bodies. These processes in fact are the outcome of combination and re-combination of EOLs dressed with consciousness of varying degree. As a matter of fact these processes or interactions become more realizable to a conscious Being, $\tilde{b} = \tilde{\mathcal{M}}^{(1)} \cup \tilde{\mathcal{G}}^{(1)}$, who can, if desires, start later enjoying the meditation of higher and higher levels. To this effect we study as to how the increasing meditation (μ) (in terms of its intensity) resolves the gross feature associated with the EOLs of b.

To start with, at low μ, the micro and gross bodies with corresponding dressed EOLs at the lowest order unite together to form a conscious Being $\tilde{\mathfrak{b}}$. As μ increases, the dressed constituents of $\tilde{\mathcal{G}}^{(1)}$, namely $\widetilde{SE}^{(1)}$, $\tilde{B}^{(1)}$, $\widetilde{WO}^{(1)}$ remain unaffected whereas those of $\tilde{\mathcal{M}}^{(1)}$, namely $\widetilde{M}^{(1)}$, $\tilde{I}^{(1)}$ **and** $\tilde{E}^{(1)}$ undergo the next order of dressing with consciousness according to the '*tri-karan*' rule and thus gives rise to a doubly dressed micro-body $\tilde{\mathcal{M}}^{(2)} \equiv \{\widetilde{M}^{(2)}, \tilde{I}^{(2)}, \tilde{E}^{(2)}\}$ (cf. eq.(7.2)). This occurs through the three quanta of interaction or *tanmātrās*, namely $t_{mg}^{(1)}$, $t_{ig}^{(1)}$, *and* $t_{eg}^{(1)}$, lebelled with mg, ig and eg corresponding to the mind-gross body, intellect-gross body and the ego-gross body interactions. Here, the bracketed superscript indicates the *tanmātrās* corresponding to interaction with simply-dressed constituents of $\widetilde{M}^{(1)}$

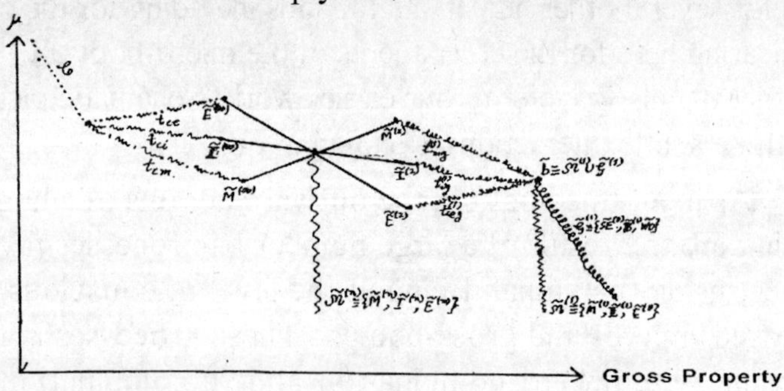

Fig. 7.1: Interactions inside the human being

The role of *tanmātrās* $\tilde{t}_{mg}^{(n)}$, $\tilde{t}_{ig}^{(n)}$, $\tilde{t}_{eg}^{(n)}$ corresponding to the nth order dressing of the constituent of $\mathcal{M}$, that of n=2,3, ... is not shown in the figure. However the effect of all these intermediate stage constructs of inner EOLs, corresponding to the dressed mind, intellect and ego is merged into the drawing of three solid lines. A cross-over of the three solid lines is for certain order n of dressing. The order of dressing at which the cross-over takes place varies from person to person. Note that after the crossover, E still continues to be little longer than before the crossover as compared to M and I. In fact in the outward actions of EOLs it is ego that starts acting first compared to the mind and intellect, where as in the inward actions the role of mind ends-up first compared to that of intellect and ego. Further, in the limit $n \rightarrow \infty$, one obtains a highly dressed micro-body which in turn perhaps becomes the source of *sankalpās*. In fact the constituents of $\tilde{\mathcal{M}}^{(\infty)}$ while ideally become the part of cosmic consciousness field, for large but not infinite values of n the causal body $\mathcal{C}$, i.e. soul interacts with $\tilde{\mathcal{M}}^{(n)}$ through another set of *tanmātrās*, namely t_{ce} , t_{ci} , t_{cm} labeled with ce, ci, cm corresponding to SO-ego, SO-intellect and SO-mind interactions.

In addition to solid lines in the figure, one can also see the dotted, wave-like, and spring-like lines representing respectively the contributions of causal, micro and gross bodies to the interaction in different domains of the meditation parameter μ. Note that at low μ, the role of gross body including that of WO remains important and at moderate μ the micro body dominates the scene whereas at high μ (intense meditation), i.e., in *Samādhi*, it is all the role of causal body of b. This is how the Being b through its micro body works between the extreme domains of SO and WO and there appears a wonderful coordination among the workings of M, I and E at the gross level.

7.5 CONCLUDING DISCUSSION

This chapter gives a final touch to the survey made in this part of the book on the subject of psychophysics or the

Science of the Self. With a view to have an understanding of the fundamental processes which take place inside the human Being prior to his performance of an action, the dynamics of inner EOLs is analyzed in this chapter at a very fine level. The role of five senses of knowledge as sensors and also as a supplier of information to inner EOLs is discussed in both biophysical and philosophical terms. The plurality of experiences so gathered by a conscious person undergoes a kind of screening by the duo of his mind and intellect. For practical purposes the process of meditation— an example of Self-interaction, is found to offer a vibrant tool for a systematic study of these intricate processes via the variable μ. In theoretical terms, it is emphasized that an intense dressing of inner EOLs with consciousness via '*tri-karan*' rule enables EOLs to overcome the subtle component of the ego E at the other end, i.e. for large μ. If one is prepared to undergo such training by way of practicing the meditation then, in due course of time, it will bring the person to the domain of spirituality.

It may be mentioned that the framework, methods, tools and terminology developed in this part of the book form the back-bone for future discussions. They will now be freely used in Part B and Part C in discussing the methods and processes of character building and personality development of an individual or of a group of individuals. In particular, in Part B we discuss as to how an individual can create his own personality by following certain systematic of positive pursuits which helps in refining the basic ingredients of a personality. Part C is devoted to analyzing, in the spirit of suggestive manner, two, three and the higher number of human Being interactions within the framework developed in this Part. To this effect, the analogies from physical theories will again come to help for further details and fine-tuning of these interactions.

Further Reading:

For the most of the material presented in this chapter we refer to (Kaushal, 2011, Chapters 8, 9 and 13).

High Skill Exercises and Projects

7.1 According to Kant, "human actions are the result of interaction of character and environment (cf. Sect.4.2)". In his philosophy while the character of a person remains poorly defined, use the patomic model of human Being to better understand the origin of actions in this phrase.

7.2 Keeping in mind the neuro-dynamics and the seer-seen chain (cf. Example 2.4.1), analyse the perception process associated with the five senses of knowledge in both biophysical and philosophical terms. Tabulate the points of similarity and difference between the two studies.

7.3 Why is the filtering of thoughts necessary? Explain how the mind-intellect duo works as a filter of thoughts.

7.4 Discuss the two ways of dressing an EOL with consciousness in mathematical terms, namely continuous and discrete. As an example of continuous dressing, explain how the mindset function evolves with the meditation variable μ through a differential equation. [Hint: See, (Kaushal, 2011, Chapter 8)].

7.5 As examples of discrete evolution of EOLs or of PMs with consciousness, write a note on '*dvi-karan*', '*tri-karan*' and '*panci-karan*' rules.[Hint: See, (Kaushal, 2011, Chapter 8)].

7.6 Define the 'faculty of understanding'. Explain how its level of development is associated with the dressings of inner EOLs with consciousness. Explain as how the different orders of dressing of each of M, I, and E with consciousness will give rise to different types of expertise in a society.

7.7 Highlight the difference, if at all, between the 'Art of living' and the 'Art of integrating the body, mind and soul'. Explain how meditation, attention or awareness play a role in acquiring expertise of these Arts.

7.8 Describe and practice the process of meditation. In some sense meditation means 'to dig and throw out something that is hidden deep inside in oneself'. Justify this statement in the light of discussions in Sects.7.2 and 7.3.

7.9 Explain and analyze the dynamics of inner EOLs (cf. Fig.7.1) that takes place inside the human Being with reference to the performance of an action in the (i) $\mathcal{G}$-domain, and (ii) $\mathcal{M}$-domain. Explain how the point of cross-over of solid-lines in this figure varies from person to person.

PART B

PERSONALITY 'CREATION': INTEGRATION OF BODY, MIND AND SOUL

Chapter 8

DO SAYINGS, STORY TELLING, PROVERBS AND ROLE-MODELS AFFECT THE PERSONALITY?

No doubt the answer to the question posed in the title of this chapter is in affirmative, yet we devote the whole chapter to justify this answer. As the force of attraction is the main binding force for inanimate objects in the Universe, so is the love for animate objects in Nature. Since love is the common factor prevailing among all these aspects of character building, we first high- light its cosmic character and make some observations. Note that whether it is a story telling, use of sayings and proverbs, or lessons from role models, they all narrate empirical aspect of certain laws (cf. Sect. 3.3.2) pertaining to human/nonhuman behavior. Therefore, we group them under the heading of behavioral facts. If these facts are devour properly, at times they can do wonders in transforming one's life. In Sect. 8.2 we discuss the origin and interpretation of these facts and highlight their role with reference to gross, micro and causal existences of the human Being. Out of the entire gamut of human experiences and actions a fact can affect only a few of them and this constitutes a 'sphere of influences', such discussions are continued in Sect.8.3. Sect. 8.4 is devoted to discuss as to what extent the 'role models' or a 'deity' if one believes in, can influence the thinking and actions of an individual. Assuming *Asthānga* yoga of Patanjali as a standard in assessing the greatness of a role model, several examples to this effect are cited here in the Indian context. Finally, concluding remarks are made in Sect. 8.5.

8.1 UNIVERSALITY OF LOVE AND THE FORCES OF ATTRACTION IN NATURE

While discussing the abstraction and proliferation aspect of knowledge the veracity of force of attraction through inverse square law is already highlighted in Sect. 3.3.1. For animate objects, however, God has perhaps translated this force of attraction into love — a characteristic of soul. In any case, the love or the force of attraction is the most fundamental entity towards the existence of Universe or in general maintaining the cosmic-order. If at all there is repulsion or hatred, it is man-made, localized and temporary. In fact, without love and affection this whole world would have been a desert. As the force of attraction for inanimate objects is quantifiable to a great extent, it is surprising that the love for living objects in the behavioral science is not quantifiable at least till this date.

As a matter of fact there exists a hierarchy of bonds for an individual in this world. First of all love and affection bind the individual to his Self and body through the functions of mind, then to his family, his society, his state, his nation and so on through one or other type of binding forces (e.g. through the terms of duties and responsibilities or via moral and ethical values). By all standards, the attachment or binding appears to be natural while the detachment or hatred is the man-made quality.

In the language of physics, i.e. in the light of many body theories these binding forces could be (i) one-to-one, (ii) one-to-many, (iii) many-to one, and (iv) many-to-many. In the context of human Beings, examples can be cited with regard to one-to-zero or many-to-zero case when an individual is interacting with the Self (i.e. when a person is sitting in meditation) or a group of persons are sitting in meditation. While we shall discuss some of these cases in Part C of this book, Vedic Science has however suggested the rules of the game in very clear terms for all the above four possibilities. As a matter of fact, particular and distinct forms of love and affection between and among persons develop different relations. They, in turn, appear as a part of their duties and responsibilities towards each other mainly for a peaceful and meaningful co-existence.

However, for humans there is another aspect of love in the form of pseudo-love and pseudo-affection or pseudo-harmony. In this case love and affection may be based on material gains and with an element of selfishness. These aspects generally are not through interior awakening and profound search of the within. This kind of love and affection could be an illusion. In fact the attributes like selfishness, greed, compassion, etc. affect the natural binding between husband and wife, parents and children, as also between friends, colleagues and the likes. However, an introspection and certain adjustments can change the things drastically. Note that love manifests its reality in deeds and not just in words.

In the language of patomic model, the love in the Being originates from soul SO, flows through the mind within the boundaries as defined by the intellect I and ego E and finally manifests through the senses of knowledge and action, SE and the body B in the domain of worldly objects WO. Conversely, in the presence of SO, SE and B of a Being b, find attachment to the objects of WO via M and decide its fineness and subtlety using I and E and realizes it finally in SO itself as the "beauty of nature". In fact it is the worldly knowledge and its applications in the day-to-day life that bind the individual even to the so called 'spiritual liberates'. Further note that there are some negative emotions like lust, pride, anger, greed, jealousy, etc., that are responsible for the distortions of love.

8.2 BEHAVIORAL FACTS: THEIR ORIGIN AND INTERPRETATION

If one goes with wisdom of old persons, passing from one generation to another generation, then it is not wrong to say that the behavioral facts must have originated with the human race and at all the levels of patomic model, namely $\mathcal{C}$, $\mathcal{M}$ and $\mathcal{G}$. Broadly speaking these facts arise due to the projection of experience of an individual at the level of Self (when the Self himself is an analyzer) or at the level of Self of other person(s) (when the other person(s) is an analyzer) in the domain of space and time. Further, at the level of space and time, these experiences could be temporal and local, or permanent and global. In fact the worth of these experiences (in terms of ethical and moral values, their multiplicity and the plurality of their interpretations) in different cultures are somehow better recognized in recent times, particularly after the advancement of means of communication.

Example 8.2.1: Suppose a person, out of his own experience, gathers a feeling that "whosoever is physically powerful, grabs his desired material things". This fact originating out of his own experience can be analyzed by his-Self and he himself phrases it as 'might is right". Note that this is only one possibility of narrating the fact; other possibility is that the person is not intelligent enough to phrase the conclusion but narrates the experience to other person who perhaps is more intelligent; and the other person analyses the experience and phrases the idiom.

One can as well note other facts about this behavioral fact as under:

(i) The experience is Universal and the conclusion can be phrased differently in different cultures and languages.

(ii) The analogy used to narrate the experience can vary from time to time, place to place and from person to person, as in (iii) below.

(iii) The level of development of faculty of understanding of the analyzer (could be the same experiencer or the other person to whom the experience is narrated) also matters in phrasing the conclusion.

(iv) Since the truth (fact) is un-manifest in physical terms, the same has to be expressed for the outer world either through words, objects, or using any other entity. Therefore, analogies, simile or parallelism have to be used for the narration of the fact. Thus, the quality of analogy (see, (Kaushal, 2003)) used in phrasing the experience differs, for example, for a common man, scientist or philosopher category of persons. They use their own specialty in designing the analogy.

From the point of view of a common man the above experience, particularly in a north Indian language (Hindi) can be narrated through "*Jisaki lathi, usaki bhains*", literally means "whosoever has stick in his hand, the wandering buffalo belongs to him". Knowing very well that there is no connection between stick and buffalo separately with the experience, but when words are put together, they make the similar sense as the experience. Thus, it is the spirit and/or the context of using the idiom which are important and not the words. This is how one should understand and devour the meanings of various other sayings, proverbs, idioms, stories, etc. in his day-to-day life.

Example 8.2.2: Suppose a person has experienced the fruits of the intricate theory of *karma* of SMBG, i.e. as to how to remain unattached to the success and failure of an action but to remain devoted in its performance only. If he finds it difficult to convey this fact to a common man, then he (as an analyzer) comes out with a phrased version of this conclusion as "*As you sow, so you reap*" or in Hindi one uses it as : "*Jaisi karani, vaisi bharani*". Now, as for the phrase in Example 8.2.1, for this case as well it is not difficult to check (i) its universality with respect to space and time, (ii) its interpretation and digestion by different users depending on the level of development of their FOUs, and (iii) its variants used in different languages and cultures, possibly with different analogies with reference to the verbs appearing in the phrase but by retaining the spirit or the purpose inherent in the phrase (idiom).

The above examples explain as to how the behavioral facts are created. Now we analyze the reverse process, i.e. the situation when a behavioral facts is narrated by a person (analyzer) and if the first time listener/reader (the so-called 'user') of it has not experienced the spirit of the fact, then the user will have lessons from this incidence. In this way, these facts can leave some impact (temporary or permanent depending on the nature of the fact and the mindset of the user) on the individual and at times can even help in transforming his life. Further, depending on the quality of the behavioral fact narrated, the impact on the actions of the individual could be in his $\mathcal{G}$, $\mathcal{M}$ and $\mathcal{C}$ domains.

8.2.1 Behavioral facts at the level of causal body ($\mathcal{C}$)

In general, all universal facts regarding the actions and behaviour of a living Being are the attributes of soul which pertain to the domain $\mathcal{C}$. As they are independent of space and time, they consistently manifest at all times and in all cultures of the world in one form or the other— sometimes in the folklore or in the wisdom of old persons through proverbs, idioms, sayings or writings, etc.

As mentioned before, all positive constructs and the characteristics thereof in the individual are the properties of soul, viz., truth, goodness, love, beauty, silence, peace, joy, etc. Negative constructs/pursuits however appear just like bubbles on the surface of water of positivity. Everybody feels that love and kindness are the best but not war and hatred, since the former pair belongs to the domain of soul ($\mathcal{C}$). In fact all behavioral facts about an individual which uplift his FOU to the level of spirituality" — a domain of $\mathcal{C}$, belong to this class.

Example 8.2.3: All the so-called eternal truths regarding an individual or Nature itself have roots in the domain of $\mathcal{C}$; e.g., *"God has provided enough for every one's need but not for every one's greed"*. Clearly, the spirit behind this saying is independent of space and time and also of the species, like human Being, i.e. a better degree of universality appears in it.

Another class of eternal facts belong to this category are those related to the phenomena of life, death and the world-order in general. Such sayings always console a person or guide him to attain peace, when one is in depression or about to die. Such sayings are normally related to the eternity of soul, its attributes, or to the intricacy of *karmic* theory (cf. SMBG).

Example 8.2.4: *"Pala kā patā nahin, barason ki ṭaiyāri"* or "when there is no guarantee of the next moment, then why to worry for future". Note that a user can extract several meanings out of it depending on his mindset or on the level of development of his FOU. For example, one can go with the spirit of "enjoy and be merry" at the level of sensual pleasure. A third (besides analyzer and user) person, who is badly attached and destroys his present for the unseen future, can have a great lesson from this simple phrase, if he so desires. For a fourth person, however, this simple saying, while can create a small sphere of influence (cf. Sect. 8.3) only, he may be capable of combining these lessons with the lessons which he draws from other sayings as well and thus he can make the best use of the aforementioned saying.

8.2.2 Behavioral facts at the level of micro body ($\mathcal{M}$)

Facts at the level of $\mathcal{M}$ are mainly attributed to the functions of mind, intellect and ego, and they are concerned with the feelings, emotions, decisions, intellectual exercises, memories, self-expressions, etc. In the literary language one can say that the first category of them belongs to the domain of heart, the second one to the domain of brain and the third one belongs to an overlap of domains of both heart and brain as the behavioral facts in the last category are selectively stored in the subconscious mind. Normally, idioms, proverbs, sayings, folklore, or wisdom of old persons, poems, etc. are the medium of expression of these facts and one applies or uses them as and when he desires in solving the problems of his day-to-day life. Sometimes these philosophical truths of life become the guiding principle in one's career or in the tenets of a cult or religion. Since the micro-body $\mathcal{M}$ links the inner (the domain of $\mathcal{C}$) and the outer (the domain of $\mathcal{G}$) worlds, the behavioral facts of this category can further be of two types, namely with subjective meanings and with objective meanings. While the whole bunch of objective sciences is devoted to find explanation(s) or to establish objective facts, many of the subjective facts are still taken as granted and sometimes without seeking any logic. But note that the facts are the facts, they have to be accepted. In what follows we list a few representative examples of various categories of subjective facts.

Example 8.2.5: Facts with reference to an individual and his Self: (i) Facts or phrases discussed in Example 8.2.2 and 8.2.3, carry a lot of subjective meaning; (ii) According to the Hindi poet, Tulsidas, in *Rāmāyan*a, "*Jāki rahi bhāvanā jaisi, prabhu mūrata dekhi tin taisi*", i.e. "in terms of faith, trust and confidence, whatever feelings one has in a deity, role model, in an individual or in an idol, he worships (or pleases) him accordingly". Another *Sanskrit* verse with parallel meaning is

Mantre, tirthe, dvije, deve, deivajne, bhesaje gurauh,
Yādrasi bhāvana bhavati siddhih bhavati tādrasi.

i.e. "in hymn, place of pilgrimage (or worship), priest, god or deity, goddess, medicine, and in teacher whatever types of feelings one has created about them, he gets success accordingly after their use in life". (iii) "*All charming people have something to conceal, usually their total dependence on the appreciation of others*" (a fact in the domain of mind) ; (iv) "*Efforts may fail, but do not fail to make efforts*" (a fact of the domain of intellect and useful for the success of an individual or a group of individuals); (v) "*To handle yourself, use your head; to handle others, use your heart*" (a fact, due to Donald Laird, which beautifully defines the self-discipline and the role of an individual while behaving with others); (vi) "*Knowledge is gained by prostrating at the feet of wise*" (SMBG:4.34) (a case of suppressing ego, clearly the experience of the "wise" is added to the knowledge available already in the scriptures), and (vii) "*All sins are crossed over by a raft of knowledge*" (SMBG:4.36) (sin often is an act of ignorance and this ignorance is inversely proportional to knowledge).

Like the facts (vi) and (vii) there are millions of facts about the life and its existence in Vedic literature (say, e.g., in *Upanisads*, *Rāmāyana* and *Mahābhārata*), however, we refrain ourselves from going into further details. One can as well note the following classified examples:

Example 8.2.6: There are plenty of facts with reference to one's relatives and family, one's friend and society, and one's citizenship and the laws of land.

Example 8.2.7: There are plenty of facts with reference to one's interaction with Nature.

Example 8.2.8: There are many facts with reference to one's existence in the world and the Universe in general.

Note that many facts of these various categories are transmitted from one generation to another, mainly by old persons. In the Indian context, epochs like *Ramayana* and

Mahabharata and the collection of stories like *Hitopadesh* and *Panchatantra* are full of above categories of examples. Sometimes their parallelisms through metaphors or similes are used to impress upon the deeper meaning of these facts.

8.2.3 Behavioral facts at the level of gross-body ($\mathcal{G}$)

Facts at the level of gross body are the creation out of the experiences gained mostly by senses of knowledge and biological body in the external environment. The facts belonging to this domain help in extracting the subjective component of reality in Nature out of the manifestly objective version of these facts. This category of facts, mainly pertain to the body or to the means of its survival (in terms of beauty, habits and maintenance) in the given environment. Some such idiomatic phrases are as follows:

Example 8.2.9: (i) "*Many people in that country live from hand to mouth*" (i.e. without any provision for future); (ii) "*He can turn his hand to anything*" (i.e. he can adopt anything), etc.

Example 8.2.10: "*Speech is silver silence is gold*" (i.e. silence is superior to meaningless or nonsensical talking).

In this case the domain $\mathcal{G}$ in fact helps in extracting the subjective component of reality in Nature out of the objective reality and the material world, which in turn is supplied to the domain of $\mathcal{M}$. The micro-body $\mathcal{M}$ is used again to establish the facts by way of analyzing the data collected using the scientific or objective methods.

8.2.4 Narrating facts through story-telling

Story telling is a wonderful art of transferring knowledge and teaching the persons of all age groups. This enables persons to learn, to grow, to find options and meanings, to heal, and to understand and to honor the world in terms of its environment, creatures and its different kinds of people. In fact a story pitches a person into a space of multiple realities in addition to the one in which he already lives.

Indian scriptures, not only *Purānās* in the religious context but also *Panchatantra* and *Hitopadesha* in the context of moral and ethical values, are full of such stories. In fact sermons, gospels or other behavioral facts for that matter communicated to a person become more effective if told or exemplified through stories. Since stories are received image by image, the characters in the story could be imagined in any form like humans, animals, birds or even the plant kingdom.

When one starts telling "once upon a time or long, long ago when animals used to speak to men or men to animals, and both to the God", etc. then such beginning toss us into another, more receptive space than the defined one we live and work in. Often it is the moral of the story which is important and not even the story teller, his words, the characters in the story or even the images for an elderly person. But for youngsters it matters a lot as to what extent the FOU of the storyteller is developed. The listener in fact gets benefitted in the same proportion. Conversely, a story can also be created in order to communicate a moral to a listener in an effective manner. While doing so, the storyteller has to keep in mind the level of understanding of FOUs of the listener. In summary, this method of imparting the knowledge while plays an invisible role in shaping the life, it helps one in creating a precious gift and also in healing and releasing him from the tension.

8.3 A Behavioral Fact and its Sphere of Influence

Whether the affected or benefited listener is an individual or a group of individuals, in either case a fact carries a "sphere of influence". Meaning thereby, out of infinitely many actions performed by an individual during the day only a selective few of them get affected by the guidance of a given fact and this defines its sphere of influence. Similarly, corresponding to another fact there is another sphere of influence among the actions of a person. At the level of inner EOLs, while these spheres of influence have somewhat hard boundaries, the same become softer or porous as they come out to the level of outer EOLs. In this domain the spheres start overlapping or penetrating into each other and thus affecting the behavior of the individual rather collectively. In fact, there is a kind of assimilation or amalgamation of different categories of facts and the diffusion of different spheres of influence takes place at different stages.

As mentioned before, certain types of behavioral facts, particularly the ones that guide at the level of $\mathcal{M}$ and $\mathcal{G}$ (cf. Sect. 8.2.2 and 8.2.3) have more than one interpretation and some of them sometimes get multiplied by the use of various metaphors and similes in different contexts, languages and cultures. This leads to proliferation of knowledge. With regard to the multiplicity of facts in the domain of $\mathcal{G}$, it has no limit in soft disciplines, whereas in hard disciplines like objective sciences and mathematics, the established facts are finite at the level of their abstraction and foundation.

Example 8.3.1: One can find infinitely many applications of a few established conservation laws of physics in day-to-day life. In general, the concepts developed in the mathematical discipline of physics (like classical mechanics, quantum mechanics, etc.) find many applications in the conceptual (like molecular, atomic, nuclear physics etc.), conventional (like heat, electricity, magnetism, optics, etc.) and engineering disciplines. This is the case of proliferation of knowledge and multiplicity of facts in physical science.

Example 8.3.2: Note that the different social or political models are the outcome of a few postulates (facts), or various religions of the world differ only in terms of the nature and interpretation of finite number of postulates (facts).

With regard to the interpretation(s) of behavioral facts, particularly when they are multiplied, it depends on the development of FOUs of users (the persons who have used or are using the fact(s)). It is not necessary that all analyzers (the person who has experienced and realized the spirit of the fact for the first time) of a fact have equally developed FOUs as the user of the fact and this makes a hell of difference in the interpretation(s) of the same fact. However, one should always go for positive/constructive interpretations, if they can be traced by the FOUs of a user. For further details on this aspect of behavioral facts we refer to (Kaushal, 2011, Chapter 5).

8.4 ROLE OF 'ROLE-MODELS' AND 'DEITIES' IN CHARACTER BUILDING

These are the actions performed and the experiences gathered at the level of $\mathcal{M}$ and $\mathcal{G}$ that have to be selectively and appropriately refined in order to have a feel for the events of domain $\mathcal{C}$, i.e. of the spiritual zone. Alternatively, if one gets a feel for the events belonging to the domain $\mathcal{C}$, then the person has learnt the Art of integrating body, mind and soul towards the constructive/positive success of an action. This, in fact, is the first step in the direction of character building or in the personality development in general. We shall return to the details of these aspects in the next chapter. However, here we highlight the roles of 'role-models' and/or 'deities', if at all one believes in them, in such of his attempts.

Before proceeding further, we start with two famous quotations in this connection, namely

"Some are born great, some achieve greatness, and some have greatness by thrusting upon them", (Q1)

and

"Lives of great men all remind us,
we can make our life sublime.
Departing souls leave behind us,
foot prints on the sand of time". (Q2)

The quotation (Q1) clearly classifies the great persons into three categories; one, who are born great; second, who achieve greatness by their efforts in this life itself, and third, who basically are not great but the greatness is thrust upon them by the followers, may be for some vested interests. Clearly, the great persons of the first and the third categories are not many and it becomes difficult to follow them whereas those of the second category are large in number and our discussions will be focused on this general class of great persons. (For a broad classification of great persons in analytical terms, see Chapter 14 and Appendix A).

According to quotation (Q2), all great persons (irrespective of their category) leave some foot prints on the sand of time by way of giving certain message to mankind which in turn can make life of other persons great. Now the question is whether the foot of an individual can as such fit into these foot prints or not? Obviously, the answer is No, as one's foot may be bigger or smaller compared to these foot prints. Therefore, an adjustment with 'positive' spirit is necessary; otherwise one can easily discard the foot prints and look for the other available in the lot. As a matter of fact the choice and the subsequent follow up of the role model is one's own desire, any imposition from outside does not work for long. Another prerequisite for this is one's faith in him, even if one wants to have only a few lessons from the life or experiences of the role model.

8.4.1 As to what extent can a role model help in character building?

One is the luckiest person on this earth if he can find a role model whose greatness can inspire and guide him in all his actions and experiences everywhere and at all times. In fact one learns only in parts from each role model and the learner himself has to do some patch-work (major or minor adjustment depending on both the role model and the person) according to his own requirements mainly to see the pieces as one whole. It is at this stage, when his own understanding of the world-order works or the external help like that of a teacher, councilor or of a guide is needed. Moreover, there is nothing wrong in gathering 'honey' from different characters and personalities.

Example 8.4.1: Recall the case of a honey bee or a butterfly. They fly from flower to flower to collect the 'nectar' and to have a taste and smell of that.

Example 8.4.2: According to Vedic scriptures there was a yogi saint of highest degree, Dattatreya. It is said that Dattatreya as such had no teacher or Guru, but he had 24 lessons from the life and characteristics each of the respective 24 different species and entities of the Universe. These are, (i) tolerance and patience, from *earth*, (ii) un-attachment from *air*, as it remains unattached while carrying the smell from one place to another, (iii) to remain unaffected from the actions of gross- and micro-bodies, from *ether*, (iv) to remain cold and pure, from *water*, (v) to have higher and higher goals in life, like the flame of *fire*, (vi) to bear ups and downs of life, like *moon*, (vii) to have a feel for all-pervading property of *soul*, like the images of *sun* in different mirrors, (viii) not to be attached with the worldly-objects, from the story of a *pigeon*, (ix) not to run after sensual pleasure, from *python*, (x) many lessons from *ocean*, (xi) to learn that all that glitter is not gold, from the life of *moth*, (xii) to have lessons from different teachers and to pass them on to others without much storage, from *honey bee*, (xiii) not to be mad after a female, from the *elephant*, (xiv) to know the limitations of wealth, the honey collected by honey bees after a hard labor, is just picked up by the *honey-extractor* in no time from the bee-hive, (xv) not to be mad after sensual pleasure like music, from *deer*, (xvi) not to be greedy, from *fish*, (xvii) to become detached from the sensual pleasure like sex, from the prostitute *Pingala*, (xviii) not to become greedy for petty small things otherwise one may face death, from a *particular kind* *of bird*, (xix) cuteness, selflessness and contentment, from a *child*, (xx) to do meditation only in solitude and isolation, from the *story of a girl*, (xxi) to see the goal of life from a distance, from the *predator*, (xxii) qualities should not be judged by the external posture, from *snake*, (xxiii) to know the generator, organizer and destroyer aspects of God, from a *spider*, and (xxiv) to know as to how an individual can achieve goodness from a company, from the story of a particular species of insect, '*Bhrangi*'. In summary, if a person understands the hints of his Self, he can always find a source of inspiration and have lessons from any object in Nature.

Example 8.4.3: It is said that God has made one specific yogic exercise (*yogāsana*) for each of the 84 lac species in this Universe as per Vedic scriptures but no exercise as such is prescribed for the human Being. Human Being, however, has borrowed his exercises from these species. One exercise from each one lac of these species is thus adopted by the human Being. Now in terms of utility, these exercises have become popular all over the world with reference to physical and mental development of an individual.

Thus, as far as the lives of great persons are concerned, it is clear from above examples that there is not a single role model who can provide guidance to an individual with regard to whole set of qualities needed either in character building or to become an ideal member of society. One has to do his own 'homework' for this purpose. Some super humans, prophets or deities can however offer somewhat more in this respect provided the person has faith in them. (cf. quotation in Example 8.2.5(ii)). We shall return to some of these discussions later in Sect. 8.4.3.

In the language of patomic model, many of the role models can guide only in the actions and experiences of $\mathcal{G}$-domain, somewhat less in number can guide in the actions of $\mathcal{M}$- and $\mathcal{G}$-domains. Further less, only a countable one, can guide in the actions of all the three $\mathcal{C}$-, $\mathcal{M}$- and $\mathcal{G}$-domains. In general, this guidance by role models to an individual can be projected in four types of actions performed by him. As per Vedic science these four types are: *Nitya* (routine) *karma, Neimittik* (obligatory) *karma*, *Kāmya* (according to one's own will) *karma* and *Nisedha* (prohibited) *karma*. Further, for a healthy and ideal living one should not ignore *Nitya karma* and one should never go for *Nisedha karma*. On the other hand, *Neimittik karma* has to be performed keeping in mind the family or social obligations in the guidance of prevailing role models and values in the society. For the guidance in *Kāmya karma*, one however needs role models of higher rank. It is not difficult to find role models for the guidance in *Nitya* or *Neimittik karmās*, normally elderly persons in the family or in society can do this job. However, as the spectrum of *Kāmya karma* is very wide ranging from $\mathcal{G}$- to $\mathcal{C}$-domains, one needs specific role models for the guidance in this case.

8.4.2 *Asthānga* yoga of Patanjali as a measure of greatness of a role model

As such there is no measure of greatness of a role model. However, if one goes by certain standards then Vedic science through *Asthānga* yoga of Patanjali, can offer a criterion for classifying the role models. In some sense this method of yoga requires a great deal of practice, however it covers the entire spectrum of experiences and actions performed by a person in all the three domains, namely $\mathcal{G}$- , $\mathcal{M}$- and $\mathcal{C}$-domains. The eight components (*asthānga*) or rather steps to be followed by the practitioners of this method of yoga are: (i) *yama*, (ii) *niyama*, (iii) *āsana*, (iv) *prānāyāma*, (v) *pratyāhāra*, (vi) *dhārana*, (vii) *dhyāna*, and (viii) *samādhi*. Each of these components has further divisions and subdivisions. Since a lot of specialized literature is available on this subject under the heading of Raja yoga, we refrain ourselves from going into the details. Here, however, we make some pertinent remarks about the categorization of these components.

(i) Another classification of these eight components is in the form of *bahiranga* (external) yoga (cf. components (i) to (v)) and *antaranga* (internal) yoga (cf. components (vi) to (viii)).

(ii) We avoid the details of the last six components, and list here further divisions of the first two components as follows. Five divisions of *yama* are: (a) truth (*satya*), (b) non-violence (*ahimsa*), (c) continence (*brahmacharya*), (d) non-stealing (*asteya*), want to accumulate of wealth with the sense of meum (*aparigrha*), and the five divisions of *niyama* are: purity (*s'auca*), contentment (*santosa*), austerity (*tapa*), self-study (*svādhyāya*), faith in God (*s'raddha*).

(iii) The entire set of eight components of this yoga represents the spirit of '*sanātana dharma*', but many religious models of the world can be seen as the particular cases of the first five components alone.

(iv) From the point of view classifying role models, one can see as to which ladder the practice of the role model has reached in his life time. In fact a role model can transmit to the follower(s) in the form of guidance in the same manner as what he has achieved. No doubt, a conscious follower can always look beyond the boundaries of the role model but only after a certain stage of development of his FOUs in accordance with the role model.

(v) When the experiences and actions of a conscious practitioner shift from one component to another, his mindset evolves and the person feels a transformed personality at his own. Note that the experiences and actions pertaining to components (i) – (iii) mostly belong to $\mathcal{G}$-domain, pertaining to components (iv) – (vi) mostly belong to $\mathcal{M}$-domain, and those pertaining to components (vii) and (viii) belong to $\mathcal{C}$-domain. Thus, when the mindset of a person has evolved to the ladder of $\mathcal{C}$-domain, he becomes a spiritual person.

This is how the Vedic science offers a clear criterion for ranking the great persons or role models. Further note that a particular quality or a group of qualities of the role model no doubt can always touch the heart of the follower, but a 'man of perfection' (who has assimilated all qualities in his Self and who could be a yogi of highest degree or a deity) can only be a true role model for him.

8.4.3 Some representative role models and deities in the Indian context

It is intensity of faith of the follower that works while he is trying to have lessons from the role model or a deity. As mentioned before, the choice of role model or of a deity may keep on changing as a child grows in age and experience. However, the impact left on the personality of the child does not change so easily, unless he comes to know certain negatives of the role model or else the 'deity' does not help him in fulfilling his desires. In such a situation, the follower instead of understanding the limitations of the role model within the framework of the above standards (cf. Sect. 8.4.2), switches on to other choices. He should rather go to the philosophy of yogi saint Dattatreya (cf. Example 8.4.2).

As a matter of fact, the gain from a role model or from a deity is directly proportional to the intensity of faith in him. At times, a role model with all appealing qualities may not solve the purpose whereas a deity with limited qualities is found to do wonders with the follower. A role model while works mostly in the finite objective (manifest) space, on the other hand, a deity takes the follower mostly to infinite subjective (un-manifest) space with a lot many supernatural powers including omnipotent qualities imposed on it with no scope of any finiteness or criticism. This feeling of the follower at times relieves him of many wrong doings and worries.

Example 8.4.4: According to a scientific experiment as reported in The Times of India 'Times & Trends', two patients suffering from identical diseases admitted to a hospital and given identical set of medicines to cure them and they were watched for a week, without allowing any interaction between them. After a week, when their progress was noted it was found that the one who was 'believer' in a deity had a better progress than the other, who was 'non-believer'. This belief or faith could be in any animate or inanimate object, but with an intensity and an imposition of all super human powers in it.

Example 8.4.5: A person remained atheist throughout his career to the extent that he had painted in all his rooms that 'GOD IS NO WHERE'. He had a child who was going to elementary school. It so happened that one day the person had an argument with his boss which resulted the person to come in depression. In the evening when the person was sitting in his room in a sad mood with his head down, then all of a sudden his child entered the room and started reading the same painting on the wall as 'GOD IS NOW HERE' instead of the spirit with which the same letters were written by his father. It was at this point of time that the person realized something beyond his belief. Not only this, the person then surrendered all his worries to the highest whatever he believed in but also noticed some relief in the depression.

Example 8.4.6: Mahatma Gandhi, after having his education in England and some crucial experiences in practical training in life in South Africa, made India as his *Karma Bhumi* (work place). It appears from his life that he learnt the *Asthānga* yoga of Patanjali but practiced truly only the first of its eight components, namely '*yama*', i.e. truth, non-violence, continence, non-stealing, etc. This made him not only the national but also international figure in the history.

In fact another superior class of role models is that of deities, whose blessings, if one has faith in them, work invariably and in an invisible form. These prophets, like Lord

Buddha, Lord Mahavira, Jesus Christ, Hazarat Mohammed and several others have, in the last two thousand years, given the messages to human race. The measure of their greatness will definitely lie somewhere within the domain of *Asthānga* yoga. Without going into the comparative study of their teachings here, one thing is clear that they were the true messengers of God. Their blessings and teachings, but within the frame work of *Asthānga* yoga, definitely work in 'psycho-space' through some kind of 'psycho-energy'.

Next to this class of role models comes the series of incarnations of God himself, like Lord Rama and Lord Krishna of Vedic literature. It is said that Lord Rama is while assigned 12 units of perfection, Lord Krishna has been assigned the 16 units of perfection, necessary for the so-called 'man of perfection', as per *Asthānga* yoga. Only a man of perfection, who has realized the truth of highest degree, can deliver the philosophy as described in SMBG.

8.5 CONCLUDING DISCUSSION

One classical method to guide a person with regard to improving his behavior is by narrating the behavioral facts before him through sayings, proverbs, storytelling, and/or lives of great persons. This way of imparting the wisdom by elderly persons to younger generation is age old, perhaps as old as the human race on this planet. The question as to what extent this method can be effective for improving the behavior is addressed in this chapter.

After emphasizing on the universality of an attribute of the soul (i.e. love in the spiritual domain), its cosmic character in the physical domain in the form of force of attraction is highlighted. It is argued that the behavioral facts originate basically from the experiences of a person at any of these $\mathcal{C}$- , $\mathcal{M}$- or $\mathcal{G}$- domains of working. The person is called 'analyzer', as he or any other person to whom he narrates the experience analyses the experience and comes out with a fact. At the next stage this fact when narrated to a person (called 'user') is used by the latter for his benefit, if he so desires, and leaves some impact. The facts so arrived at, in their own right while are independent of space, time and culture, but their impact towards improving one's character or behavior, however, varies from user to user. In fact, the quality of analogies used in narrating the fact to the user also depends on the level of development of FOUs of both the analyzer and the user. Some further remarks on the role of behavioral facts in improving one's behavior are as under:

(i) There is some kind of imperfection in the person and to restore the perfection the person needs guidance or education. If one learns the 'Art of living' then this imperfection can be converted into strength. The guidance from the behavioral facts is a step in this direction of learning the Art of living. It overcomes the negativity and leads to success. Further, note that (a) the person alone is responsible for his attitude, (b) as is his attitude, so are his perceptions, (c) as is his perception, so is his interaction with the world, (d) as is his interaction, so is the experience of life, and (e) as is the experience, so is the quality of his life and actions. Further note that whatever is the quality of his life, the same he transfers to coming generation(s) and the same in fact leads to a downfall or upliftment of a family or society. This is how the attitude of an individual, derived from a fact, affects the community as a whole.

(ii) Note that both, analyzer as well as user of a fact are living Beings who are equipped with the faculties involving uncontrollable parameters. Therefore, in the process of transferring the experience to newer generations, the distortion of facts is natural and sometimes they are multiplied to the extent that the original spirit of the fact is lost.

As these facts help in improving the behavior of a person only in parts, after sometime he starts looking for a role model, who perhaps is equipped with a bigger set of qualities in one entity itself. However, in view of the standard set by the *Asthānga* yoga of Patanjali, the role models also show limitations as far as an overall development of one's personality is concerned. Then the person switches on to a deity for the guidance. It is a common experience that if one surrender himself totally before "someone", then that "someone" is expected to take care of all liabilities of the person who surrenders, provided that "someone" is capable enough for this purpose. It does not mean that the surrendering person becomes weak or handicapped by doing so, rather he draws power by remaining in the shadow of that "someone" and thereby when the person is in trouble physically or mentally, he can approach the "someone". By doing so the person passes a peaceful life — a motto of life. Imagine! How would be the life of a person in the absence of that "someone"; it will continue except for the fact that the person now might feel more insecure and worried (cf. Example 8.4.5).

As a matter of fact, the devotee is benefitted from a deity only up to a certain extent even if the latter is a 'man of perfection'. Then, after a great devotion a stage comes when the devotee develops his own FOU sufficiently so that he himself starts feeling as a part of deity as far as the omnipotence of the deity is concerned.

Further Reading:

This whole chapter is a condensed version of Chapter 5 of (Kaushal, 2011); for a discussion on *Asthānga* yoga see (Kaushal, 2011, Chapter 12) and for a discussion on Deities see (Kaushal,

2011, Chapter 13); for further details of Example 8.4.2, see (Acharya, 1995).

High Skill Exercises and Projects

8.1 Imagine and discuss the possibility of existence of a world which is bereft of love among living Beings and force of attraction among inanimate objects, i.e., full of hatred and the force of repulsion. Can such a world maintain its order and existence?

8.2 Analyze the phrase, "All that we are, is a result of what we have thought" in view of the Universality of law of force of attraction.

8.3 Note the chain of 'desire', 'prayer', 'faith' and 'success' in the experience "Whatsoever things you desire, when you pray, believe that you receive them and you shall have them", and accordingly discuss the nature of forces of attraction that come into existence at different stages in the whole process.

8.4 "What one radiates outward in his thoughts, feelings, mental pictures and words, one attracts them into his life". Analyze this law of attraction through the dynamics of EOLs.

8.5 Elaborate with examples on the meaning of the phrase, "Love manifests its reality in deeds and not just in words". Analyze the underlying process of this manifestation with an example.

8.6 Write a note on the creation of a behavioral fact at different levels of development of FOUs of an individual out of the same experience. Discuss the roles of 'analyzer' and 'user' in the process of implementing this fact.

8.7 Discuss and differentiate the impacts left on a listener by a behavioral fact as narrated by a 'user' and also by a storyteller with the help of an example.

8.8 What do you mean by the 'sphere of influence' of a behavioral fact? How can one avoid the clashes between two and more distinct influences during the period of their practice?

8.9 List and elaborate on one behavioral fact (not listed in the book) from Hindi poetry for each category of human existences (namely causal, micro and gross). Repeat this search from English poetry as well.

8.10 Analyze the idiom, "As you sow, so shall you mow' (i.e. "*Jaisi karani veisi bharani*") and search its other analogues in Hindi, English and in your own mother tongue, with reference to actions performed at all the three (namely causal, micro and gross-body) levels.

8.11 Discuss the wonderful lesson which one draws from the folk-saying, "*Oot ke ghar ki pāti, bānche satyānāshi*" (i.e., "a confused person analyses the proceedings of an immoral family"). Clearly, the level of development of FOUs of the analyzer will matter a lot in the quality of analysis. Keeping this situation in mind, discuss in detail the cases when (i) the proceedings of a family with morals are analyzed by an enlightened person, (ii) the proceedings of a family with morals are analyzed by an immoral person, (iii) the proceedings of a family with immorals is analyzed by an enlightened person, and (iv) the proceedings of a family with immorals is analyzed by an immoral person.

8.12 Keeping in mind the multiplicity of behavioral facts and their influence in the life, discuss once again the abstraction and proliferation aspects of knowledge (cf. Exercise 3.3).

8.13 Write a note on the role of 'role models' and of a 'deity' in the character building of a person. Spell out the advantages and disadvantages of the two choices. Prepare a summary of morals which one draws from Example 8.4.2.

8.14 Explain how the *Ashthânga* yoga of Patanjali can be used as a standard to measure the greatness of a great person or of a role model. Also discuss the role of the last six components of this yoga in such a categorization.

8.15 One remembers God during the trouble: When a person was wandering on the ground near a multistoried building, another person was watching his movement from the top, say, from 11-th floor of the building. The latter started dropping one Re coins from the balcony of the 11-th floor. The person on the ground started collecting the coins without really watching as from where these coins are coming. When the person on

11-th floor started dropping pieces of stone (some of which might have had hit the former) instead of coin, then the person on the ground started looking up as to where from and how these stones are falling and hitting him. This is how a common man remembers God, when he is in trouble; otherwise does not care for Him. What moral do you draw from this story?

8.16 Peculiarity of a saying sometimes inspires a person to remember it and subsequently to have lessons from it: Here is a mathematically designed saying which beautifully connects the $\mathcal{G}$-domain functioning to the $\mathcal{C}$-domain functioning, viz., "*2get and 2give create many problems, (just double it), 4get and 4give solve all the problems.*" Analyze this saying and discuss in detail the moral one draws from it.

8.17 To realize as to how much important is the 'attitude'-component in one's personality, see Exercise 14.13 and justify the concluding remarks made on it in Sect. 8.5 (i).

Chapter 9

CHARACTER BUILDING AND PERSONALITY DEVELOPMENT

Whether it is character building or the personality development, both mechanisms are mostly individual based in the sense that the external environment only offers a standard to judge their merit and not the method of their creation. While the former is somewhat subjective, like the inner garments of soul, the latter is objective like the outer garments. Further, the character focuses on the distinctive human qualities, the personality, on the other hand, is an extreme adulation of the individual. The character gives a boost to moral strength, the personality, however, invites both moral and physical strength in a varying proportion. However, both these aspects of human behavior originate from the same dynamics of inner EOLs, termed here as the 'personality creation mechanism' (PCM). In this chapter, after presenting a brief survey of these aspects of human behavior studied in thc modern context, the basic ingredients necessary for their creation are discussed in Sects.9.2. and 9.3. In Sect.9.4, we explore the possibilities of analyzing different personalities within the framework of patomic model and suggest some tips towards their improvement in Sect.9.5. Further, in Sect.9.6 we demonstrate a correspondence between two akin mechanisms, namely 'personality creation' and the 'art of integrating the body, mind and soul'. Finally, concluding remarks are made in Sect.9.7.

9.1 STUDIES ON PERSONALITY AND ITS DEVELOPMENT IN MODERN TIMES

Personality development has been a subject of study and research in psychology departments for more than a century now. In view of the downfall of moral and ethical values in the society as also an increase in the psychic diseases not only among young generation but also among professionals, the subject has become the thrust area of study in recent times. The subject has gained further momentum in its new incarnation under the names of 'individual processes' or 'self-management' in the institutes of management. In either situation, the methodology adopted is the one that is based on statistical analysis of data or on a vast variety of case-studies. This leads to empirical theories for the subject. Unless an individual is defined and analysed at the most fundamental level in terms of EOLs and EFLs, a formal theory for the subject remains a far cry. In its new incarnation, no doubt, the subject has started dealing with very subtle and somewhat intriguing cases, but the approach remains an empirical one, mainly because the case-studies supply the basic facts only in a piece-meal manner towards the development of theories. In spite of all this, there still remains a need of a formal theory of personality. In the forthcoming sections an attempt will be made on this front using the patomic model of human Being.

In its new incarnation, the subject has grown mostly in the West where there have been frequent industrial revolutions and the problems were cropping up between employers and employees. When studying the behavior of employees in an organization, one broadly considers five heads corresponding to five categories of processes that take place, namely (a) individual processes, (b) inter-personal and group processes, (c) organizational processes, and (d) change processes, over and above them is the (e) environment, in which the employees are working. For an analysis of these processes within the framework of patomic model, we shall return in Chapter 14. However, here we make some brief observations on the prevailing studies in the institutes of management, carried out now mostly in a scientific spirit.

9.1.1 Personality and individual processes

Obviously, the personality of an individual plays an important role in the dynamics of the organization as a whole. In addition to personality, the other aspects of study under the caption of 'individual processes' pertain to one's perception, values and attitudes, learning capacity and its reinforcement or implementation, work motivation, and the last but important one is the capacity of bearing the work stress. Many of these aspects clearly rely on the fact as to how an individual has created his personality out of its subjective content, i.e., the character of the person. Before proceeding further, let us look at some modern definitions of the personality of a person.

As such there is no unique definition of personality. However, according to Engler (1991), personality of a person represents personal characteristics that lead to conscious patterns of behavior. One analyses these behavioral patterns when the person interacts with other persons. According to another definition by Hogan (1991), personality refers to the relatively stable pattern of behaviors and consistent internal states that explain a person's behavioral tendencies. Further, the personality is considered to have both internal and external elements. The external traits in fact are observable behaviors that help in identifying one's personality. The internal states, on the other hand, represent the thoughts, values and genetic characteristics that one infers from the observable behaviors.

One way to understand the personality of an individual is to understand both internal and external elements that the individual has in common with others and what makes that particular individual unique. Thus, each employee in an organization is unique but may or may not respond as others do in a given situation. In fact, the theories of personality are developed mainly on this ground. Since the behavior is an outcome of stable personality traits, some social scientists do not accept the notion of personality as such instead they argue that the behavior can be determined exclusively by the external conditions. Moreover, stable traits do exist and these lead people to behave consistently with time and in different settings. In such descriptions, though the concept of personality appears illusive, but in reality it is not so; it remains in the background while understanding the traits of the individual. Like this, there are many other aspect of one's personality which have been the subject of study in behavioural science. However, we refrain ourselves from going into these details here. Yet, some pertinent points are worth mentioning here:

(i) Hogan's definition of personality is somewhat more intriguing in the sense that it accounts for internal states and that too the consistent ones. This clearly points to the dynamics of inner EOLs in the present context.

(ii) When the behavior patterns of a person are compared with those of others, it still remains a case of relative studies, may be good for an organization but not on a absolute scale. For the absolute scale, every society or culture, however, has certain standards to judge the merit of one's personality. This standard is normally defined after keeping in mind the social and/or religious norms. For example, one such standard, namely Raj Yoga, is already discussed in the previous chapter (cf. Sect. 8.4.2).

(iii) The external environment in general may consist of humans, nonhumans and inanimate objects. The interactions of a person with them will, however, differ from person to person. Thus, an account of external environment, when comparing the personalities is not that simple as considered in the organizational studies.

(iv) Hofstede's framework (1980) can be presented as follows: In tune with point (ii) above, culture also provides more than an understanding of personality development. In fact, without a cultural-religious framework, the behavior of a person and hence his personality has no meaning and without meaning behavior has no purpose. It is the culture that provides people with a set of values and assumptive beliefs as well as implicit inferences about how the world operates. Thus, the culture of the society or the country a person lives in also has an impact on the personality.

9.1.2 Understanding personality traits and dimensions

With a view to differentiating, ordering and naming the differences in people's behavior and experience, the concept of personality factor has been introduced in the multidimensional model of personality. Pertaining to human qualities, the words which were semantically similar (synonyms) were grouped in some minimal number of 16, as antonyms pairs. These sixteen personality factors so found are as follows: (i) apprehensive vs. self-assured, (ii) assertive vs. humble, (iii) conscientious vs. expedient, (iv) controlled vs. casual, (v) emotionally stable vs. unstable, (vi) experimental vs. conservative, (vii) happy-go-lucky vs. sober, (viii) imaginative vs. practical, (ix) more intelligent vs. less intelligent, (x) outgoing vs. reserved, (xi) relaxed vs. tense, (xii) reserved vs. warm, (xiii) shrewd vs. forthright, (xiv) suspicious vs. trusting, (xv) tough-minded vs. sensitive, and (xvi) venturesome vs. timid.

At the time of recruitment or when one judges the personality of a person, a questionnaire prepared on the basis of these factors is used in personnel selection. Further, for analysis purposes these 16 factors are reduced to five which, in turn, have helped in developing the so-called 'Big-Five' (multidimensional) personality theory. These Big Five factors identified are: (a) extraversion (comfort level of individual), (b) agreeableness (individual's behavior towards others), (c) conscientiousness (extent to which one shows consistent and reliable behavior while working in organization), (d) emotional stability (ability to control his emotions at the time of crisis), and (e) openness to experience (ability to be open to any kind of experience that helps him to do the job). Each of these factors helps in understanding the behavioral patterns in one's personality.

Another approach for the personality test, based on cognitive styles of psychology and very widely used in business organizations, is due to Jung (1933). Cognitive style describes the way in which an individual perceives and processes information. According to Jung, individuals develop, mostly unconsciously, preferred ways of gathering information and evaluating it to make decisions. The two opposite ways of gathering information are through a sensing method and by intuition, and the two opposite ways of evaluating information are thinking and feeling, as depicted in Fig.9.1. These different ways of gathering and evaluating information combine to form matrix of four problem-solving behaviors in cognitive psychology, namely sensation thinkers (ST), intuitive thinkers (IT), sensation feelers (SF), and intuitive feelers (IF). Fig.9.1 demonstrates as to how these four personality types emerge. Each type has its merits and de-merits, but in a complex organization all are necessary. Further, note that while using these types in the analysis of personalities of individuals, the roles of personality of managers, judges, or recruiters cannot be ruled out, and the same does not appear clearly in the theory of Jung. In the next section we make some more observations on this theory.

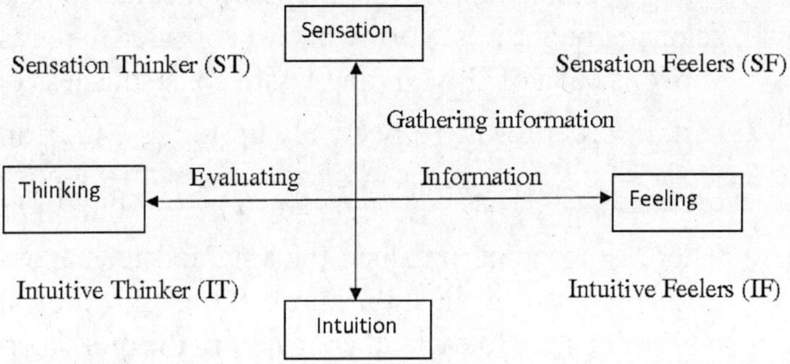

Fig.9.1: The framework of Jung for handling information. In this representation, the four quadrants depict the four cognitive styles of analyzing the personality of individuals.

9.2 PERSONALITY THEORY OF JUNG: REMARKS AND POSSIBLE MODIFICATIONS

In what follows, we make some observations on the personality theory of Jung and suggest some possible modifications to it in the light of patomic model of human Being.

(i) The basic requirement to develop preferred ways of gathering information and evaluating it to make decision by a person is that he has to be conscious. A dead body can not undergo the processes of sensation, feeling, intuition and thinking. The respective agencies responsible for these processes also have to be functional and conscious. This consciousness or awareness may vary from person to person but cannot be zero.

(ii) In fact, in Fig.9.1, a simple replacement of 'sensation' by the biological body and senses of knowledge (B+SE = G), 'feeling' by the faculty of emotion, i.e. the mind M, 'intuition' by the faculty of memory, i.e. the ego E, and 'thinking' by the faculty of decision, i.e. the intellect I, as displayed in Fig.9.2, will help a lot in understanding and implementing the theory of Jung.

(iii) Since a person looking for an opportunity has to be conscious enough, it is worthwhile to consider the dressed versions each of G. M, E and I with consciousness up to certain orders, say, respectively up to s , m, r and n orders as $\tilde{G}^{(s)}$, $\tilde{M}^{(m)}$, $\tilde{E}^{(r)}$ and $\tilde{I}^{(n)}$ (cf. Fig.9.2).

(iv) There is no point in calling thinking and feeling as opposite ways of evaluation information, they are rather complementary to each other in view of the dressing rules (cf. Eqs.(7.1)-(7.3)). Moreover, if they are the opposite ways, then there will never be a stability— emotional or otherwise (cf. Big-Five theory). Therefore, not only I and M as also G and E pairwise have to be in harmony but also each of the four has to be in tune with the source of consciousness SO.

To illuminate or make functional all the four agencies constantly with consciousness let its source SO be placed in the centre as in Fig.9.2.

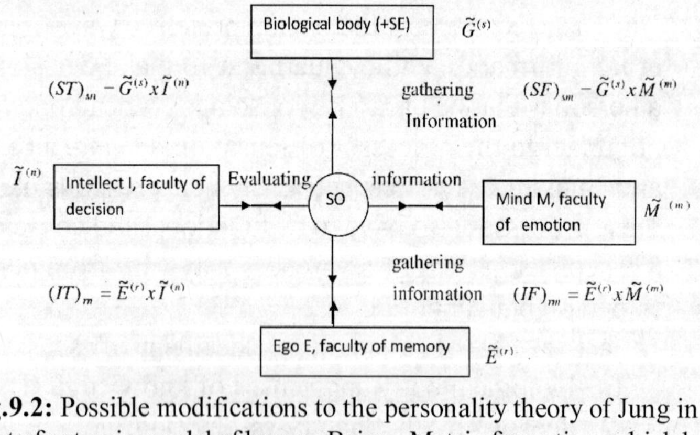

Fig.9.2: Possible modifications to the personality theory of Jung in the light of patomic model of human Being. Matrix formation, which helps in distinguishing the personalities, can clearly be seen in this picture in all the four quadrants.

Such a scheme of study will not only give a better understanding of the theory of Jung but also suggests a way out to construct four-style matrices in cognitive psychology in precise mathematical terms, viz.,

$$(SF)_{sm} = \tilde{G}^{(s)} \times \tilde{M}^{(m)}; \ (IF)_{mr} = \tilde{M}^{(m)} \times \tilde{E}^{(r)},$$

$$(IT)_{nr} = \tilde{I}^{(n)} \times \tilde{E}^{(r)}; \ (ST)_{sn} = \tilde{G}^{(s)} \times \tilde{I}^{(n)},$$

where $\tilde{G}^{(s)}, \tilde{M}^{(m)}, \tilde{E}^{(r)}$ and $\tilde{I}^{(n)}$ are the dressed versions of the corresponding agencies as discussed in Sect. 7.2. Next we discuss the subjective aspect of personality, which, in turn, pertains to the character building of an individual.

9.3 PERSONALITY AND ITS INGREDIENTS: A SCHEMATIC PICTURE

As we have seen in the previous section, the personality tests of individuals are carried out on the basis of gross features of human qualities. In this section we proceed to analyse these features within the framework of patomic model of human Being, particularly with reference to the dynamics of inner EOLs. A flowchart to this effect is shown in Fig. 9.3, which in some sense is the modified version of the one discussed by Parthasarathy (1992). If a person is conscious enough to undergo self-observation and watch the nature of *sankalpās*, then this chart works, otherwise for a common man engaged badly in worldly objects, Parthasarathy proposes another broad classification of personalities as shown in Fig.9.4.

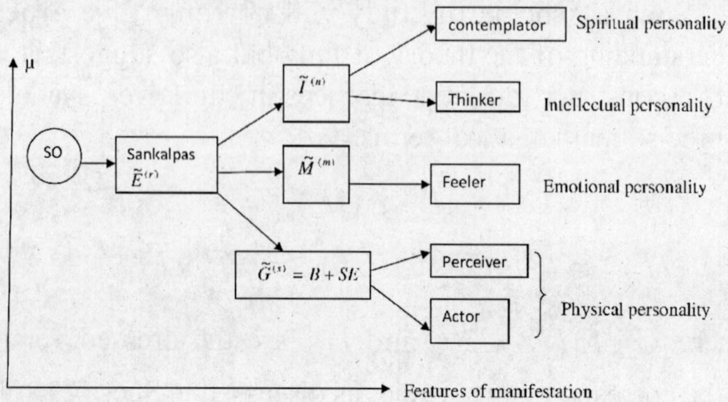

Fig.9.3: A flow chart explaining the creation of different types of personalities in an individual depending on the levels of development of his FOU.

In a broad sense personalities can also be classified on the basis of *sankalpās* (cf. Fig.9.4). A *sankalpa* allows two choices to follow–passive and aggressive. Each of them again follows either the systematic of positive pursuits (goodness) or of negative pursuits (badness). Thus, there are four distinct natures covering the entire range of inner personalities of persons characterized by aggressive goodness, aggressive badness, passive goodness and passive badness (cf. Fig.9.4). For example, a passive person works according to the fancies of his mind without the intervention of his intellect. He follows a routine, mechanical and traditional pattern of life. His actions originate out of his feelings and emotions rather than his determination. On the other hand, an aggressive person is just the opposite; his actions originate out of his judicious decisions of merit and demerit of actions before actually performing them.

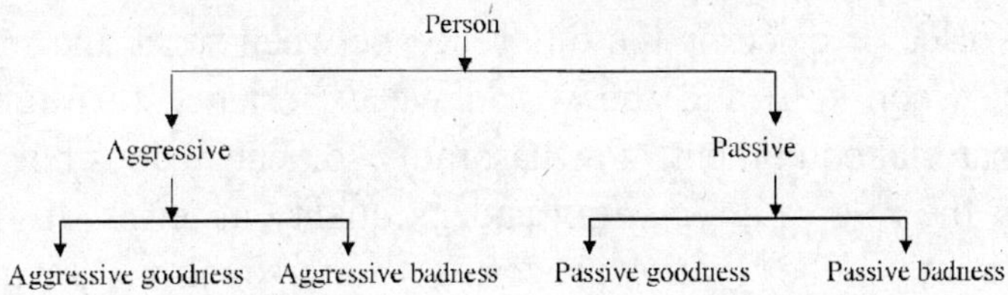

Fig. 9.4: Four possible ways of classifying the personalities in a broad sense with reference to a common man.

In the schematic picture of Fig.9.3, the role of each EOL is clearly demonstrated in creating a personality of an individual. The process starts at the level of E through the nature (in terms of *gunās*) of a s*ankalpa* and accordingly the gross body G(=B+SE), mind (M), or intellect (I) come into action, though not in isolation but in a dominating manner. For example, if G dominates over M and I, then it leads to a personality rich in bodily qualities which manifest through his actions and perceptions but in a limited sense. Similarly, if M dominates over G and I, then it leads to an emotional personality through feelings and other such emotions. However, the role of I is important in bringing the spiritual content in the personality.

In fact, if the intellect I is tuned to think dominantly over G and M and to the acceptance of spatio-temporal character of the outer world, then such a thinking would lead to intellectual personality (say, that of scientist-category of persons). On the other hand, if I is tuned to think beyond the spatio-temporal character of the outer world by way of realizing (i.e. using its subtle component) the transcendental reality behind its working, then such a contemplation leads to a spiritual personality (say, that of yogi-category of persons). According to Parthasarathy (1992), the subtle intellect is the discriminating faculty which contemplates upon and distinguishes the transcendental reality from the terrestrial world. It discerns the difference between spirit and matter, between soul and the world we experience through our material equipment. Parthasarathy somehow does not bring in the role of a *sankalpa* and its quality in terms of *gunās*, directly in the creation process of the personality. As a matter of fact no creature other than human Being can nourish this last category of personality.

9.4 HOW DO PERSONALITIES DIFFER?

Whether it was the scheme of study of Jung (cf. Fig.9.1) for the personality test or the original description due to Parthasarathy (1992) for the creation of personality, both define four types of personalities in a broad sense. Of course they are not independent of each other. Even among these four types, there can be further sub-divisions of personalities and to account for them both schools of thought offer certain possibilities. Here, however, we have suggested a simple way to account for these differences, i.e., by replacing the nascent version of EOLs by the dressed ones. It is the order of dressing of an EOL with consciousness or the extent of evolution of one's EOLs with meditation that will further make a difference among the personalities of a given category. For example, there may be a variety of each of spiritual, intellectual, emotional, and physical category of personalities (cf. Fig.9.3) and the same can be understood if one considers different orders of dressing or the development of the corresponding EOL with reference to meditation. In fact, this evolution of EOLs differs from person to person.

Another aspect emphasized in Fig.9.3 which may help in differentiating the personalities is to view the personality creation scheme as a whole in the positive quadrant of μ vs. features of manifestation plane. Clearly, as the intensity of meditation (self-observation) enhances, then the personality of a person may change from the physical to emotional, intellectual and then to the spiritual level. Similarly, features of manifestation in the personality increase as one proceeds from the zones of subtlest (soul), subtler (E, I and M), subtle (their functions), and finally to the gross and grossest features as shown in Fig.9.3. In fact, such considerations in the creation aspect suggest the ways to improve one's own personality.

Example 9.4.1: Even among spiritual persons there is a spectrum of their realization, among scientist and philosopher category of persons or among the so-called skilled workers there is spectrum of their intellectual evolution, and thus each common man has a varying view of the world-order; all this creates sub-division of personalities.

In some sense, the *Asthānga* yoga of Patanjali can again help in explaining the sub-divisions of personalities. Depending upon the practice aspect of the components and the sub-components of this system of yoga and their follow-up or creativity aspect in the daily life, the sub-division of personalities can be understood. As a matter of fact, the sub-components of *yama* and *niyama* and their further sub-divisions at a subtle level are full of human qualities that one needs for character building.

9.5 IMPROVING A GIVEN PERSONALITY: CHARACTER BUILDING

Character building means inculcating the human values in one's way of life as defined by a society in terms of moral and ethical values and at a given point of time. While it is not a difficult task for an individual to do so, yet there is a limit on this as suggested by the Vedic science. As far as the nature and fruit of actions of a person are concerned, there are three basic reasons to classify them, namely *prārabdha*, *sancit* and *kriyamāna* which respectively means, destined out of the previous or past birth(s), performed in this birth itself and the ones performed in the present. Thus, the efforts can be made to build the character or to improve the personality and accordingly the success can be expected to the extent that the actions pertain to the domains of *sancit* and *kriyamāna* category. Hardly any change is possible with regard to the fruit of actions of *prārabdha* category, as it is all destined in advance to a great extent.

To this effect, first of all there has to be a desire to improve upon the character. If it is there, then there is a huge list of human qualities towards the improvement of all the three $\mathcal{G}$-, $\mathcal{M}$- and $\mathcal{C}$-domains of a personality. Some such qualities, which a conscious person can inculcate in his character and also include the *yama* and *niyama* components of Raj yoga, are: truth, nonviolence, non-stealing, continence, abstaining from vilification, modesty, un-haughtiness, artlessness, purity, contentment, endurance, spirit of service, sacrifice, charity, austerity, study of religious scriptures, mind-control, sense-control, humility, straightforwardedness, compassion, faith, discrimination between true and false, dispassion, living in seclusion, non-accumulation of wealth and property, lack of doubt and distraction, minimization of desire, forgiveness, patience, absence of malice, fearlessness, pridelessness, peace, faith in a deity, etc. One can adopt some or all of them at a time and try to improve his character and subsequently the personality. Note that this spectrum of human qualities includes those of all the three $\mathcal{G}$-, $\mathcal{M}$- and $\mathcal{C}$-domains and one can pick any or all of them conveniently to go from the level of physical personality to that of the spiritual one (cf. Fig. 9.3) .

Note that for these changes in the personality space and time considerations are immaterial, i.e. the change can occur anywhere and at anytime as and when a person is inspired by an event or incidence of the outer world, and develops a will power for the change, or when opts for a better *sankalpa*, or when certain events constantly pinch him during the process of self-observation.

Example 9.5.1: As an example of change in personality, recall the story cited in Example 1.5.2.

Now we discuss another method based on Vedic science to improve the personality. For this purpose recall Example 1.5.3, where it is demonstrated that the senses in the body are very powerful, as discussed in this example through an analogy with horses as far as their attachment to sense-objects is concerned. Mind joins this attachment and moulds the intellect accordingly.

Example 9.5.2: Just as the wind carries away a barge upon the waters, even so the wandering senses, the one to which mind is attached takes away the intellect of the person (SMBG: 2.67).

Conversely, if the intellect is powerful enough, downward (towards the outer world) flow of energy can be controlled and the working of the (body) system becomes ordered from the so-called the chaotic one. Even this orderliness of the whole body-system can be of different categories depending upon the nature of intellect I and that of *sankalpās* in terms of three *gunās*, namely *sātvik*, *rajas* and *tamas*. We analyze this in the next section and argue as to how a particular case of this mechanism yields the integration of body, mind and soul.

9.6 PERSONALITY CREATION MECHANISM AND INTEGRATION OF BODY, MIND AND SOUL

As discussed in Chapter 1, the words body, mind and soul in the phrase 'integrating body, mind and soul' respectively stand for the gross ($\mathcal{G}$), micro ($\mathcal{M}$) and causal ($\mathcal{C}$) existences of the human Being. When one talks about their integration it is in the spiritual sense and the same in fact, is an idealized situation which is not easy to achieve by an individual everywhere and at all times. No doubt, there is always a coordination of body, mind and soul towards fruit or success of actions but their integration is a particularized case of this coordination in the sense that what one thinks, so he expresses in words and acts in practice accordingly. In fact, the word integration is used in two related senses, namely (i) in the sense of strengthening the body, mind and soul towards the success of an action, and (ii) to have straightness in all activities of mind, senses and the body. Any way both these purposes are useful as far as the development of personality is concerned. Any departure from this policy does not justify the integration of body mind and soul. It is only in this situation that one can make best use of the energies associated with his body, mind and soul. In fact this creates an ideal condition to ensure success in the actions so performed.

Now the question arises as to what type of actions need to be performed with reference to the maintenance of world-order and the value system in a society? Naturally, one does not want to spoil the world or the Universe as a whole– a beautiful gift of Mother Nature. Thus, the above idealized situation should be the goal of one's life and the integration of body, mind and soul should be taken in the spirit of positive pursuits and spiritual sense. In what follows, we discuss a personality creation mechanism (PCM) in the light of Vedic science and argue that the integration aspects of body, mind and soul are just a particular case of this general theory.

Although one can start with the dressed versions of inner EOLs and analyse the case of the finest possible processes taking place inside the human Being, but here we restrict ourselves only to the nascent versions of EOLs. However, as we consider the role of three *gunās* in the mechanism, this in some sense will bring in certain orders of dressing of EOLs with consciousness. Here we discuss a Jung-type (cf. Sect. 9.1) matrix formation but at the character level, which at a later stage of course manifests in the correspondingly developed personality.

Note that either due to *prārabdha* or due to certain inborn qualities of an individual a *sankalpa* (S) can come in three colors or is influenced by the three *gunās*, namely *sātvik* (s), *rajas* (r), *tamas* (t) to furnish three possibilities S_s, S_r, S_t. On the other hand, the guiding agency (intellect) I, which for an ordered system plays an important role in the actions performed by the body G through the mind M (cf. Example 1.5.3), this also comes in three abstract colors as I_s, I_r, I_t (cf. SMBG: Verses 18.30 to 32) . Now, in this order to account for all the possibilities, one can construct the so-called personality matrix P from the *sankalpa* matrix S and the intellect matrix I, viz. **P=S x I**, as

$$P = \begin{pmatrix} S_s - I_s & S_s - I_r & S_s - I_t \\ S_r - I_s & S_r - I_r & S_r - I_t \\ S_t - I_s & S_t - I_r & S_t - I_t \end{pmatrix} \equiv \begin{pmatrix} (SI)_{ss} & (SI)_{sr} & (SI)_{st} \\ (SI)_{rs} & (SI)_{rr} & (SI)_{rt} \\ (SI)_{ts} & (SI)_{tr} & (SI)_{tt} \end{pmatrix}.$$

Following remarks are in order about the nature of this construction:

(i) Note that s, r, t are the independent variables and constitute a space (may be Cartesian in mathematical sense) in which both *sankalpa* and intellect are projected.

(ii) There are three zones of integration of body, mind and soul: The nine elements of the matrix P=SI represent nine types of characters or personalities, out of which the diagonal ones, namely $(SI)_{ss}$, $(SI)_{rr}$ and $(SI)_{tt}$ correspond to the integrated body, mind and soul of an individual. The integration can be there for all the three category of persons, namely, (i) for a *sātvik* person, this in turn will take him to the spiritual zone, (ii) for a *rājasik* person, this in turn will make him a successful person in worldly matters by maintaining no harm to Nature, and (iii) for a *tāmasik* person, this in turn will take him to a downfall with reference to the world-order and society.

(iii) In general, it is the *sankalpa* that influences the intellect and not the vice versa. Therefore, SI ≠ IS, i.e. the matrices S and I do not commute. However, for a man of perfection or for a yogi of highest degree both S and I stand in the same zone of consciousness and they can commute, i.e. SI=IS, only for this exceptional case.

Table 9.1: Classification of personalities on the basis of Vedic science.

S.No.	Category of personality	Nature of personality
(a)	Integrated personalities	(1)Satoguni sātvik persons (2)Rajoguni rājasik persons (3)Tamoguni tāmasik persons
(b)	Non-integrated personalities	(4)Rajoguni sātvik persons (5)Tamoguni sātvik person (6)Tamoguni rājasik persons (7)Satoguni rājasik persons (8) Satoguni tāmasik persons (9) Rajoguni tāmasik persons
(c)	Ideally integrated personalities	(10) Satoguni sātvik persons with zero nonintegrated component (11) Rajoguni rājasik persons with zero nonintegrated component (12) Tamoguni tāmasik persons with zero nonintegrated component

(iv) Nonintegrated personalities: There are six categories of nonintegrated personalities corresponding to six off-diagonal elements in the personality matrix P, which are (1) persons improving from *rājasik* to *sātvik* zone correspond to $(SI)_{sr}$; (2) persons improving from *tāmasik* to *sātvik* zone — a bit difficult task, correspond to $(SI)_{st}$; (3) persons improving from *tāmasik* to *rājasik* zone correspond to $(SI)_{rt}$; (4) persons degrading themselves from *sātvik* to *rājasik*, correspond to $(SI)_{rs}$; (5) persons degrading themselves from *sātvik* to *tāmasik*, correspond to $(SI)_{ts}$, and (6) persons degrading themselves from *rājasik* to *tāmasik*, correspond to $(SI)_{tr}$. These categories are further listed in Table 9.1 (cf. category (b)).

(v) Integrated personalities of Remark (ii), in whichever zone they are, have stable mind at least for a certain period of time and at a given place. On the other hand, the non-integrated personalities of Remark (iv) are of fluctuating mind, always undergoing transitions from one type nature to another type.

(vi) In view of Remarks (iv) and (v), the personality matrix P is not symmetric i.e., $(SI)_{ij} \neq (SI)_{ji}$, where i,j=s, r, t and $i \neq j$. As a matter of fact when a person undergoing transitions from one zone of *gunās* to another zone, the circumstances and environment of the person change. Therefore, a change in personality is bound to exist in spite of the forward and backward transition of the same nature.

(vii) A better lot of integrated personalities: Integrated personalities of remark (ii) correspond to the fact that the nature of person in terms of *gunās* whether *sātvik*, *rājasik* or *tāmasik* is sharply defined; otherwise most of us are born with mixed, but dominated by any one or two of them. Therefore, it is worthwhile to look for the diagonalized version of the matrix P as P_D, viz.,

$$P_D = \begin{pmatrix} (\bar{S}I)_{ss} & 0 & 0 \\ 0 & (\bar{S}I)_{rr} & 0 \\ 0 & 0 & (\bar{S}I)_{tt} \end{pmatrix},$$

where the integrated personalities corresponding to $(\bar{S}I)_{ss}$, $(\bar{S}I)_{rr}$ and $(\bar{S}I)_{tt}$ are truly the integrated ones in practical terms. In fact one can attempt to find the diagonalizing matrix whose elements will be the appropriate mixtures of different *gunās*. Further, this mixing can be attributed to the effect of circumstances and environment in which the individual is placed. We can place this class of personalities in ideally integrated personalities as there is no energy loss in any other dimension of human activities.

9.7 CONCLUDING DISCUSSION

With a view to giving a better foundation to the subject of personality and its development in a person, several suggestions are advanced in this chapter within the framework of patomic model. To this effect, commonly used theory of Jung for the personality test takes a new look when the agencies of gathering information and evaluating information in the work of Jung are pairwise replaced by gross body ($\mathcal{G}$) and ego (E) and by mind (M) and intellect (I), respectively. Latter are the basic entities of the patomic model which contribute to the dynamics that takes place inside the human Being not only before but also during his performance of an action. Further replacements of these EOLs by their dressed versions with consciousness (cf. Sect. 9.2) clearly explain in a general manner the matrix formation corresponding to the four cognitive styles of psychology namely sensation feelers, intuitive feelers, sensation thinkers and intuitive thinkers.

Using another approach of Parthasarathy which is also based on Vedic science, the ingredients of a personality are identified schematically and their role in the dynamics is analyzed (cf. Sect.9.3). This suggests an alternative to classify the personalities and their test. It is further argued that the personalities of persons differ on the basis of different orders of dressing of their different inner EOLs with consciousness. Using again the concepts of Vedic science, some ways to improve the character and subsequently the personality of a person are highlighted (cf. Sect.9.5). In particular, the role of *gunās* of Vedic science in the functioning of inner EOLs is explored. It forms the basis for the newly proposed personality creation mechanism. In mathematical terms, a personality matrix is formed to this effect, whose nine components accordingly define nine types of personalities in general (cf. Table 9.1). Out of these nine, three are the integrated ones and the rest six are the non-integrated. One can as well classify the personalities on this basis and prepare a questionnaire to this effect. Compared to the scheme of Jung, this kind of personality test will definitely reflect a long-term stability in the nature of a person. As far as the integration of body, mind and soul towards the performance of an action is concerned, it appears that this is a particular case of this general analysis. It is emphasized that a mixed nature of *gunās* in the personality will give rise to a better integrated personality as far as the stability of mindset function is concerned. Further, note that such an integration of EOLs is suggested to exist in different psychic zones corresponding to *sātvik*, *rājasik* and *tāmasik* nature of a person. The subject matter in fact requires further studies and we do not intend to deliberate on this here.

In the next chapter we shall analyze some of these personalities and discuss other alternative ways towards improving and developing the personality of a person, namely by following a systematic of positive pursuits.

Further Reading:

For further studies on personality and its role in organizational behavior, see (Singh, 2010) and for the Vedanta view on the personality development, see (Parthasarathy, 1992, Part B); For the role of trinity of *gunās* in personality studies, we refer to the recent work (Singh et al, 2012) and the references therein.

High Skill Exercises and Projects

9.1 Differentiate between the empirical and formal theories of personality. Explain how the personality theories developed in the West remain empirical in the absence of the knowledge of the Science of the Self.

9.2 Explain how the character building and the personality development of a person in some sense correspond to the vertical and horizontal components of complete personality. (Hint: Also, see Sect. 14.4].

9.3 Discuss the Personality Theory of Jung. What possible modifications to it are suggested here in the light of patomic model of human Being?

9.4 Considering (a) your school, (b) your college, and (c) the administrative block of your university as organization, analyze and discuss all the four pillars of study of organizational behavior, namely (i) the individual processes, (ii) the inter-personal and team processes (iii) the organization processes, and (iv) the change processes with reference to these organizations.

9.5 Consider a mob of students protesting against certain decisions of the authorities. Analyze the conditions under which there will be an order or a chaos in the mob after listening to the authorities or to a message from them on the concerned issue. Explain how the human dynamics changes from individual to a collective one in terms of the working of EOLs.

9.6 Discuss in detail the role of parameters associated with inner EOLs in differentiating the different personalities.

9.7 As a project, carry out a study on the organization culture from a reference book. What suggestions would you like to propose to improve the culture of your institution? What role does culture (traditions) have to play in sustaining the viability of your institution?

9.8 Discuss the similarities and differences between the 'personality creation mechanism' and the 'art of integrating the body, mind and soul' towards the success of an action. Elaborate on the ideally integrated personalities.

9.9 As a project, carry out a study of questionnaire for the assessment of the personality trait self-esteem, in a person. Categorize the answers according to the actions performed in the $\mathcal{G}$-and $\mathcal{M}$-domains.

9.10 On the basis of personality creation mechanism analyze the personality profile of (a) your subject teacher, (b) your best friend, and (c) one of your parents. Has the knowledge of their personality profile influenced your decision in determining your behavior towards them?

Chapter 10

SYSTEMATICS OF NEGATIVE AND POSITIVE PURSUITS

In this chapter, we discuss an alternative route which, if followed, a person automatically develops a personality in a rather natural manner. In fact, once the nature of *sankalpās* in terms of *gunās* takes a form, then certain sequences of human characteristics automatically start playing their role in shaping the behavior. In the ambit of shaping the guidance of these suggested characteristics, all sorts of actions, first of **M** -domain and later of **G**-domain, are performed by the individual. These sequences of characteristics, termed here as the 'systematics of pursuits', perhaps have come out of deep and long experiences of great seers of the past. After analyzing certain categories of personalities, particularly the ones listed in Table 9.1 within the framework of these natural trends of human tendencies, we discuss a fundamental principle, the so-called 'the principle of minimum efforts' in human behavior and experiences in Sect.10.2. In Sect.10.3, we discuss the roles of systematics of negative and positive pursuits towards the development of a personality. As to how the actions motivated by following the systematics of positive pursuits lead to a spiritual personality is discussed in Sect.10.4. Finally concluding remarks are made in Sect.10.5.

10.1 NATURAL TRENDS OF HUMAN TENDENCIES

We have seen in the previous chapter (cf. Sects. 9.5 and 9.6) that after the *Prārabdha* (destiny), it is the nature of *samkalpa* at the inner-most level in conjunction with the nature of intellect that affects the development of personality of a person and subsequently his actions in the outer world. Note that besides one's own determination, the other possible factors which matter in influencing his *sankalpās* are (i) pleasant or bitter experiences that he gathers from the outer world, (ii) circumstances and environment he lives in, and (iii) the knowledge he obtains from teachers, elders, friends, or from the prevailing religious scriptures. Once the *sankalpa* is shaped with a particular *guna*, say *satva*, *rajas* or *tamas*, then the intellect also (influenced independently by these *gunās*) comes in operation and suggests a path to follow towards the success of an action. A person, who is once trapped in this path, certain sequences of characteristics are automatically followed by him as per Vedic science. Next we analyze the role of trinity of *gunās* in the personality creation and in the choice of systematics of pursuits.

10.1.1 Trinity of *gunās* and the nature of human personalities

Before proceeding further we briefly analyze here the personalities listed in Table 9.1. Note that the nomenclature of a personality in this Table refers to both the innermost, i.e. at the level of *sankalpa* and the exterior, i.e., at the level of intellect aspects of a personality. For example, a *rajoguni sātvik* personality (cf. case b4)) means the *sankalpa* and intellect of a person are enveloped respectively in *rājasik* and *sātvik gunās*. Further, the trinity of *gunās*, namely *sātvik, rajas* and *tamas* in some sense are in the spirit of superlative, comparative and positive degrees of an adjective, respectively. It is well accepted that the inner EOLs or the human characteristics enveloped in *sātvik guna* are the best from the point of view of both maintenance of world-order and ethical as well as moral values in a society. In fact, the inner EOLs enveloped in *sātvik guna* lead to actions in the outer world which are the best in the maintenance of world-order. Contrarily, the roles of EOLs or of human characteristics enveloped in *tāmasik guna* in human behavior and actions are not well appreciated in a society and also not considered to be good in the maintenance of world-order. In a nut-shell, it is not wrong to say that the positivity at any level leads to order in the Universe whereas the negativity leads to chaos in the Universe.

The three categories of personalities of Table 9.1, namely integrated, nonintegrated and ideally integrated can be analyzed further in terms of their stability with respect to space and time. In the first category, the *satoguni sātvik* personality is supposed to be the best where as the *tamoguni tāmasik* personality is considered as the worst with reference to values in a society or with regard to the world-order. In these cases there is an occasional stability in the nature of such persons and the equilibrium among the trinity of *gunās* keeps on changing with circumstances and environment. Nonintegrated components also manifest occasionally in these personalities, but for most of the time there is definitely some correlation between their thinking and doing.

The second category concerns the nonintegrated personalities which are 6 in number. Among them the *tamoguni rājasik* and *rajoguni tāmasik* personalities (cf. (b6) and (b9)) are considered to be on the worse side whereas the *rājoguni sātvik* and *satoguni rājasik* personalities (cf. (b4) and (b7)) are on the better side in a relative sense. This category of persons never notices a stability of mind and thus the question of equilibrium among the trinity of *gunās* does not arise. Often there appears a kind of nonlinearity between their thinking and doing. These personalities keep on changing the decisions with environment and circumstances.

Clearly, the third category of ideally integrated personalities is the most stable ones with respect to space and time. Also, they are not affected easily by the changed environment and circumstances. This is mainly because a kind of equilibrium among the trinity of *gunās* is already established in an ideal and appropriate manner prior to the final achievement. Even in this category, *satoguni sātvik* personality is the best and the *tamoguni tāmasik* is the worst with regard to the standards set in a society in spite of the fact that there is a linearity and simplicity between the thinking and the doing of the persons of all the three cases.

Further, it is noticed that the personality of a person is not stable during his learning stage, i.e., when he is a student or becomes a youth. However, only after attaining the adulthood, his personality tends towards stability or the changes, if at all they are there, are slow but steady. Many examples of these categories can be found in the society. However, we are restraining ourselves from citing them here.

10.1.2 Nature of *sankalpās* vis-à-vis systematics of characteristics

In some sense, one can identify the nature of a *sankalpa* with that of the so called ultimate 'doer' of an action inside the body. Lord Krishna in SMBG (Verses 18.26 to28) has characterized this 'doer' in three distinct categories in accordance with the trinity of *gunās*. Once the *sankalpa* of a person with regard to a particular action and a particular *guna* takes a form then according to Vedic science a definite sequence of human characteristics (termed here as 'systematics of pursuits') need to be followed by the person. Corresponding to the nature of *sankalpa* or doer, whether *sātvik*, *rājasik* or *tāmasik*, such sequences are already fixed by the Vedic seers and surprisingly these sequences still work successfully even today. It appears that these sequences of Vedic seers are derived out of their long experience of life and reflect the stages through which the mechanism of inner EOLs, when influenced by *gunās*, works toward the success of an action.

For example, as per SMBG (cf. Ch. 18) the three colors in which the same intellect can separately envelope itself to give *sātvik* intellect, *rājasik* intellect, and *tāmasik* intellect, are as follows:

(i) In the *sātvik* mode, the intellect is capable of knowing what is right action and what is right cessation of action, what must be done and what ought not to be done, what is fear and what constitutes fearlessness, what is bondage and what is liberation.

(ii) In the *rājasik* mode, intellect understands incorrectly what is right and what is wrong, what must be done and what ought not to be done, etc.

(iii) In the *tāmasik* mode it is, however, enveloped in ignorance, thinks the wrong to be right and regards all the above things contrary.

On the other hand, a *sankalpa* when identified with the ultimate doer of an action (in the sense of ego) then it also appears in three colors as per SMBG, namely the *sātvik* doer is the one freed from attachment, un-egoistic, endowed with firmness and vigor, and unaffected by success or failure of an action. The *rājasik* doer is the one who is passionate and greedy, seeks the fruits of action, is given to violence and of impure conduct, and is affected by joy and sorrow. Contrary to these features, the *tāmasik* doer is the one who lacks self-control and piety, vulgar, arrogant, deceitful, inclined to rob others of their livelihood, slothful, despondent and procrastinating, etc. With these possibilities of virtues and vices in a *sankalpa* and in an intellect one can trace a wide spectrum of personalities. Also, it is not difficult to trace the sequences of virtues and vices which need to be followed by an individual towards his upliftment or downfall with reference to the standards of a society or to the maintenance of world-order.

10.2 THE PRINCIPLE OF MINIMUM EFFORTS AND THE SYSTEMATICS OF PURSUITS

For a conscious human Being, the principle of minimum efforts is a key to the success in both long-term and short-term goals in life. Note that the minimization of efforts in the mental domain takes place with respect to certain variables, like the intensity of attention/meditation/ concentration (all are the manifestations of the same consciousness in a person in different working domains of EOLS) and the 'span' during which this intensity is used to perform the task. In fact, one can talk of the Heisenberg-like uncertainty principle of quantum physics between this pair of variables, namely the intensity of attention and the time span. However, we avoid these discussions here, but it is worthwhile to remind of other similar principles of physics here, namely the Hamilton's principle of least action or the Fermat principle of least time which are defined with respect to space-time variables. All this shows the Nature's liking for the principle of minimum efforts. As a matter of fact this universal principle is found to work in all personalities in the form 'do less accomplish more' – a common practice found with all persons.

Now the question is as to how it is possible to have concerted but minimum efforts to achieve the maximum success, particularly when there are so many distractions at the levels of mind, body and senses of perception. In other words, it is a rather difficult task to become the man of 'stable mind' or the 'man of wisdom' in the present circumstances.

One line answer to this difficult question, as suggested by SMBG is to meditate on higher goals by way of adopting certain systematics of virtues or else face the downfall in the natural course of time which too follows certain systematics of vices. A possible way to proceed towards higher goals is by censoring the actions of lower strata of EOLs, namely mind, body and senses. To this effect, one should control the mind and simultaneously withdraw the senses from their respective sense-objects. Again a key to achieve this stage for an individual is the meditation and self-observation.

While one can physically withdraw the senses of perception from their respective sense-objects, their withdrawal at the mental level is a difficult task. For a person to become the man of stable mind, one should control SEs at the mental level, i.e., by discarding both attachment to and detachment from their respective sense-objects at the mental level as a part of positive pursuits. As a matter of fact, with whichever sense of perception the mind flows, the same is found to control the intellect I as well mainly due to the turbulent nature of mind. Therefore, the control of senses through the rein of mind in the guidance of intellect I is necessary to achieve the state of stable mind. This mechanism becomes clear from the following example.

Example 10.2.1: The above situation is similar to the process of rowing a boat in a river, particularly upstream. Note that the down-stream rowing is easy and even in the absence of efforts the movement of boat naturally goes with the flow of river. Further, in the absence of flow, i.e., in static water, it is the wind direction which controls the movement of boat in the same way as a sense attached with a sense-objects controls the intellect with the help of mind.

Thus, the principle of minimum efforts deals with the directed efforts which subsequently lead to directed (judicious) actions of various EOLs. The system as a whole is made to work in a regulated manner so that the efforts are minimized by resorting appropriately to the space-time variables in the physical domain and the meditation variable μ in the mental domain.

10.3 SYSTEMATICS OF PURSUITS

10.3.1 Systematics of negative pursuits (SNP)

If the mind is not controlled by an individual from its wandering in senses and sense-objects and also the senses of knowledge and action are not withdrawn from their sense-objects, then this results in the negative pursuits and arbitrary actions. This later situation disturbs the peace of mind of a person. As per SMBG Verse 2.62, "the man dwelling on sense-objects develops attachment for them; from attachment springs up desire; and from (unfulfilled) desire ensues anger" and corresponding to Verse 2.63, "from anger arises infatuation; from infatuation, confusion of memory; from confusion of memory comes loss of reason; and from loss of reason one goes to complete ruination". Clearly this is the sequence of qualities that start appearing in the personality of a person and leads to his downfall.

During this course of negative pursuits, the fundamental processes keep on going inside the individual and often without coming to his notice but they reflect in the behavior. The end-product, however, is the loss of reason which results either into arbitrary actions against the principle of minimum efforts or with a wastage of efforts. In fact this is not the end of vices, the sequence further continues. "He who has not controlled his mind and senses can have neither determinate reason nor can such an undisciplined man have belief (in the Creator or God). The unbelieving man cannot have peace. And how can there be happiness for one lacking peace of mind?"

Thus, the effect of the systematics of negative pursuits is some sort of vicious circle— starts from **M**-domain, shifts to **G**-domain, and from **G**-domain again affects the **M**-domain of a person.

10.3.2 Systematics of positive pursuits (SPP)

Contrary to the systematics of negative pursuits discussed above, one who has controlled his mind and senses of knowledge and action enjoys the fruits of positive (directed) efforts. This is what SMBG emphasizes in Verses 2.64 and 2.65: "The self-controlled practitioner, while enjoying the various sense-objects through his senses, which are disciplined and free from likes and dislikes, attains placidity of mind. Further, with the attainment of such placidity of mind, all his sorrows come to an end; and the intellect of such a person of tranquil mind, soon withdrawing itself from all sides, becomes firmly established in higher goal (God)."

Whether or not one realizes the above sequence of processes that is followed under different systematics, its effect however reflects in the personality at different places, timings and circumstances in one form or the other. Here we present some examples demonstrating the symptoms of a man with stable mind.

Example 10.3.1: Case of a tortoise: As one knocks or hits the shell of tortoise, he withdraws his limbs or organs from all directions inside the shell immediately. In the same way, a person of stable mind or the one who has controlled his body, mind and senses withdraws his senses from the sense-objects even if there is some hint of them.

Example 10.3.2: A lesson from ocean: As the water of different rivers enters in the ocean, the ocean, which though full on all sides remains undisturbed. Likewise the man of stable mind merges in himself all enjoyments and pleasures drawn out of sense-objects without any disturbance at the mental level and restores the peace in no time.

10.4 POSITIVE PURSUITS MOTIVATE ACTIONS TO SPIRITUAL ZONE

It is true that only a conscious person with active EOLs notices the occurrence of the above mentioned processes taking place inside him; otherwise these processes are universal. They do take place in all human Beings irrespective of their caste, color, creed or country, and in some nonhumans as well. Vedic science in fact has attempted to quantify them through systematics of negative and positive pursuits. Many of these processes form part of a self-consistent mechanism that is taking place constantly in each of us as far as the Karmic theory of SMBG is concerned (see, (Kaushal, 2011,Chapters 4 and 8)).

In general, the actions of a common man are focused around any one, two or all the three objectives as per his *sankalpās*, namely (a) desiring of sense-objects, (b) desiring of talent, and (c) desiring of (true) knowledge. In fact, there is a connection between these objectives and they correspond to the three domains of human actions, namely **G**, **M** and **C** domains. Note that as one proceeds from the objective (a) to (c), the quality of desire becomes better from the point of view of social values and positive pursuits. In what follows, we elaborate on each of these objectives to demonstrate the working of EOLs towards a successful pursuit in spite of the fact that the underlying mechanism for all the cases remains more or less the same.

(a) As long as one is carrying on with an active body, it is rather impossible for him to discard the actions necessary for the survival of the body itself at least at the physical level. Actions need to be performed in an optimum style to maintain the body fit. Not only this, a viable and dynamic body is also the basis for all sorts of development of FOUs or EOLs. In this respect nonhumans are wiser than man in the sense that their actions are confined according to their (minimum) body requirements for their survival since they have limited *sankalpâs*. On the other hand, human Being gifted with extra sense, i.e. intellect, makes full use of it to fulfill maximum (perhaps unlimited) requirements for his survival. As a result of this he keeps on running after the sense-objects or in arranging accessories for this purpose.

Example 10.4.1: Suppose that a person decides (at the level of intellect I) to have a taste of a particular dish and accordingly takes *sankalpa* (at the level of mind M) to arrange the things for this purpose, sometimes by taking extra pains or by using his particular resources. For arranging necessary ingredients he makes repeated use of SE, B, and WO as also of other EOLs until he succeeds in attaining the desired sense-object, i.e., the taste of his liking or the enjoyment of the same by M but with a reference to I in this regard. In enjoying the dish, the person must have used his past experience or has stored a liking for this new taste in E. If the taste or the fruit of action is not up to the mark, he takes lessons from this task for future preparation(s)/arrangements. Similar examples can be narrated with reference to other single or multiple sense-objects. If these actions (or the fruit of actions) are performed to keep the body fit and are in accordance with the norms of a society in ethical terms, then they are the cases of positive pursuit; otherwise they are very likely the case of negative pursuits from the point of view of social norms or the maintenance of world-order.

(b) For a person who is desirous of talent (say a position in an office or society) in absolute or relative terms, the role of gross body (i.e., of SE, B and WO) of the type discussed above in (a) remains only optimum whereas that of micro-body (i.e. of M, I and E) becomes maximum. In this case *sankalpās* belong to higher hierarchy and correspond to somewhat long-term goals as compared to the one's belonging to the case (a) above (where the goals by and large are the short-term ones). In quest of talent, the individual hardly bothers about the *sankalpās* of lower hierarchy (i.e., of domain **G**). The fulfillment of the latter becomes necessary but not sufficient unlike that in case (a) above. No doubt, the same sequence of steps has to be followed to fulfill these necessary *sankalpās* but always with an eye on the *sankalpās* of higher hierarchy. Moreover, the roles of EOLs, M, I and E now become more crucial at times, respectively in terms of concentration, short- and long-term decisions, and the use of past experiences.

(c) A person who desires knowledge goes ahead with *sankalpās* of the highest order at the level of SO, particularly when he is in quest of true knowledge (see, (Kaushal, 2011, Sect.4.1)). Knowledge of any form in this world is said to be pure but the purest one is that which belongs to the Self itself. Such knowledge is achieved by keeping the (fulfillment of) *sankalpās* of lower-hierarchy, i.e., those belonging to the domains of micro- and/or gross-body at low pitch as they now become necessary but not sufficient. These *sankalpās* of highest order now, however, need to be fulfilled by following the same steps as in (a) or in (b) above but with a spirit of constructive and positive pursuits. Again, one can have a desire of knowledge either of the man-made world (in terms of scientific methods) or of the God-made world (in terms of the methods suggested to enter the spiritual zone) or of both, but the basic steps to be followed to this effect remain the same as far as the methodology is concerned.

10.5 CONCLUDING DISCUSSION

Once again using the tenets of Vedic science two alternative prescriptions which, at their end-points, provide two extreme personalities in a person, are suggested. In this context, certain systematics in the human qualities are traced by analyzing the personalities listed in Table 9.1. Further, it is found that these systematics have some connection with a proposed fundamental principle, the so-called 'the principle of minimum efforts'. This principle, on par with other minimalism principles in physics, however, prevails in an unnoticeable manner in the behavior of all human Beings and at all space-time points and in all circumstances. It is also emphasized that this is the systematic of positive pursuits which takes a person to spiritual zone by keeping the *sankalpās* corresponding to **G** and **M** domains at low pitch.

With regard to the systematic of pursuits, further additional remarks may be made as follows:

(i) Whether the systematic corresponds to a positive or negative pursuit is decided by the third party observer, or as guided by the social norms or by the question of maintenance of world-order. While the performer of actions often remains unaware of the changes in the personality, an outsider does notice these changes and decides on the nature of the systematic that the performer is following.

(ii) These systematics may work at all the three, **G**, **M** and **C** levels; but only the role of parameter(s) makes them to differ, i.e. positive or negative. For example, for the causal domain, the subtle component of ego E has to be suppressed, for the micro domain, it is the mind M that has to be controlled and for the gross domain, these are the senses and body which need to be withdrawn from the sense-objects, for the case of positive pursuits, otherwise these EOLs are free to follow the systematic of negative pursuits.

(iii) In fact the source of these negatives of a systematic is the subtle component of ego which prevails in the form of 'I-ideology' or in the 'I-ism' that leads to a feeling of pride and fuels greed, selfishness, and later anger for a common man. However, a conscious performer of an action is capable of overcoming these negatives of a personality.

Further Reading:

For further details on the nature of *sankalpās*, the principle of minimum efforts and the systematics of positive and negative pursuits, see (Kaushal, 2011, Chapters 4 and 8). On the role of trinity of *gunās* in the personality, see (Singh et al, 2012).

High Skill Exercises and Projects

10.1 Justify and comment on the statement, "positivity at any level of human actions, behavior, experiences and knowledge lead to order in the Universe whereas the negativity of any type contributes to chaos in the Universe in one form or the other".

10.2 On the basis of Table 9.1 and discussions in Sect.10.1 identify some personalities out of your friend circle and relatives.

10.3 Define systematic of pursuits. Following the concepts of SMBG (cf. Verses:18.26-18.33) write a detailed Note on the three types of 'doer' with reference to their actions and three types of 'intellect' with reference to the quality of their decisions.

10.4 Explain how the integrated body, mind and soul of a person leading to success in his actions conform to the 'principle of minimum efforts'.

10.5 Explain how the systematic of negative pursuits completes the vicious circle for actions, i.e., from **M**-domain to **G**-domain and then from **G**-domain back to the **M**-domain as far as the peace of mind is concerned.

10.6 Using examples from your different working domains in the day-to-day life, justify the statement, "positive pursuits always m otivate a person to spirituality".

Chapter 11

AN INDIVIDUAL IN A GROUP: MULTIPLE ROLES

With reference to an individual the word 'circumstance' is used essentially in a localized manner and in a subjective spirit, whereas the word 'environment' stands for non-local or global surroundings and largely used in an objective sense. Parameters generally responsible for creating the circumstances are time, place, cause, manner, occasion, etc. but those for the environment they are surrounding objects, region or other physical conditions. Circumstances and environment both influence the human actions and subsequently the personality of a person in one way or the other. In some sense, the former influences the mental state characterized by the so-called 'mindset function' (see, (Kaushal, 2011, Chapter 8)), the latter, on the other hand, affects the personality at the gross-body level. To provide a background for Part C of this book, this chapter is devoted to discuss quantitatively the effects of circumstances and environment in which an individual is left to interact with. Further, note that the environment in general consists of both animate and inanimate objects and their associated interactions. But here we shall focus our attention mainly on human environment and the corresponding interactions. After elaborating on this subject, in Sect.11.2 we discuss as to how a given personality influences a group or gathering of persons or vice-versa. In Sect.11.3, we highlight as to how the different types of human interactions take place or how an individual plays multiple roles in the changing environment. A discussion on as how an individual is responsible for creating a good or bad environment is presented in Sect.11.4. Finally, concluding remarks are made in Sect. 11.5.

11.1 AN INDIVIDUAL AND THE ENVIRONMENT

In a philosophical spirit, the environment can be considered as consisting of animate as well as inanimate objects as listed in Fig.11.1. While the inanimate ones are further divided into P-matter and EP-matter (cf. Sect. 2.4.1) categories, the animate ones can be put broadly into human and non-human categories. To further make the classification finer, the humans are divided into four major categories as mentioned earlier (cf. Example 1.2.2), namely common man, scientist, philosopher and yogi, according to their outlook towards the world-order. Non-humans, on the other hand, could be of two categories, namely domestic and wild, which can further be sub-divided in biological terms.

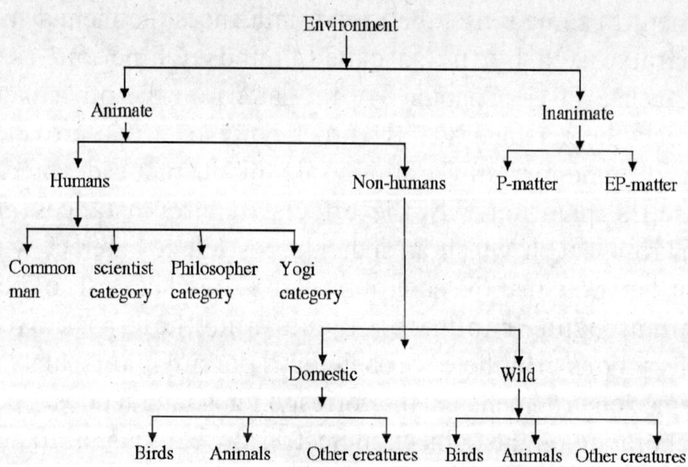

Fig.11.1: A philosophical way of defining and classifying the constituents of environment.

Now an individual, as described in the patomic model, is placed in such an infinitely extended environment. Imagine how many and what varieties of interactions between the human Being and the external world will come into play! As a matter of fact, each end-point of the classifying chart of Fig.11.1 is capable of interacting with the human Being. As a whole, it is a highly complicated process of interaction with environment. More complicate than this are the rules of the game at both gross and subtle levels, which actually maintain the world-order. As far as an interacting individual is concerned, these interactions do take place in all the three of his **G, M** and **C-** domains. Yet there exists an order in Nature in spite of all these apparent disorders at different levels. Individuals, however absorb this reality differently through a broad spectrum of experiences depending on the levels of development of their FOUs. Further, the nature and quality of these experiences keep on changing as a person grows with age. This is how the same individual plays multiple roles while living in this world. Here onwards, we shall deal with the case of human environment in general, consisting of a variety of persons.

11.2 HOW A PERSONALITY INFLUENCES A GROUP OF PERSONS OR VICE VERSA? : SOCIALIZATION

It has been observed that there exists a sign of love and affection, cooperation and co-ordination as well as the efforts for co-existence among the members of a particular species of living Beings. On the other hand, the negatives of this systematic are also observed among these members as and when there is a question of their survival. While this kind of socialization is universal for all species separately, sometimes different species are also found to follow this systematic. For human Being, however, the exception to this law is more frequent mainly due to the presence of extra sense, i.e., intellect in them. Even a single person in a group of persons is capable of influencing the entire gathering by his presence or the presence of a group of persons (or for that matter even that of a single person) which does not take much time in changing the mindset of a person. All these are attributes of the extra sense— intellect, present in the human species. In fact, since birth until the death a person undergoes this kind of socializations on different occasions in life through one-to-one, one-to-many, many-to-one, and many-to-many types of human interactions. These interactions in fact are necessary to establish and re-establish the human values from time to time and from place to place and to nourish and enrich the experiences of an individual at all the three **G**, **M** and **C**-levels.

It may be mentioned that with age, the fronts of socialization of a person increase in terms of his relationship, citizenship, professionalism, religion and the like. In general it is found that the FOUs of a person develop with age and accordingly different fronts of socialization emerge and come into existence. In what follows, we briefly review the development of socialization on different fronts in the life of a person as he grows with age, naturally by way of undergoing variety of human interactions at different space-time points during this journey.

11.2.1 Interactions during childhood

A newly born baby interacts with his mother for his various needs and survival. As he grows, he starts interacting with his father and other family members and later with friends of the same age group. Note that first these interactions are mostly at the level of B and soon thereafter the child learns the 'mother-tongue' which need not be a formal verbal language or script; he starts reacting and interacting through SE not only with humans and pets but also with Nature. While all this continues in the 'school' of his family, at the same time his FOUs start developing in a particular way in the sense that the family traditions are inculcated in him at the level of M and I. Since E is still not very active till this time, M and I also function 'linearly' and this is the reason for the innocence and simplicity built in the child's behavior in general. As E is not fully developed by this time, the child has the tendency to forget and ignore the effects of many of the interactions temporarily or permanently. Although the *prārabdha* also plays a role in this case but some of the *sanskārās* (tendencies) in the child, germinated at this age, do stay throughout life.

At the next stage, when the child is admitted to a school and later to a college, he is exposed to a variety of personalities for interactions. The FOUs including the EOL, E, of the child start working at a fast pace during the schooling. The FOUs are trained in various ways for digesting the preliminaries of the existing world-order. By this time the child along with his contemporary friends becomes prepared to survive properly in this world. In some cases, even in the absence of formal education, the child only on the basis of training from his 'family school' becomes capable of doing wonders. In this case he gets opportunity to learn many lessons from the interactions with society of which he himself becomes a part later. These lessons also supply a feedback constantly for further development of his FOUs. In nut-shell, the child learns at a fast rate from the circumstances in which he is left and starts behaving accordingly.

11.2.2 Interactions during adulthood

Once the child becomes adult, his socialization increases. Besides the educational (if attached to a centre of higher learning) two more fronts of his interaction open. These are the extended domains of interactions at the family level through his marriage and a new front of interaction at the work place for the sake of livelihood in future. Note that by now family *sanskārās* become more or less static and remain only in the background. The marriage front, however, offers only limited personalities to interact with, but of sensitive nature in the sense that they matter a lot in maintaining peace at home and at work. When the married person has a child, then no doubt history repeats for the child as per his father or mother. However, for the latter it is an altogether new experience in terms of interactions with the child at every stage of his growth. This experience in terms of interactions becomes richer when the parents have more than one child.

The livelihood front, on the other hand, brings in countless personalities for interaction of the adult. In fact the individual adult becomes the nodal point of many and sometimes diverging fronts of interaction with various organizations and societies. Now, he automatically becomes an important member of the society in the same way as he was an important member of the family during his childhood. At every stage and point of time his FOUs keep on enriching in terms of experiences and the same in turn also supply a feedback to his EOLs for further improving the lifestyle or behavior. This is the period in one's lifetime when all the EOLs are most active. The person is capable of leaving certain impact on the society or the foot prints on the sands of time in whatever form it may be.

11.2.3 Interactions during middle-age

During the adulthood the interactions of an individual with other persons reach a peak mainly because of the maximum activity of his EOLs at this point of time. Then comes the period of middle-age during which already developed interactions are just maintained with a possibility of certain new interactions with third generation whether it is at home or at work. With the experiences becoming richer and richer with time, the behavior of the person accordingly becomes more refined. As a result, the middle-aged person develops a natural tendency to share and express himself through these experiences now and then, and again at home and at work. This sometimes further enhances his domain of interactions with persons other than those of family and work place. As the experiences about the world-order by this time are highly refined in terms of universal values, a natural tendency develops in some persons to enter the domain of spirituality. During middle-age, both inner and outer EOLs in general remain equally active. In some cases, however, B and SE start showing symptoms of decay.

11.2.4 Interactions during old-age

In the old age, while inner EOLs, namely M, I and E continue to remain active as in the case of middle-age, but may be at low pace, and outer EOLs, namely B and SE now start decaying fast in most cases. As a result, the interactions with other persons, which at one time achieved the peak during adulthood and a constant level during the middle-age, now, however, start decreasing because of the limitations on the efficiency of body parts and the senses of perception and action. If a person has been a true observer of his conscious and serious actions during earlier stages of his life, then his experiences gained so far out of interactions with other persons and with the world, now indeed become the 'wisdom of old persons'. They not only become the source of inspiration to new generation but sometimes the person himself becomes the role model for the society as a whole.

Next, we pinpoint some typical events, which occur during the above journey of a social person, as the examples of one-to-one, one-to-many, many-to-one and many-to-many human Being interactions.

Example 11.2.1: (i) Discussions between husband and wife, mother and child, father and son, between two friends are some examples of one-to-one human Being interactions, (ii) A teacher delivering his lecture in the class room, a politician addressing a gathering, a trade union leader giving an impressive speech to the members, a saint delivering sermons to his devotees, etc. are some examples of one-to-many interactions, (iii) A group of councilors counseling the chairperson, family members jointly guiding their child, a group of students complaining to the principal, etc. are some situations of many-to-one human Being interactions, (iv) Two groups of persons with rival motives standing face to face in arms, armies of two countries facing each other in a battle field, etc. are some examples of many-to-many human Being interactions.

Note that in all the above four situations the mindset of the participating member(s) in the interaction, plays an important role in producing the output and also to understand the underlying process of interaction. We shall attempt to quantify and identify some of these processes using the patomic model of human Being in Chapter 12.

11.3 INTERACTIONS OF EOLs AT DIFFERENT LEVELS: EXISTENCE AND CO-EXISTENCE IN A GROUP

All through the journey of life described in the previous section, a person exerts and works for his existence and co-existence, otherwise his survival in a society becomes difficult. In the early part of his life, one exerts for the essentials for life and in the later part for the values in a family or society if he has remained conscious of his actions in the past. In this case it matters a lot whether the person has grown up with systematic of positive pursuits or with that of negative pursuits.

For most of the time, many of us (barring some lucky souls) exert for the essentials for life, namely food, clothing and housing and for this an average but professionally trained intellect suffices. In order to get specialty or super-specialty in a profession, an innovative intellect is required in addition to a huge stock of experiences. For this purpose, education and training whether formal or informal although work but by and large they only show a map. In real life, however, a person has to travel on his own following this map and he should be prepared to face all sorts of challenges which appear at every step to perform the journey of life.

In this real-life journey of a person, the role of his EOLs appears in two distinct forms: Firstly, in the vertical development of his personality in which he prepares himself to survive and serve the society. The art of such a preparation, in fact, has already been described in preceding chapters. Secondly, the role of EOLs also appears in the horizontal development of the personality of a person in which he interacts with other persons towards his existence and co-existence in the society. In both the cases, no doubt, the interactions inside the human Being are common and play important roles, but for his horizontal development of personality a new dynamics evolves through the same set of EOLs, particularly for his coexistence in the society or a group.

In this new dynamics the EOLs of a person interact with the EOLs of other persons under the given circumstances (in terms of necessity, demand and supply towards EFLs) and environment in terms of man-made and God-made external conditions. These interactions do occur at the levels of both inner and outer EOLs of the patomic model. In fact, the nature and quality of this interaction very much depends on whether two or more persons interact through outer EOLs or inner EOLs or through their cross possibilities. Note that unlike the atomic model of matter, here in the patomic model of human Being these are the WO, B, SEA and SEK EOLs which are readily available to interact with and their participation in the interaction corresponds to the 'inside out' (ISO) case, whereas that of the

SO, E, I and M EOLs corresponds to the 'outside out' (OSO) case and the participation of the latter generally appears only at a later stage. Thus, in a broad sense one arrives at the four possibilities of interactions between persons, namely (i) ISO-ISO type, (ii) ISO-OSO type, (iii) OSO-ISO type, and (iv) OSO-OSO type. It is needless to say that ISO-OSO type interactions are not the same as OSO-ISO type ones as each participating member (person) has different levels of development of his FOU (or the so-called 'treasure of experiences' of life). In this regard, at the finer level if one accounts for the different orders of dressing of EOLs with consciousness of each person, then there may arise infinitely many varieties of interactions between two or among more than two persons.

Example 11.3.1: The case of ISO-ISO type interactions: A discussion between two persons or among a group of persons who have not much developed their inner EOLs about the world-order, say about EFLs, weather, political system or any other similar topic for that matter.

Example 11.3.2: The case ISO-OSO type interactions: A discussion between a common man and an intellectual or a group of intellectuals, say about anything related to the world-order.

Example 11.3.3: The case of OSO-ISO type interactions: A discussion between an intellectual and a common man or a group of such persons with an intention to imparting good to the latter about world order, viz. teacher-taught interactions, religions discourses by a saint, etc.

Example 11.3.4: The case of OSO-OSO type interactions: A discussion between two intellectuals or among intellectuals on anything related to world-order, including the spiritual personalities.

Very often the discussions are meaningful if they take place between or among like-minded persons or in the case when the delivering person is at a higher potential (in terms of the development of his FOUs) and the rest are at lower potential but with good intentions and balanced or controlled mind and senses. Alternatively, one can as well have another, rather precise, way of classifying the interactions among human Beings, namely in terms of the exchanges at the level of three **G**, **M** and **C** domains of their working towards the understanding of world-order. We shall carry out some of these analyses in quantifiable terms in Chapter 12.

11.4 HOW CAN AN INDIVIDUAL VITIATE THE HARMONY IN A GROUP?

There is a lot of truth in the popular saying, "a rotten apple in the basket spoils the whole pack of apples". In other words, for the upliftment of a group or society the collective efforts of all its members are necessary whereas for its downfall just the efforts of a single individual are sufficient. If this individual happens to be a teacher or the head of a family, group or of a society, then this downfall becomes even faster. Note that this individual is capable of vitiating both circumstances and environment in the group. Of course, the extent of this downfall depends on the efforts of the spoiling person and the development of his FOUs as also on the degree of prevailing harmony among the remaining members of the group. It is observed that if the coordination or harmony among the members of a group is very strong, it does not take time to corner out the spoiling person; otherwise the single spoiling individual finds ways to dominate over the group but not for long. In fact, there is a limit to it and it is a bit difficult as well to achieve positivity and become constructive in the life by way of following the systematic of positive pursuits as compared to achieving the negativity and become destructive by following the systematic of negative pursuits. As a matter of fact, one can become destructive to any extent and there is no limit to it.

With a view to analyzing the extent of vitiation by the spoiling (destructive) person here we revisit the human interactions that appear at all the three **G**, **M** and **C** levels of the person. We, however, consider the case when the spoiling individual is active in the group and the remaining members are not active against that individual. Normally **C** level interactions are highly suppressed in such persons due to strong hold of ego E on their mindset. This helps in moulding their *sankalpās* accordingly and also makes weak the faculty of emotion, i.e., mind M. If at all some emotions are present, they are just of superfluous nature. Thus, the interactions are mainly dominated at the levels of B, SE and I and that too in a destructive spirit in the group. While the spoiling person keeps on working in the group through his body, senses and intellect, he always keeps an eye on his vested interest rather than on the interest of the group or society.

Next comes the question of time duration during which such a person remains harmful to the society. This can be better understood in terms of the nature of his personality as defined in Sect.9.6 (cf. Table 9.1). To this effect, both integrated and nonintegrated personalities can be proved to be harmful. But the fact is that the personalities with *satoguni sankalpās* can never think of harming anyone, and if at all they do so it will be for a very short period or mainly to teach lessons to others. The personalities with *rajoguni sankalpās,* however, can do harm for a longer duration and vested interests but with a possibility of reformation thereby, provided they are guided properly and at appropriate time. For the persons with *tamoguni sankalpās*, the negativity is built-in in their character. There is no chance of their improving unless they have something good in their fortune or *prārabdha*. However, the extent to which these *tamoguni sankalpa* persons can do harm to the society can be guessed easily from Table 9.1. The harm is maximum by ideally integrated *tamoguni tāmasik* personalities, little less by integrated *tamoguni tāmasik* personalities and further less by nonintegrated category of persons but with *tamoguni sankalpās.* Even among the last case, the persons with *tamoguni sātvik* nature may turn out to be better than persons with *tamoguni rājasik* nature. Further, as far as the reformation in the character, possible in whichever category, is concerned it also depends on the circumstances and environment prevailing in the group.

11.5 CONCLUDING DISCUSSION

With a view to carrying out a qualitative analysis of interactions which an individual can have in a family, group or in a society, the patomic model of human Being is exploited once again. An individual in fact plays a multiple role while interacting with other persons in a family, work place or society. To this effect, an overview of possible interactions which an individual can have at different stages of his journey of life, is presented. It is emphasized that there are two distinct but related types of human dynamics which emerge for the existence and co-existence of an individual in a group. These are the interactions inside the human Being, particularly those among the inner EOLs, which contribute to the existence of an individual in a group whereas an understanding of interactions between the EOLs of a person with those of another person in thc group define his co-existence. In a broad sense, four possible types of interactions between interacting persons corresponding to their inner and outer EOLs are also suggested (cf. Sect.11.3).

An answer to the question as to how and to what extent a single individual can vitiate the existing harmony in the working of a group is sought within the framework of Vedic science. The cases when the spoiling person appears in different personalities as a member of the group are analyzed under the assumption that this person is active in the group and the remaining members do not react to his actions.

In the next chapter, we shall give a quantitative flavor to some of these studies and analyses.

Further Reading:

For further discussions on the material given in Sects.11.2 and 11.3, see (Kaushal, 2011, Chapters 8 and 9).

High Skill Exercises and Projects

11.1 Compare the chart of Fig. 11.1 with the one used in the studies of environmental science. Discuss and analyze the interactions of the end-products of the chart with the human Being of patomic model in the two cases.

11.2 "A rotten apple in the basket spoils whole pack of apples", discuss the spirit of this behavioral fact in the light of discussions in Sects.11.2 and 11.4 with some examples from your (a) class-room, and (b) neighborhood.

11.3 With reference to Exercise 11.2, analyze the possible ways and methods which a spoiling person can adopt in vitiating the atmosphere. Is the reformation in the character of such a person possible? If yes, then to what extent?

11.4 Write an essay on the interactions which a person can possibly have during his life time as (a) a family member, (b) a member of society, (c) a person working in an organization, and (d) a retired person. Discuss in detail as under what conditions the actions of such a person can become the examples for the generations to come.

11.5 Classify the actions and interactions associated with the four cases discussed in Exercise 11.4 under the heads of vertical and horizontal components of a complete personality. Explain what role the interactions inside the human Being play in the development of both the components of personality (cf. Sect. 7.4).

11.6 Corresponding to the four categories of interaction among the human Beings (cf. Sect. 11.3), namely (i) ISO-ISO type, (ii) ISO-OSO type, (iii) OSO-ISO type, and (iv) OSO-OSO type, pick up one example of each and discuss in detail as to how the underlying human dynamics works.

PART C

HUMAN INTERACTIONS: ROLE OF INDIVIDUAL IN A SOCIETY

Chapter 12

TWO, THREE AND MANY HUMAN BEING INTERACTIONS : A QUANTITATIVE APPROACH

An attempt is made in this chapter to give a possible quantitative flavor to two, three and many human Being interactions using the framework of patomic model of human Being. For this purpose, the concepts, models and theories of atomic physics are freely used in an analogous manner. In fact the use of the latter via patomic model suggests a new dimension of study of human dynamics. After having some lessons from physical theories in general, we analyze the interactions between two human Beings in Sect.12.2. In Sect.12.3 we discuss as to how this interaction gets affected in the presence of environment consisting of both animate and inanimate objects (cf. Sect.11.1). Three and many human Being interactions are discussed respectively in Sects.12.4 and 12.5, after having some more lessons from physical theories. Finally, concluding remarks are made in Sect. 12.6.

12.1 LESSONS FROM PHYSICAL THEORIES III

Symbolically, a 'reaction' or a 'process' in physical sciences depicted on a board or on a piece of paper and further going on in the mind of a scientist, is represented conventionally by

$$A + B \underset{\text{conditions}}{\overset{\text{Physical}}{\rightleftarrows}} C + D \,. \tag{12.1}$$

The objects A and B on the left are termed as 'reactants' and C and D on the right as 'products'. Note that this is the simplest and the first step to understand a complicated underlying reaction mechanism. This also represents a variety of processes taught in different branches of physics and chemistry, except for the fact that the meanings of reactants and products, the nature of underlying reaction- mechanism and interactions, and energy scales at which these processes occur, keep on changing in different disciplines. They appear mostly in an analogous manner. To be more specific, (i) the 'objects' A, B, C, D change with regard to their nature, shape, size, structure, etc., (ii) the 'rules of the game' change with regard to the nature of interaction between and among A, B, C, D in terms of their strength and range, etc., and (iii) the 'scales' change with regard to space and time and at the level of mind of the scientist as well (for details, see (Kaushal, 2003, Chapter 5)).

Other remarks about the process (12.1) that are relevant in the present context are as follows:

(a) The arrow towards right (left) in (12.1) is the 'time arrow' representing the process in the forward (backward) direction. The phrase(s) above and below the arrows represents the physical conditions (like temperature, pressure, etc.) favoring the occurrence of the process.

(b) Only two objects in the initial and final states are shown in (12.1), mainly for simplicity; otherwise one can as well have more than two objects in either of the initial or final states. Some particular cases of process (12.1) are the 'production' process in which either D or C is absent and (12.1) becomes 'decay' process when either B or A is absent.

(c) Note that the objects A, B, C, D can be composite as well and their constituents can also participate in the process. In that case, one can question the elementarity of the objects A, B, C and D and also the fundamentality of the process as the compositeness leads to several other sub-processes which, in turn, correspond to different types of interactions and energy scales.

(d) It may so happen that the reactants and products could be the same but are in different (excited) energy states after the reaction, viz. $A + B \rightarrow A^* + B^*$.

(e) Whether such a process occurs in physics or in chemistry, the interactions involved are the space-time meditated ones, i.e., they could be gravitational, weak, electromagnetic or strong. In other words, these interactions are generated only out of space and time and not from anything beyond like consciousness; secondly their nature is considered only as action-at-a-distance (AAD) type or at the most contact-type in case of the physical contact of the participants. Participating members in the process, in fact, are assumed not to carry any memory, i.e., there is no scope of any action-at-a-time (AAT) or action-at-a-distance time (AADT) type forces.

(f) At certain energy scales and for certain class of reactants the process (12.1) can also be expressed as Feynman-like diagram shown in Fig.12.1.

(g) In view of Remark (e) the entire process consisting mainly of inanimate (participating) objects proceeds as a 'closed' system, i.e., it does not interact with the surroundings except for those factors which are accounted for in the process.

As lessons from the above concepts of physical science, we rewrite below all the seven Remarks for the case of two interacting human Beings, which are now identified with the objects A, B, C and D of (12.1) and each of them is described by the patomic model.

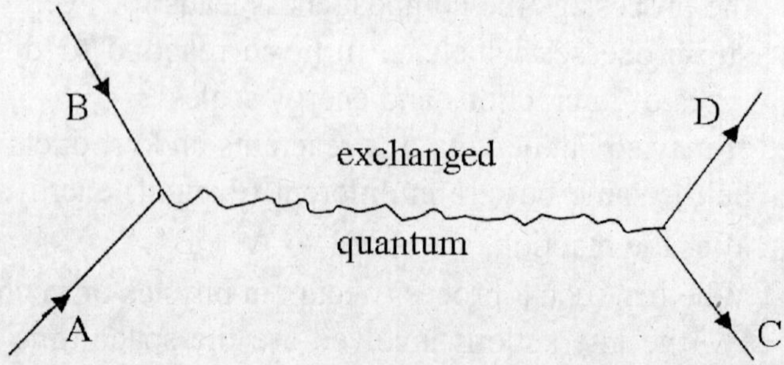

Fig.12.1: At certain energy scales and for certain class of reactants the process (12.1) can also be represented by a Feynman-like diagram.

(a') The place of 'time arrow' is now taken by the meditation variable μ which accounts for the evolution of consciousness of each of the participants. For a common man the processes, however, remain irreversible.

(b') For simplicity we consider the interaction between two persons. Husband and wife trying to conceive a baby or a mother giving birth to a baby can be considered as examples of 'production' or 'decay', respectively in the present context.

(c') Note that each participating member A, B, C and D is now composite; at crude level in terms of gross, micro and causal bodies and at subtle level in terms of detailed EOLs of each. Note that the interactions are going to be different at different levels.

(d') In physical terms, the process, $A+B \rightarrow A^*+B^*$, always remains but A^* and B^* now differ from A and B in infinitely many ways due to the dressings of their different EOLs with consciousness as a result of interactions.

(e') In addition to the contact and AAD-type forces, the possibility of AAT and AADT type forces is always there for conscious participants.

(f') Feynman-like diagram can still be drawn but with reference to the μ-variable instead of the time variable. As a result, there arises a new class of *tanmātrās* (the quanta of interaction) in addition to the ones postulated in Vedic science for the interaction of a human Being with PMs.

(g') As the consciousness associated with an individual cannot be localized, hence the interacting system in the present case always remains an 'open' system. Therefore, there is no question of using existing physical laws as such in the present case in view of Remark (e').

12.2 INTERACTIONS BETWEEN HUMAN BEINGS

It is a common experience that when a single person is left in the field of PMs or in general that of WO, he alone feels and realizes the interactions with them, first through B and SE and later through M, I and E depending upon the development of his FOU. However, when two or more than two persons are present in a given environment then, in addition to individual's feeling and realization, there is also a tendency for sharing these feelings and realizations with other persons about the same WO. If the sharing persons are strange to each other (i.e. they are not biased or do not have any prejudice) then the same sequence of interactions follows; otherwise the interactions can start at any subtle level and the same depends on the development of FOUs of the sharing person. Although the interactions initiate at the most fundamental level through EOLs (bare case), the presence of PMs in the form of environment just dresses them up (dressed case). This enables the interactions to become more effective and the same leads to a success of the outward action. With a view to quantifying these interactions, we employ here the patomic model of human Being.

12.2.1 Interactions at the crude level

Consider two human Beings b_1 and b_2 each of them having described in terms of gross, micro and causal bodies (i.e., by the reduced version of patomic model of Sect.6.3.2), viz., $b_1 \equiv \{\mathbf{C}_1, \mathbf{M}_1, \mathbf{G}_1\}$, $b_2 \equiv \{\mathbf{C}_2, \mathbf{M}_2, \mathbf{G}_2\}$. These persons are now placed within the range (!) of interaction. Unlike the physical forces, the range here is not defined in the space-time domain, rather it is characterized by the meditation variable μ. In fact they have to have something common in their thinking in order to interact with each other. For example, the persons sitting next to each other in a train or bus may not interact for hours or even days unless the environment forces them to do so. On the other hand, the persons living far apart (distance-wise) can interact with each other either through thought process or through the material means like phone calls, etc. Similar is the case with the time variable. Persons sitting together may or may not go in the past and future but, if they wish, they can as well share their experiences of infinite past or infinite future (though rare but it might include their past or future births provided they are capable enough) depending on the development of their FOUs. In case of distant persons while M, I of **M** play the important role, it is E of **M** which plays the role in case of persons sitting together.

The interactions between b_1 and b_2 are shown in Fig.12.2 within the framework of reduced version of patomic model and with meditation variable μ in the upward direction. While the consciousness of each of the interacting persons is separately evolving through their corresponding variables μ_1 and μ_2, the variable μ accounts for the evolution of consciousness of the observer (Reader!). Before analyzing the possible quanta of exchanges in this figure, following points are worth noting:

(i) Since $\mathbf{C}_1$ and $\mathbf{C}_2$ represent the second quantized version of the same all-pervading cosmic consciousness field, they separately or combined together will only provide the background for a cognitive b_1-b_2 interaction in general.

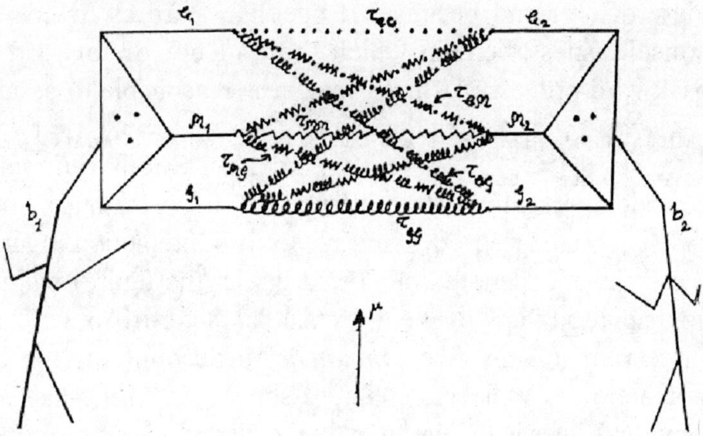

Fig.12.2: Interactions between human Beings at the crude level, i.e., at the levels of **C** ,**M** and **G.**

(ii) In view of (i) $\mathbf{M}_i$,$\mathbf{G}_i$ jointly or separately for i=1 and 2 are active in the presence of $\mathbf{C}_1$ and $\mathbf{C}_2$ respectively.

(iii) In view of (i) and (ii) above, for the interaction of $\mathbf{M}_1$ with $\mathbf{M}_2$ or $\mathbf{G}_2$, or of $\mathbf{G}_1$ with $\mathbf{M}_2$ or $\mathbf{G}_2$ (or vice versa) $\mathbf{C}_1$ and $\mathbf{C}_2$ separately remain in the background. Similarly, for the interaction of $\mathbf{G}_1$ with $\mathbf{G}_2$ (or of $\mathbf{G}_2$ with $\mathbf{G}_1$), $\mathbf{M}_1$ (or $\mathbf{M}_2$ in the reverse case) remains in the background (cf. seer-seen chain in Example 2.4.1).

(iv) Note that { $\mathbf{C}_i$, $\mathbf{M}_i$, $\mathbf{G}_i$} for i=1 and 2, separately constitute individuals who can be in general in different mind sets. For a noticeable interaction between them there has to be an overlap in certain domains.

In general there are nine quanta of interaction (*tanmātrās*) which can exchange between b_1 and b_2 at crude level, namely τ_{C1C2}, τ_{C1M2}, τ_{C1G2}, τ_{M1C2}, τ_{M1M2}, τ_{M1G2}, τ_{G1C2}, τ_{G1M2} and τ_{G1G2}. Further universality of $\mathbf{C}_1$ and $\mathbf{C}_2$ implies $\tau_{C1C2} = \tau_{C2C2} = \tau_{CC}$. In view of (iv) and because of peculiar features of cosmic consciousness field in which the concept of forward or backward processes is irrelevant, it is reasonable to assume $\tau_{M1C2} = \tau_{C1M2} = \tau_{CM}$; $\tau_{G1C2} = \tau_{C1G2} = \tau_{CG}$; $\tau_{M1M2} = \tau_{M2M1} = \tau_{MM}$; $\tau_{G1M2} = \tau_{M1G2} = \tau_{GM}$; $\tau_{G1G2} = \tau_{G2G1} = \tau_{GG}$. Such symmetry considerations thus imply existence only of six quanta, namely τ_{CC}, τ_{CM}, τ_{CG}, τ_{MM}, τ_{MG} and τ_{GG} for b-b interaction. Out of these six; τ_{CC} (denoted by dotted line in the figure) will not contribute in view of the universal character of soul. Thus, there remain only five *tanmātrās* to account for the b-b interaction. While τ_{GG} and τ_{MM} shown by spring-like and wave-like lines in the figure, τ_{CM}, τ_{CG}, and τ_{MG} are respectively shown by correspondingly mixed line segments.

Note that while the human Beings will interact accordingly to their own μ_1, μ_2 parameters (or, the levels of development of their FOUs), the observer will evaluate this interaction according to his own μ or the development of his own FOU, however, remaining only as a spectator. Further remarks about the exchanged quanta between b_1 and b_2 are as follows:

(i) The *tanmātrā* τ_{CC} may correspond to *turiya* state (a state of the human Being beyond the three commonly known aspects of consciousness on the substratum of Self, namely awaking, dreaming and deep-sleep).

(ii) The *tanmātrās* τ_{CM} and τ_{CG} correspond to the case when the micro- or gross-body of b_1 is in direct communion with the SO of b_2 or vice versa. Similarly, τ_{MM} and τ_{MG} correspond to the cases when the micro-body of b_1 is in communication separately with the micro- and gross-bodies of b_2 or vice versa, i.e., when b_1 can imagine/dream the gross body actions of b_2.

(iii) In the b-b interaction, it is the τ_{GG}-type exchanges that lie within the purview of physical and biological theories; otherwise as μ increases any or all nonphysical interactions corresponding to $\tau_{MG}, \tau_{MM}, \tau_{CG}$ and τ_{CM} start manifesting and come into existence as a result of fine tuning of the interaction in the lowest order.

(iv) Only experts can visualize the dynamics arising out of higher order fine-tuning, which is attributed to the constituents of **M** and **G** of each of the interacting persons. We demonstrate this in the next sub-section.

In summary, the conscious mind of one person is capable of activating different EOLs of the other person. In fact the mind sets of b_1 and b_2 as a function of their individual μ_1 and μ_2 play a crucial role in the whole process of interaction.

12.2.2 Fine and hyperfine tuning of the b-b interaction

Next we use the finer details of **G**, **M** and **C** as **G**≡{B, SE}, **M**≡{M, I, E} and **C**≡{SO} to analyze the "reaction" (or, the interaction process),

$$b_1 + b_2 \rightleftarrows b_1' + b_2' + \tau_{b_1 b_2}, \tag{12.2}$$

essentially in the spirit of diagram 12.1. Here b'_1 and b'_2 are the enlightened versions of b_1 and b_2 after the interaction(s).

The *tanmātrās* $\tau_{b_1 b_2}$ satisfies $\tau_{b_1 b_2} = \tau_{b_2 b_1}$ for the reasons given before and correspond to the earlier composition of b as b≡ {**C**, **M**, **G**}, will now correspond to the composition of each of the Being b as b≡{B, SE, M, I, E, SO}. This will lead to twenty varieties of interactions mediated through $\tau_{B,B}$, $\tau_{B,SE}$, $\tau_{SE,SE}$ (correspond to τ_{GG}); $\tau_{B,M}$, $\tau_{B,I}$, $\tau_{B,E}$, $\tau_{SE,M}$, $\tau_{SE,I}$, $\tau_{SE,E}$ (correspond to τ_{GM}); $\tau_{B,SO}$, $\tau_{SE,SO}$ (correspond to

τ_{GC}); $\tau_{M,M}$, $\tau_{M,I}$, $\tau_{M,E}$, $\tau_{I,I}$, $\tau_{I,E}$, $\tau_{E,E}$ (correspond to τ_{MM}); $\tau_{M,SO}$, $\tau_{I,SO}$, $\tau_{E,SO}$ (correspond to τ_{MC}). Note that the interactions of the type $\tau_{SO,SO}$ do not form the part of this classification since it provides the basis for all the above interactions as argued earlier for τ_{CC}. Further each of these 20 interactions accounts for certain aspect of behavior arising out of the interaction of two human Beings. While for the details we refer to (Kaushal, 2011, Chapter 9), here in what follows we cite five examples —one corresponding to each of the five gross *tanmātrās*.

Example 12.2.1: (τ_{GG}): Case of body-body interaction without prejudices: certain instances can be traced for example in the wrestling of two wrestlers, meeting of husband and wife or of two drunkards.

Example 12.2.2: (τ_{GM}): Case of body-mind interaction without the roles of I, E and SE (i.e. only emotions) : Many examples one can find in a family but the most ideal one is that of mother-baby or at times of husband and wife interactions.

Example 12.2.3: (τ_{GC}): Case of body-soul interaction: A person in *Samādhi* receiving the salutation of another person.

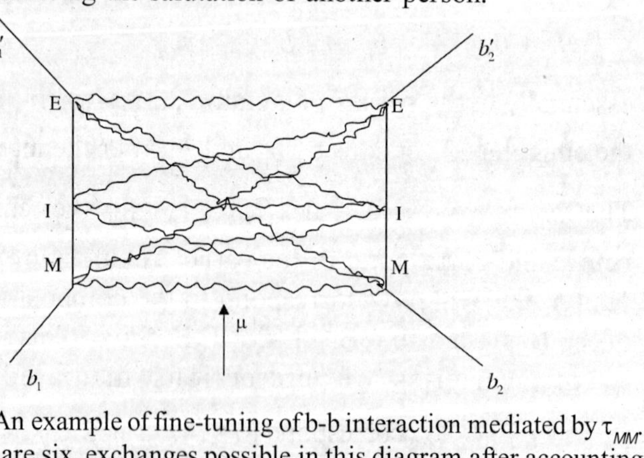

Fig. 12.3: An example of fine-tuning of b-b interaction mediated by τ_{MM}. In all there are six exchanges possible in this diagram after accounting for the symmetry considerations.

Example 12.2.4: (τ_{MM}): Case of mind-mind interaction $(\tau_{M,M})$: Imagination of or dreaming the emotional exchanges between two persons like weeping of a lady when she watches the other weeping lady.

Example 12.2.5: (τ_{MO}): Case of mind-soul interaction $(\tau_{M,SO})$: A person in *Samādhi* noticing the emotions of the other.

In fact Feynman-like diagrams can be drawn for each of the interactions described above and through Examples 12.2.1 to 12.2.5, but here we elaborate only on τ_{MM} class of exchanges, as shown in Fig. 12.3.

Note that the above discussed exchanges are between bare EOLs (not dressed and enriched with environment) of b_1 and b_2. The examples cited above are accommodated only in a crude manner in the scheme of classification. In fact they suggest the cases of ideal interactions as far as the real life is concerned. In the next section we shall account for the effect of environment and circumstances on these bare interactions in order to bring them to a more realistic situation.

The process (12.2) in general evolves with respect to space, time and consciousness variables and the latter is accommodated through μ. Here, however, we have proceeded with the evolution of the system with respect to μ only, as the scales of space-time and of non- space-time mediated interactions are quite different. Moreover, the process (12.2) is just a symbolic representation as far as the physics content of reactants and the products is concerned.

Lastly, we make a few remarks about the hyperfine-tuning of b-b interactions. This feature, for example, for the τ_{MM} class of exchanges described in Fig.12.3, can be understood as follows. Note that each constituent of **M**, namely M, I and E has subtle and gross components as argued in Sect. 3.1. If one considers such sub-divisions of M, I and E in the present

τ_{MM} class of exchanges, it will further increase the number of exchanges to 36 in general at the next hyperfine level. However, symmetry considerations will reduce this number to 21. In fact such hyper-fine tuning of exchanges is also possible for other fine classes of exchanges, namely those corresponding to τ_{GG}, τ_{GM}, τ_{GC}, and τ_{MC} with $\mathbf{G} \equiv \{B, SE\}$. Such details of **G** and also that of B (in terms of different inner and outer organs) and that of SE (in terms of different SEA and SEK) will lead to a huge list of exchanges which in turn can account for further finer aspects of two human Being interaction. We restrict ourselves here from going into further details. However, an example pertaining to τ_{MM} would suffice in this respect.

Example 12.2.6: If a person has some prejudices against the other it is all due to the storage of certain past memories in the subtle component of E, and this accordingly materializes the interaction between b_1 and b_2. As a result the person feels joy or becomes angry out of this interaction depending upon the good or bad memories of the past stored in subtle E.

12.3 DRESSING-UP OF b-b INTERACTION: THE EFFECT OF ENVIRONMENT

What has been discussed above in Sect. 12.2 is the (bare) b-b interaction generating basically from the bare EOLs of b_1 and b_2. These interactions (or their measure in the form of associated *tanmātrās*, namely τ_{GG}, τ_{GM}, τ_{GC}, τ_{MM}, τ_{MC}) get dressed up in the presence of WO in general or PMs in particular. Actually the external environment consists of two aspects, namely the presence of kith and kin (or a third person) and/or the PMs. In either case, the b-b interaction gets modified or dressed up and may enrich the awareness of both b_1 and b_2 according to the level of development of their individual FOUs and hence affects the interaction. Note that the presence not only of PMs, but also of a third Being (human or nonhuman), if that happens to be a relative, a pet or even a stranger, affects the b-b interaction accordingly. Although, the latter forms the case of three-Being interaction (which we shall take-up in the next section) but as long as the third human Being remains a spectator the b-b interaction will only be marginally affected. Thus, in the presence of environment all the five exchanges τ_{GG}, τ_{GM}, τ_{GC}, τ_{MM}, τ_{MC} get dressed up to become $\tilde{\tau}_{\mathbf{GG}}$, $\tilde{\tau}_{\mathbf{GM}}$, $\tilde{\tau}_{\mathbf{GC}}$, $\tilde{\tau}_{\mathbf{MM}}$, $\tilde{\tau}_{\mathbf{MC}}$. It may be mentioned that the 'dressing' here means enriching the quota of sharing between b_1 and b_2 or enriching the FOU of each b_1 and b_2.

Dressing up of b-b interaction, in fact, is a two step process: In the first stage each of b_1 and b_2 gets enriched by the presence of WO through $\tilde{\tau}_{ea},\tilde{\tau}_{w},\tilde{\tau}_{a},\tilde{\tau}_{f},\tilde{\tau}_{et}$ (i.e. through the *tanmātrās* associated with the interaction of a human Being with *panca mahabhūtās*) and then in the next step such enriched FOUs of b_1 and b_2 interact mutually via $\tilde{\tau}_{\mathbf{GG}}$, $\tilde{\tau}_{\mathbf{GM}}$, $\tilde{\tau}_{\mathbf{GC}}$, $\tilde{\tau}_{\mathbf{MM}}$, $\tilde{\tau}_{\mathbf{MC}}$ or in the language of Sect. 7.2.1 via $\tau_{\mathbf{\tilde{G}\tilde{G}}}$, $\tau_{\mathbf{\tilde{G}\tilde{M}}}$, $\tau_{\mathbf{\tilde{G}C}}$, $\tau_{\mathbf{\tilde{M}\tilde{M}}}$, $\tau_{\mathbf{\tilde{M}C}}$. In other words, the mindset functions of b_1 and b_2 (see, (Kaushal, 2011, Chapter 8)), namely $\mathbf{M}_1(m_1,i_1,e_1)$ and $\mathbf{M}_2(m_2,i_2,e_2)$ now become $\mathbf{M}_1(m_1,i_1,e_1;\sigma)$ and $\mathbf{M}_2(m_2,i_2,e_2;\sigma)$, respectively. In fact, for the dressed case the mindset function, $\mathbf{M}$, of each individual starts depending on a fourth variable σ accounting for the effect of environment in addition to its dependence on m, i, e responsible respectively for the roles of mind, intellect and ego. In a more realistic computation this function also depends on space (q) and time (t) variables in addition to all the four above, viz., $\mathbf{M}$ $\mathbf{M}(m_1,i_1,e_1;\sigma, q,t)$. For details we refer to (Kaushal, 2011, Kaushal, 2012).

It may be mentioned that the bare *tanmātrās* whether they are τ_i's (with i= ea, w, a, f, et) or τ_{ij}'s (with i, j=b_1,b_2)

could be more or less the same for all human Beings but the dressed ones $\tilde{\tau}_i$'s or $\tilde{\tau}_{ij}$'s may differ from individual to individual or for pair to pair of human Beings. This is mainly because the EOLs of each of us react with the environment differently even if B and SE may appear to be the same at the gross- level but the personalities are definitely different at the levels of M, I and E. If one also accounts for such differences (which at times are very crucial) then the assumption, $\tilde{\tau}_{b_1b_2} = \tilde{\tau}_{b_2b_1}$ breaks down in spite of $\tau_{b_1b_2} = \tau_{b_2b_1}$. We shall consider some real-life applications and examples of these situations in the next chapter.

12.4 THREE HUMAN BEING INTERACTIONS: BRIEF REMARKS

12.4.1 Interactions at the crude level

After a detailed analysis of b-b interaction in the previous section, here we briefly extend the discussion to the case of three-human –Being interactions. No doubt, the methodology in this case remains the same but the number of situations to be analysed in terms of exchanged quanta becomes rather large. If one resorts to the pair-wise interactions (by assuming the third person as a spectator) for a three-human-Being-system, then the life becomes simple as it happens in physical theories where the contribution of three and higher-body forces (particularly in nuclear physics) are found to be small. However, in case of human Beings this is not the case, three- and many-human Beings interactions are equally or even more important, as we are now dealing with an 'open' system whose sub-systems again are no more the 'closed' systems. Therefore, we continue the analysis of an interacting three-human-Being-system described by

$$b_1 + b_2 + b_3 \rightleftarrows b_1' + b_2' + b_3' + \tau_{bjb_k} + \tau_{b_j b_k b_\ell} \quad (12.3)$$

under some simplifying assumptions. This in some sense will suggest a guideline to analyse more realistic situations. Here in process (12.3) τ_{bjb_k} are the quanta corresponding to pair-wise interactions and $\tau_{b_j b_k b_\ell}$ are the quanta corresponding to three-human-Being exchanges with j, k, l=1, 2, 3; but j is not equal to k and not equal to l.

Further note that in the language of reduced version of patomic model each of b_1, b_2, b_3 in the subscript of τ can be **C, M** or **G** but by barring the cases like τ_{CCC}, τ_{CMC}, τ_{MCC}, τ_{CCM}, τ_{CGC}, τ_{GCC}, τ_{CCG} for the reasons given in the case of b-b interaction in terms of the universality of soul. This results into twenty possibilities of three-human–Being exchanges, namely τ_{CMM}, τ_{CMG}, $\tau_{CG,M}$, τ_{CGG}, $\tau_{M,CM}$, $\tau_{M,CG}$, $\tau_{M,MC}$, $\tau_{M,MM}$, $\tau_{M,MG}$, τ_{MGC}, $\tau_{M,GM}$, τ_{MGG}, τ_{GCM}, τ_{GCG}, τ_{GMC}, τ_{GMM}, τ_{GMG}, τ_{GGC}, τ_{GGM}, τ_{GGG}, contrary to the five exchanges for the case of two human Being interactions, namely τ_{GG}, τ_{GM}, τ_{GC}, τ_{MM}, τ_{MC}.

12.4.2 Fine tuning and dressing of b-b-b interactions

We first demonstrate here as to how the mind, M, initiates the interactions in a group of three human Beings. Recall that it is the presence of SO (or, of self-awareness or of the source of consciousness) in a human Being that makes him an SEP-matter from the EP- or P-matter (cf. Sect.2.4.1) existing already inside b. Let b_1, b_2, b_3 be the three human Beings characterized by

$$b_1 \equiv \{SO,\ E_1,\ I_1,\ M_1,\ SE_1,\ B_1\} \ ;$$

$$b_2 \equiv \{SO,\ E_2,\ I_2,\ M_2,\ SE_2,\ B_2\} \ ;$$

$$b_3 \equiv \{SO,\ E_3,\ I_3,\ M_3,\ SE_3,\ B_3\}$$

where E_j, I_j, M_j , SE_j, B_j, for j=1,2,3 are various EOLs present in b_j. Note that the EOL SO is the same in all the three because of its cosmic character and the same offers a basis for their interaction. However, other EOLs are different and in general they are different in all human Beings for not completely independent reasons, namely (i) each Being has different *sanskārās* (tendencies) generated out of his *Prārabdha*, *Sancita*, and *Kriyamāna* components of actions, (ii) each has different levels of development of his FOU, and lastly (iii) each is affected differently by Nature-born three *Gunās* (or each lives in different environment and circumstances). In principle, one should analyze the b-b-b interaction with these reasons in mind but it has been found that it is the EOL, M, while acting as a bridge between **M** and **G** , also plays a

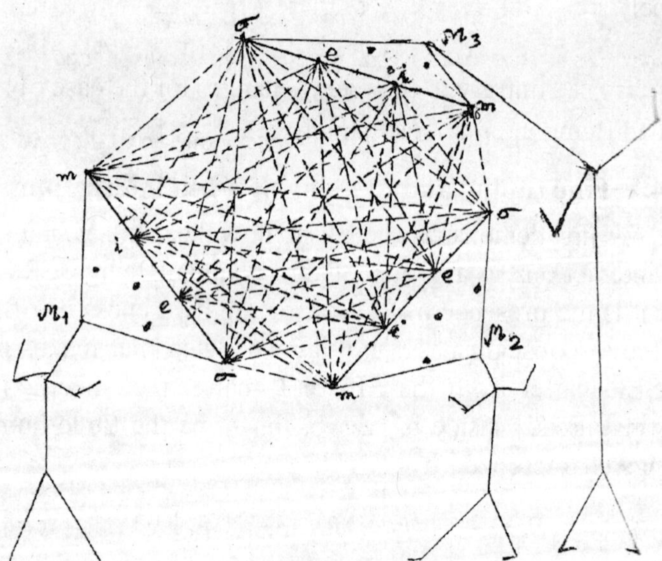

Fig. 12.4: An example of the fine tuning of b-b-b interaction. Possible 48 pair-wise exchanges among the three mindsets $\mathbf{M_1}$, $\mathbf{M_2}$, $\mathbf{M_3}$ are shown here corresponding to the three-human-Being exchange quantum τ_{MMM} .

dominant role in these interactions. As mentioned before (cf. Example 10.2.1), to whichever SE, the mind M is attached, the same SE controls I of that person and accordingly his behavior gets affected.

As for b-b interaction, the fine tuning of b-b-b interaction in terms of constituents of each **G** and **M** corresponding to each interacting person can also be carried out in principle but as a whole it becomes a very complicated dynamics. In fact, this complexity increases further if one wants to analyze the dynamics of four- and higher-human –Being interactions. With the result there is a need to follow other methods for this case. We shall refer to one such method based on statistical description of the system in the next section.

The bare exchanges discussed above between three individuals take place only under ideal conditions as was the case for the b-b interaction; otherwise in real life it is the superposition of different exchanges out of 20 *tanmātrās* that need to be considered. Alternatively, one can as well use the dressed versions of these 20 *tanmātrās* with consciousness as discussed before for the b-b-case. Equivalently, in the use of mindset function for the three interacting persons, viz. $\mathbf{M}_j(m,i,e;\sigma)$ where j=1,2,3, the parameter σ also accounts for the effect of environment. In fact, the same environment is perceived differently by the three interacting individuals depending upon the level of development of their respective FOUs and this also suggests a basis for the interaction among them.

In order to have some glimpses of complexity of b-b-b interactions, we display possible exchanges among the constituents of three mindsets $\mathbf{M}_1$, $\mathbf{M}_2$, $\mathbf{M}_3$ in Fig.12.4. This represents the fine tuning of the interaction described by the *tanmātra* $\tau_{\mathbf{MMM}}$ of the previous subsection but in the presence of environment.

Next, we present a classification of b-b and b-b-b interactions based on the mood of the interacting persons.

Recall that each person can be in any of the three modes while interacting with the other, namely SEP-mode (with an alert self-awareness), EP-mode (conscious but without self-sense) and P-mode (unconscious or may be dead). Clearly, for a meaningful b-b or b-b-b interaction the last mode is ruled out. Therefore, for b_1-b_2 case we have EP-EP, SEP-EP, EP-SEP, SEP-SEP varieties of interactions whereas for the b_1 - b_2 - b_3 case, the following choices emerge:

(i) EP-EP-EP type interaction: when all the three persons are in light moods.

(ii) SEP-EP-EP (or, EP-SEP-EP; EP-EP-SEP) type interaction: when one person is in serious mood and other two are in light moods.

(iii) SEP-SEP-EP (or, SEP-EP-SEP; EP-SEP-SEP) type interaction: when two persons are in serious moods and one person is in light mood.

(iv) SEP-SEP-SEP type interaction: when all the three persons are in serious moods in which case the inner most existence, SO, is manifesting maximum.

12.5 MANY HUMAN BEING INTERACTIONS

We have seen that the magnitude of complexity of interactions among human Beings increases with increasing number of interacting members. No doubt, for these many-human-Being systems, the starting b-b interaction, in its general form, still remains in the background but at the same time the environment and circumstances demand many-human-Being interactions to be equally important. Social and ecological sciences are full of such examples of interacting many-Being systems (cf. next chapter). In fact, the knowledge of b-b or b-b-b interactions as such cannot be extrapolated to a system of many-human Beings in a straightforward manner.

The many-human-Being features that evolve are co-existence, co-operation, coordination and the like and the same at a higher level are more pronounced in the present case than for a physical many-body system. To analyze an interacting many-human-Being system once again we borrow certain concepts and methodology from physical sciences and employ the same to the present situation, though with appropriate modifications.

12.5.1 Lessons from physical theories IV

Here we highlight some physical aspects from atomic and nuclear theory which we plan to use in the next subsection for the case of many-human-Being systems in an analogous manner.

(a) Core-valence picture: When a many-body system (like an atom consisting of electrons or a nucleus consisting of nucleons) in physics interacts with the surrounding (like an external field) or with another many-body system, then the so-called weakly bound particle(s) in the outer periphery of the system (an electron in the case of atom or a nucleon in the case of nucleus), termed as 'valence' particle, participate actively in the interaction after leaving behind the remaining part, the so-called 'core' which is considered more or less as inert during the interaction. No doubt, all this is a modeling game which has a basis in the specific nature of the constituents (as they are the Fermi particles) but the fact is that the model works and explains a variety of data in both atomic and nuclear physics. Such a picture also explains excited states of both the systems within their respective mathematical frameworks and has also been employed to many-atom or many-nucleus systems but with a limited success.

(b) Statistical approach to many-body systems: The core-valence picture discussed above also suggests a statistical approach to study many-body-systems. In fact, not only the collection of atoms or nuclei but also that of valence particles contributed by each atom (or each nucleus) in the assembly of atoms (or nuclei) to constitute a 'new' many-body system. The quantum statistical methods are employed to study the latter. Further, various considerations like spin of the constituent members of the system or whether the members are treated as free or interacting with other members, etc. have helped in explaining different properties of microscopic many-body systems. The free electron gas model for metals or Fermi gas model of nucleus are some examples of such analyses.

(c) ***Saha's ionization theory for hot gaseous systems:*** About eighty years ago, Indian physicist M.N. Saha studied ionization of gases by thermal excitation. In particular, the question as to what happens when the gaseous mass consisting of atoms is heated to very high temperatures (like the ones appear in the formation of stars) was discussed by Saha (see, (Saha and Srivastava, 1931)). To this effect, a formula for computing the fraction of the number of (r+1)-times ionized atoms to r-times ionized atoms was derived in terms of pressure, temperature and internal energy of the system. Here, within the framework of patomic model, we use this formula for a system in which the gaseous mass containing many atoms is replaced with a system of conscious human Beings in an analogous manner.

12.5.2 Patomic model and interactions among human Beings

Statistical methods are expected to provide only limited success when they are used to describe many-Being systems in general or many-human-Being systems in particular, and this is mainly because the constituent of the system are not the inanimate objects but they are (i) living Beings, (ii) having will-power and self-sense, and (iii) having sensitive dependence on the environment provided, or in general they are the open systems. Further, the statistical laws derived using an inanimate dice are expected to be viable only for inanimate objects as in physics, but not in the present case. In spite of all this, it is worthwhile to try them for the systems of living Beings for their quantitative studies in the absence of availability of any other alternative method at present. In fact, the use of analogous patomic model of human Being proves an asset in this regard.

In order to use the core-valence picture through patomic model, note several points of differences from atomic model, e.g., (i) the excited state here are the EOLs, which are going to be different in each excitations of the Being b in terms of scales and other contents of analogy (see, (Kaushal, 2003)), (ii) the core left behind after the excitation does not remain inert as such but in general it becomes more and more active than before in each excitation, (iii) unlike atoms and nuclei where the particle(s) in the outer periphery participate first in a reaction or in a two-body interaction (a case of 'outside out' (OSO)), in the present case, however, it is the picture of 'inside out' (ISO) that actually works. In this case the EOL B, deep inside and close to WO in the schematic picture (cf. Fig.6.1), first comes out to interact with surroundings or another system, provided the mind is in the passive state. Therefore, the actions at the B-level can be considered as the result of the lowest excitations of b. However, B is not isolated but the set of senses of knowledge and actions (SEK and SEA) are attached to it. Thus, in the next stage these are the SEA, namely hands, feet, etc. and later the SEKs, namely eyes, ears, etc. that immediately join B to perform an action.

During all this period (on the scales of both time and meditation variable μ) when M, I and E are still working through the passive mode of consciousness (a departure from the conventional core-valence picture of physics), at the next stage of excitation active mode of consciousness through M,

I and E starts manifesting in the action. At any stage, the remaining core(s) do not remain inert; rather they prepare the ground for the next stage of excitation. Thus, the excitations of b that started with the level B, continue through that of SEAs, SEKs, M and I and finally leave behind certain experiences in E. For a conscious person, these different stages of outward excitations in fact enhance the orders of dressing of his remaining EOLs, with consciousness. Further, unlike atoms and nuclei, here the exchanges (synonym of excitations) in the beginning are ISO-type and much later (on the scale of μ) they become that of OSO-type.

The above prescription of excitations of EOLs leads to formation of various groups, castes and sub-castes in a society and the same we shall take up in future chapters. Here, however, a few examples would suffice for the sake of elucidation.

Example 12.5.1: *Groups on the basis of sharing at B- and SEA-level*: The groups of wrestlers or manual laborers are the befitting examples of this category. In society there are both skilled and non-skilled workers. While the actions of a non-skilled worker are dominated by B and SEA, his other EOLs work under the passive mode of consciousness. His capability of performing an action is defined to this extent only, whether he is a domestic help, a factory worker, or a manual laborer. A skilled worker, who can perform the same set of actions as that of the non-skilled one but he also uses some of his other EOLs in the active mode of consciousness. This, in fact, brings in his deeds some sort of creativity and guiding capacity.

Example 12.5.2: *Groups on the basis of sharing at SEK-level* : Groups and subgroups formed in a society on the basis of exchanges at the SEK-level are plenty. Each sense of knowledge (such as ear, eye, nose, tongue, skin) separately or jointly with other SEKs or in conjunction with B and/or SEA is capable of creating an expertise in a human Being. Further, the degree of expertise is defined by the order of dressing of that particular SEK with consciousness or in terms of experience gained over a period of time. This also becomes a criterion for the formation of further subgroups or sub-castes.

12.5.3 Cases of one-to-many human Beings and many-to-one human Being interactions

Like in Saha's theory the collection of atoms in a hot gas consists of atoms in their different mode of excitations, the same is the case here in a mob of persons. The persons in the mob or gathering, in general, are not like-minded, i.e., they are not in the same degree of ionization. When such a mob or gathering is exposed to the same external stimulant, then the constituents of this system of living Beings react differently. Note that this stimulant can either be a human Being (like a teacher, political leader, sermon delivering saint, etc) or a nonhuman Being (like lion or any other wild animal) or an inanimate object (like storm or cyclone etc.). Individuals in the mob react differently according to the level of development of their respective FOUs and thus undergo different excitations. Life is easier for all the situations except when the stimulant is a human Being in the sense that during or after the reaction with stimulant the mob maintains order or else it becomes disordered. In case of human stimulant, this in fact depends on the development of his FOU to guide the mob accordingly. In return some persons in the mob will derive the inspiration to work at the level of B, some at the level of SEA, some at the level of SEK, some at the level of M, and so on while exposed to the same stimulant and in the given circumstances.

Again a physics-law enters here, i.e., when the external forces are strong (i.e. in terms of pressure and fear in physical sense or in moral sense) then the mob will attain orderliness over a period of time, of course after a continuous exposition to the stimulant. If the internal forces become strong (compared to those created by the stimulant) then the many-human-Being system becomes disordered and may reach to a stage of break down.

Here we demonstrate the application of a Saha-like formula to compute the evolution (excitation) of a single EOL as a result of imposition of such a collective thinking expressed by a collective meditation variable, μ_c (on par with the external temperature in Saha's theory). The fraction α, defined as $\alpha = N_+ / N_0$, where N_+ is the number of beneficiaries in terms of evolution of any one of their EOL and N_0 be the number of persons in the mob initially ready to undergo such an exposition at a given space-time, can be written as follows (see, (Kaushal, 2008)):

$$\alpha(\mu_c,\sigma) = -\phi(\mu_c,\sigma) + [\phi^2(\mu_c,\sigma) + 2\phi(\mu_c,\sigma)]^{1/2} \qquad (12.4)$$

with $$\phi(\mu_c,\sigma) = \left(\frac{\mu_c}{\mu_c^0}\right)^{3/2} \exp(-\chi_s^\sigma / \mu_c) \quad .$$

Here χ_s^σ is the measure of negative efforts (in appropriate units consistent with μ_c) made by an individual in the given circumstances σ to achieve the s-th level in the patomic model (in the spirit of ISO-type interactions) and μ_c^0 is the measure of initial mindset of the human stimulant (transmitter) prevailing and derived by judging the nature of the mob (receiver).

The behavior of the fraction of beneficiaries in the audience is shown in Fig. 12.5 as a function of the collective meditation variable μ_c (in the units of μ_c^0) for three typical values of χ_s^σ, namely solid, dashed and dotted curves correspond to $\chi_s^\sigma = 0.1$, 1.0 and 10.0 respectively in the units of μ_c^0. Note that (i) in general α increases with μ_c and then slowly attains the value unity rather asymptotically irrespective of the nature of efforts. (ii) For a given μ_c, α is large for small values of χ_s^σ, implying that if μ_c is compatible with μ, i.e., if there is a matching of mindsets of the transmitter and of the receiver, then most beneficiaries are those who have never made an effort (or made negative effort) in the past but now they are conscious to learn or to gain from the given transmitter. (iii) The limiting value of α as unity is an ideal situation and the same is hardly attained by a group of audience, but for those who have small χ_s^σ, such a limit is achieved rather quickly.

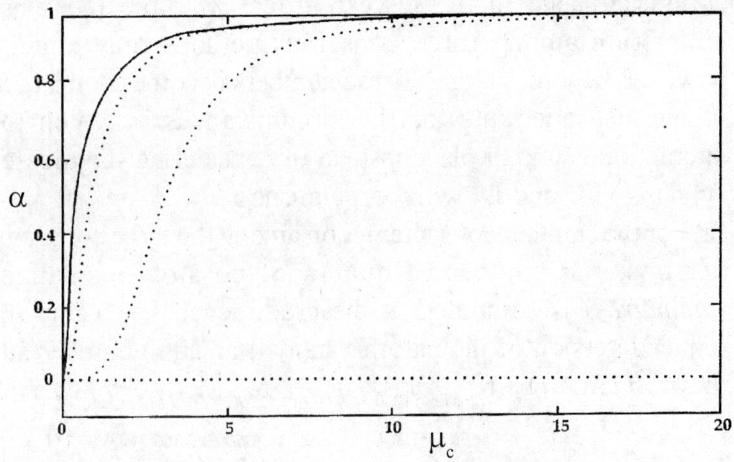

Fig.12.5: Behavior of α as a function of (μ_c / μ_c^0) for different efforts of individual. Solid, dashed and dotted curves respectively correspond to χ_s^σ =0.1,1.0,10.0 (in units of μ_c^0).

12.6 CONCLUDING DISCUSSION

With a view to understanding the nature and other finer details in a quantitative spirit, two-, three- and many-human-Beings systems are analyzed in this chapter using the framework of patomic model. Many concepts and theories from physics are freely used for this purpose in an analogous manner. It is argued that like in physical theories, the three- and higher-human-Being interactions in a many-human-Being system can not be neglected, rather they become more important. In spite of all this the viability of certain concepts and tools of many-body physics is demonstrated in the present case. Some important results arrived at in this chapter are as follows:

(i) At crude level there arise five quanta of exchanges (*tanmātrās*), namely τ_{CM} , τ_{CG} , τ_{MM} , τ_{MG} , τ_{GG} which mediate the interaction between conscious human Beings and are capable of covering their entire gamut of experiences and actions at least in the lowest order. For the pair-wise interaction among three conscious persons this number, however, becomes large. These numbers become even larger, if one also accounts for the circumstances in which the interaction is taking place instead of considering the dressed versions of **G** and **M** with consciousness.

(ii) For the simultaneous interaction among the three conscious persons, the number of quanta of possible exchanges (*tanmātrās)* is computed at the crude level (i.e., using the reduced version of the patomic model) as 20 in number and they turn out to be τ_{CMM}, τ_{CMG}, $\tau_{CG,M}$, τ_{CGG}, $\tau_{M,CM}$, $\tau_{M,CG}$, $\tau_{M,MC}$, $\tau_{M,MM}$, $\tau_{M,MG}$, $\tau_{M,GC,}$ τ_{MGM}, τ_{MGG}, τ_{GCM}, τ_{GCG}, τ_{GMC}, τ_{GMM}, τ_{GMG}, τ_{GGC}, τ_{GGM}, and $\tau_{,GGG}$.

(iii) Mainly to demonstrate the underlying complexity in understanding the fundamental processes in human behavior and experiences, the fine tuning of the interactions mediated only through $\tau_{M,M}$ in the b-b case and $\tau_{M,MM}$ in the b-b-b case are analyzed and discussed (cf. Figs.12.3 and 12.4).

(iv) A new basis for the socialization of persons in a society is suggested in this work at the most fundamental level within the framework of patomic model of human Being.

(v) If one goes with the core-valence picture of physical theories and its use in the present case, then the formation of various groups, sub-groups and further sub-divisions of sub-groups or that of castes, sub-castes, etc. in a society becomes transparent on the basis of valence-sharing mechanism among the interacting members.

(vi) A basis for finding the fraction of beneficiaries in the case of one-to-many human Being interactions is suggested here using the Saha-like ionization formula for a collection of conscious (excited) human Beings.

In summary, keeping the analogies with physical theories in mind many other aspects of the proposed theory need to be explored in future. In the next chapter, however, we switch over to a discussion on some typical examples of these studies in real-life situations.

Further Reading:

For further discussions on various topics listed in this chapter see (Kaushal, 2011, Chapters 8 and 9).

High Skill Exercises and Projects

12.1 List the points of difference in the following cases when the reactants and products in the process (12.1) are: (i) inanimate point objects, (ii) inanimate but extended objects, (iii) animate objects like human Beings, and (iv) animate objects like nonhumans.

12.2 Explain how the all-pervading property of cosmic consciousness field suggests the equivalence of forward and backward processes with regard to the exchanges corresponding to *tanmātras*, namely $\tau_{M1C2}=\tau_{C1M2}$; $\tau_{G1C2}=\tau_{C1G2}$; $\tau_{C1C2}=\tau_{C2C1}$

12.3 For the τ_{MM} -class of exchanges between the two persons draw a diagram like Fig.12.3 when each of the three M, I, E appears with their gross and subtle components.

12.4 Explain how the presence of circumstances and environment enables one's EOLs for dressing with consciousness. [Hint: Recall dressing rules]. Explain how this individual dressing code gets modified by the presence of interactions with another person and leads to a new class of *tanmātrās*.

12.5 Explain and discuss as how the dressed *tanmatras* $\widetilde{\tau}_i$, $\widetilde{\tau}_{ij}$ can differ from person to person and from pair to pair of persons, respectively whereas their bare (nascent) versions τ_i , τ_{ij} remain the same for all individuals and pairs of persons.

12.6 Account and compute for the possible exchanges corresponding to τ_{MMMM} for the case of four human Being interactions using the analogy of the three human Being case as in Fig.12.4.

12.7 Keeping in mind that a many human Being system deals with life-based parameters (like will power, consciousness, etc.) discuss and analyze the phrase, "the statistical laws derived using inanimate dice are expected to be viable only for a system of inanimate objects but not for a system of living Beings". Should one use a dice of living matter, then explain how the derived laws will be affected.

12.8 Discuss the excitation mechanism of the being b in the patomic model (cf. Fig. 6.1) and compare it with that of an electron in the atomic model.

12.9 Discuss and study the formation of groups, castes, sub-castes, etc on the basis of sharing at the B, SEA, SEK, M, and/or I levels in the patomic model among human Beings. How will the nature and quality of these sharings at different levels add to the nature and quality of experiences that one stores in E out of these many human Being interactions (cf. Examples 12.5.1 and 12.5.2 and also see (Kaushal, 2011).

12.10 Study and analyze the Saha-like ionization formula (12.4) and the corresponding Fig.12.5 with reference to the cases. (i) teacher-taught interactions in the class room at the primary school, post-primary school, college and university levels, (ii) a researcher addressing specialists in a conference hall, and (iii) a politician addressing a mob at a public place.

Chapter 13

SOME TYPICAL EXAMPLES OF TWO, THREE AND MANY HUMAN BEING INTERACTIONS

In the previous chapter, we have discussed a theoretical frame-work to analyze two, three and many human Being interactions in a society. These interactions, in fact, essentially take place at a crude level from all the three, namely **C**, **M** and **G** domains of working of an individual. Fine tuning and hyperfine tuning of these interactions do offer explanation for subtlety of fundamental processes which take place during the character building and personality development of an individual. In this chapter we look for justification and support for these theoretical prescriptions and developments by way of analyzing a number of typical examples relating to daily life and also from all the four fronts, namely family, friends, profession and organization. Note that the discussion of examples by and large will take place here in the same order as the theoretical concepts are presented in the sections of the previous chapter. However, before that we once again emphasize the universality of love in the spirit of Sect. 8.1 which, like consciousness, remains in the background of all human interactions to start with.

13.1 THE ENIGMA OF LOVE

13.1.1 The love and its variants

As mentioned before, the love is an attribute of soul and so is that of cosmic consciousness since it plays a dominant role in the existence and maintenance of world-order (cf. Sect.

8.1). As far as its role in human dynamics is concerned it appears in several incarnations and forms. While it is not difficult to notice its role in many-human-Being interactions, but it predominantly manifests in two and three human Being interactions perhaps with its highest and higher intensities, respectively. It is observed that this intensity of love further enhances and manifests in a variety of ways when the pair or trio of interacting persons consists of opposite sex. This is not only true with humans but according to scientists peculiar are the ways of creating, expressing and receiving the love in various nonhuman species and in some species of plant kingdom as well. One can say that in this case the inclusive character of love converges to its exclusive form. In some sense the love,. as a synonym of consciousness, offers a background for all the interactions between and among the human Beings. With regard to the world-order it is capable of accommodating both negative and positive aspects of interaction as they belong mainly to its outer garments. Of course, it is the positivity with which the love is finally aligned at the end-point at the cost of temporal negativity.

In historical perspective, another version of love, termed as 'platonic love' has been described in various contexts and scriptures of the West. Platonic love is a type of love that is chaste and nonsexual. The term is named after Plato who philosophized about the nature of love. Initially, the term was used for the divine aspect of love, but later it was used in the context of creation and evolution of both sexual and nonsexual love.

Now we look at another aspect of love, i.e. expressing and receiving of love by the interacting pair of participants. As true love (and not the pseudo-love) is the characteristic of soul, the interactions between the two human Beings start with and end-up in the love itself. In between the starting and the ending, however, other variants of love appear through systematics of positivity and negativity against each other, more in a temporary manner. In this regard it is worthwhile to quote the sayings of Albert Einstein and Amy Bloom, viz.,

> "*How on earth are you ever going to explain in terms of chemistry and physics so important a biological phenomenon as first love*?" – Albert Einstein

> "*Love at first sight is easy to understand; it is when two people have been looking at each other for a life time that becomes a miracle*" – Amy Bloom

Clearly, both these sayings hint to the limitations of the tools and working of objective sciences as far as the explanation and understanding of the phenomenon of love are concerned. However, it is not difficult to find answer to the queries posed in these sayings in terms of the above remarks and also within the framework of patomic model. Though it is already detailed in the previous chapter, however, in the next section we shall elaborate on the underlying 'physics and chemistry' of love through real-life examples. In what follows we elaborate on the basic processes which take place when a person is proposing to other, or else he is wishing and greeting another person.

The processes of 'greeting' and 'wishing' as expression of cosmic love: In different cultures and civilizations, different phrases and body actions, jointly or separately, have been used by a person to greet or wish to the other person on different occasions. But when the meanings of these actions are extracted in philosophical terms, they all end-up either in the cosmic zone or at least in the SO zone of love. However, by doing so the ego of either of the interacting persons or of both of them is suppressed. This, in principle, opens the door for the direct interactions of **C**-level; or at least a situation is created to realize the boundary lines of their individual self with a minimum stress on intellect and that too after controlling mind, senses and body. In practice, however, the life does not go like this.

The notion of the word 'greeting or saluting' in some sense brings in a feeling of gradation (like in a family, in a defense agency, etc.), whereas that of the word 'wishing' is used at equal level between the persons. No doubt in both the processes there are roles of both gross (i.e., of EOLs B and SE) and micro (i.e., of EOLs M, I and E) bodies in the presence of SO, but the fact is that in the process of greeting someone, the role of **G** and the associated processes dominates. While in the process of wishing someone, the role of **M** and the associated processes dominates.

The meaning of the phrase 'I love you' or its analogues: When a child becomes adult the inclusive form of his love in the family starts converging to its exclusive form for a person of opposite sex. As a result, a natural instinct starts developing in him for the latter. It is at this stage the adult starts looking for a partner of opposite sex often within the frame-work of prevailing traditions in a society or culture. In fact, there are different ways for such a search of partner in different societies and culture. Not only this, once the search is over, then again there are various ways for formalizing and solemnizing the binding, i.e. the marriage between the partners so that the same becomes approval of the society for a longer survival in the life. In this connection it is rather befitting to mention a mythological story of the East in the following example.

Example 13.1.1: According to this story, God created man and woman together not as two Beings but as a single entity— they are joined in one body, but then there were conflicts. The woman wanted to go to the East and the man was not willing to do so. Or, the man was ready to do something and the woman wanted to take rest. They complained and God separated their bodies. Since then, every man is searching for his woman, and every woman is searching for her man. Now it is such a big crowd that it is very difficult to find your woman or man. The myth says that if you can find, everything fits; you can again become one. But it is very difficult to find.

According to a modern Indian saint, Osho, there are ways to find woman of the above story, because woman is not outside. There are only parallel similarities outside. What happens when one falls in love with a woman? Somehow the outside woman fulfills your inner woman's image, may not be 100 percent, but enough to fall in love. What happens when one falls in love with a man? Something inside you clicks and says, "Yes, this is the man, the right man".

It is not that woman finds all the pros and cons about the man and then decides or compares the man with all other men in the world then she decides. Something (!) happens out of the blue. Suddenly she sees that this is the man (or the woman for a man) whom she (he) was waiting for. In other words, she carries an image of man, he also carries an image of woman inside. In fact you are both man and woman and still you go on looking outside for the counterpart. Nobody is going to fit 100 percent, because the woman you find outside has her own image about you and you have your own image of her. It is very difficult to fit with each other. So marriages are always on rocks, and people, by and by, learn how to carry on peacefully.

The story of Example 13.1.1 and its interpretation by Osho provide a good moral and an important essence relevant to the society. Also, there seems to exist a plausible answer in it to Einstein's query about the first love and an explanation to the so-called miracle, described by Amy Bloom. Further lessons from this story can be summarized through following points in the present context of patomic model:

(i) According to *karmic* theory, the phenomenon of creating, expressing and receiving love does involve the roles of *prārabdha, sancit* and *kriyamāna* components of an action.

(ii) Note that the role of first love is common to both the so called love marriages and arranged marriages. The situation is, however, marginally different in the two cases. In the love marriage, the b-b interaction starts immediately at the level of SO, then sequentially continues through E, I, M over a period of time; both the partner's (man and woman) analyze the case keeping all pros and cons along with the past experiences (memories) in mind, slowly get attached emotionally, finally ending up with the interactions first at the SE level and then at the B level. Ideally, since both the man and the woman have been parts of the same SO (as per above story) and so are their micro-bodies, certain matching frequencies between the working of EOLs, E, I and M of one person with that of other, are expected. This will help them to co-exist peacefully in life. If the matching becomes impossible, then marriages break-down. In the arranged marriages, in Indian context, the b-b interactions start at M level, then continue through I and E by way of imagination to which feedback comes as a result of listening from elderly persons, relatives and friends and also reading advertisement in the newspaper or by meeting each other. Of course SO-level interactions also start simultaneously but temporarily until all rituals related to marriage are completed.

(iii) There also exists a basis for the platonic love in the story.

Next, we elaborate on the underlying meaning of the phrase 'I love you' used generally in the Western culture at the time when a boy proposes to a girl or vice versa. When boy proposes to a girl (normally girls do not propose but they definitely help in creating an environment for this act from the boy side), there is a particular style of doing this. Firstly, both boy and girl tune their mindsets for understanding each other for days, weeks, months and sometimes for years (this varies from case to case) and one fine day the boy comes and sits with knees at a lower level and proposes to the girl (who is sitting on a higher level or standing in front of him) by saying 'I love you'. In return the girl also says these words after a thought. This act is normally witnessed by a priest/ father and may be by a few more witnesses for the name sake, otherwise they both go by their inner voice. These three words bind them together at least for sometimes or even for the entire life span. In fact, this is a kind off *sankalpa* (pledge) they take to remain together forever. In philosophical terms, this is the occasion when they realize by saying these words from the core of their hearts that each of them is the part of the same cosmic consciousness and they want to join now to become one in the spirit of the story of Example 13.1.1. The boy as a representative of the cosmic man (*purusa*) surrenders his SO by suppressing his ego E to another SO of the girl, who acts as a representative of the cosmic woman, i.e., *prakriti* of the Vedic science in front of the Supreme showering his blessings through the word 'love'. This corroborates the meaning of the phrase "I (one soul SO) love (Supreme) you (another soul SO)".

In the context of Indian style of marriages again there are similar rituals during the ceremony of marriage when the boy and the girl undergo several of such *sankalpās* or pledges, whose meanings are equally, if not much deeper than the above phrase. We shall discuss other incarnations of love in future sections.

13.1.2 Creative love and the concept of new humanity

Material adjustment with a person or with a group of persons is only a part of the wider problem of establishing spiritual adjustment. In fact the latter requires elimination of the self not only from material aspects of life but also from those spheres which affect our intellectual, emotional and cultural lives. To identify the problem of humanity merely with the problem of bread is equivalent to reducing humanity to the level of animalistic nature. But, even when person sets himself to the limited task of material adjustment, he can succeed in this attempt provided he has spiritual bent and understanding. What one gets, in the identification with a narrow group or section or with some limited ideal, is not a real merging of separative self but only an appearance of such merging. A real merging of the limited self (love) in the ocean of universal life (cosmic love) involves complete surrender of separate existence in all its forms. Often this is missing and it becomes the main source of bitterness between persons or lovers.

Humanity, as some saints feel, is expected to come through release of love in measureless abundance; and this release of love can come through spiritual awakening brought about by spiritual masters or by self-realization. Love cannot be born of mere determination; through the exercise of will, one can at best be dutiful and such actions lack the inward beauty of spontaneous love. Love has to spring spontaneously from within, and it is in no way amenable to any form of inner or outer force.

According to a saint, love and coercion can never go together; though love cannot be forced upon any one, it can be awakened through love itself. Love is essentially self communicative; those who do not have it, catch it from those who have it. True love transforms every one whom it touches.

Devine love is unassailable by the onslaught of duality and is an expression of divinity itself. It is through this love that the new humanity will emerge in tune with the divine plan. The saint further expects that once the new humanity emerges through divine love, the same will learn the art of cooperative, peaceful and harmonious life.

Example 13.1.2: Love as a binding force in a family: There was a prosperous family consisting of four sons, daughters-in-law and children in addition to the Head (an elderly person) of the family. The members were always in a quarrelsome mood and hardly have peaceful communication among themselves. One night, the Goddess of wealth came in the dream of the Head of family and warned him that she is going to quit his house as there was no peace in the house and all members always remain in a fighting mood. She continued, "however, before leaving I want to bless you with one and only one boon, which you can ask for after due consultation with other family members". The Head discussed the matter with other members in the family. Different members suggested differently. Somebody suggested to ask for more money, some body for property, etc.. But, the youngest daughter-in-law came out with a suggestion to ask for '"love among family members" from the Goddess. Next day, the Head again has Goddess in the dream who was reminding him about the promised boon. Good sense prevailed on the Head of the family and as per suggestion of the daughter-in-law, he just requested the Goddess to give love and affection in the family. Hearing such a request from the Head, the Goddess changed her mind and promised to stay back with the family. Thus, wherever there is love and peace, wealth and prosperity are bound to come automatically.

13.2 EXAMPLES OF b-b INTERACTIONS

As examples of the fundamental processes taking place in b-b interactions, we shall highlight here some representative cases from the real life situations.

(a) Husband-wife interactions: Only an ideal couple offers a typical case of b-b interaction in which all the exchanges outlined in Sect.12.2 and displaced in Figs.12.2 and 12.3 are possible, of course at different space-time points and over a period of time. Keeping in mind the universality of sexual processes (see, (Kaushal, 2011, Sect.8.11)), the words "husband" and "wife" can be considered as synonyms of "male" and "female", respectively for different living Beings while discussing the entirety of b-b interaction. With regard to the reproduction process in living Beings, peculiar are the ways of creating and expressing the love between male-female members of a species. In the process, in fact, the whole set of EOLs participate in one form or the other. As a matter of fact, the first love starts at the level of SO (i.e., OSO case) in its purest form. By the time it comes down to the level of B and WO (i.e., ISO case) it all gets polluted by the interplay of exchanges at the levels of SE, M, I and E. However, a link is always maintained in terms of exchanges at the level of SO but only in case of an ideal couple.

Moments also come in the life of husband and wife when the interactions are highly confined to the levels of B and SE in the field of WO. Such exchanges are unhealthy and they might result into an unhappy relationship, which is full of stress, anxiety, hostility, etc.

(b) Mother-baby interactions: Whether a baby is in the womb or has taken birth, in either case, the mother-baby interaction starts taking place at the level of SO. And why should it not be? After all it is the same SO of mother which is now just partitioned into two Beings. Not only this, when the baby is in the womb even then mother continues to interact with the baby for nine months rather unilaterally in a variety of ways. Only because of these features, the mother-baby interaction is unique in this world and there is no parallel to it. For this reason people say that for the baby, after God, mother is the only next entity in the world who deserves the worship from his heart.

Also, this interaction is unidirectional since all the EOLs of the baby are not yet developed except for a few like SE and

B. The interactions generally start at the level of M, i.e., with emotions, often keeping aside the interactions at levels of I and E. In fact, the M-level interactions are so strong that they are hardly affected by the presence of other Beings or from the environment. This aspect of mother-baby interaction is universal—true for most of the living Beings.

(c) Mother-child and Father-child interactions: When the baby grows up, some of his EOLs, like B and SE develop and start enriching themselves from the worldly objects like from the environment and from the one-sided interactions of mother. At this stage, the EOLs I and E of the mother also start showing their roles as far as the interactions with the child is concerned. This is in addition to the roles of her EOLs M, B and SE. Now the child has enough time to interact not only with other family members but also with environment including pets and toys. As a result, the interactions with mother in a reciprocal manner increase and thereby dilute their unidirectional nature. At this stage, if father has enough time for the family, then father-child interactions also come into existence and the same can be considered on par with mother-child interactions except for the fact that the latter are dominated by emotions and the former by intellect/reasoning.

These three examples of b-b interactions are the ones in which the individual (child or baby) has no choice. Now we list the cases in which the choice of the individual matters, particularly in intellect- dominated interactions. In this category we start with another universal case of mother-in-law and daughter-in-law interactions, well-known all over the world.

(d) Mother-in-law and daughter-in-law interactions: Like mother-baby and husband-wife cases, the mother-in-law (MIL) and daughter-in-law (DIL) interactions are universal only for humans. These interactions, in fact, start from soul, remain in soul and end-up in the soul itself, of course after covering a long journey of life. The interactions in the MIL-DIL duo are unavoidable due to a common male in-between the two females, who is the son on one side and the husband on the other. While this common male factor has emerged from the (polluted) soul of one but he is going to be the part of the (polluted) soul of other. (No doubt, the pure soul is basically of cosmic character in nature, the polluted version of it, however, involved more in WO). This provides the root-cause of MIL-DIL interactions. Thus, the MIL-DIL interactions cover the entire range, i.e. they start from **C**-level, continue a little longer at the **M**-level and finally prolonged further into the **G**-level exchanges. During the journey of life both MIL and DIL undergo both the extremes, namely love and affection on the one hand and hatred and jealousy on the other. Note that the nature of interaction between father-in-law and son-in-law is totally different from that of the present case.

(e) Friend-friend interactions: Before discussing the exchanges in the friend-friend interactions we highlight certain norms which are necessary for an ideal friendship. Generally, the friendship in modern times is for vested interest and as soon as these interests are met, the friendship dies. However, there are cases of ideal friendship in the history and also in modern times. It is said that friendship continues longer if it is extended to a 'like-minded' person and certain norms are observed during its maintenance/pursuance. Here 'like-minded' means that there exists some compatibility between them not only at the micro-body level but also on certain factors at the gross-body level. Some other norms which need to be observed for an ideal friendship are: (i) compatibility of views and mindsets of the two persons, (ii) certain degree of sacrifice and forbearance from both sides, and (iii) a clear understanding of each other. In some sense, in friend-friend interactions all these exchanges exist which are necessary for an ideal couple of husband and wife except for the fact that certain exchanges at the soul level are missing in the present case. The strong binding between the friends through τ_{GG} and τ_{MM} in an ideal case can serve as an example of a diatomic molecule in physics.

(f) Teacher-taught (one-to-one) interactions: Like ideal friends, a lot has also been said in Indian scriptures about an ideal teacher and an ideal disciple. Still for a meaningful interaction between the two, following analogies from physics will appeal.

(i) In the class room, the teacher and taught are like 'transmitter' and 'receiver' (of radio signals), with certain matching frequency ranges. Although the exchanges of Fig.12.2, in the present case are unidirectional (i.e., from teacher to taught, as is the case with the mother-child interactions) but certain prerequisites in terms of competence of both teacher and taught (may be in a particular domain) are essential for a meaningful transmission in that domain. Clearly, during teacher- taught interactions, there are exchanges of quanta at the levels of micro-body and SEK, but by suppressing the interactions at the levels of B and SEA. While emotions remain in the background of the teacher, the EOLs, I and E dominate the teacher-taught exchanges. Other norms to maintain the unidirectional flow of energy are like disciple should have faith and confidence in the teacher in order to qualify himself as the best receiver.

(ii) According to the second law of thermodynamics, the energy flows from source to sink and the opposite is prohibited. The same is the case here, teacher acts as a source and disciple as a sink and the former should be at a higher potential by way of developing his FOU up to the mark. Accordingly a disciple is expected to be at lower potential by way of suppressing his ego, so that there is a meaningful flow of energy from source to sink.

Example 13.2.1: In order that the water from an over-head tank flows to a bucket, note that (i) the bucket should be kept at a lower level as compared to that of tank, and (ii) the bucket must be empty for its meaningful filling. If it is already filled, it has to be made empty for its meaningful filling of better water.

(g) Boss-subordinate interactions or the interactions between business partners: Boss-subordinate interaction is a particular case of employer-employee interaction and is a very delicate one as far as the source of livelihood of an employee is concerned. Both the boss and subordinate work within certain set of rules, yet the human component comes in the way from either side but at the secondary stage. In practice they both work in an isolated manner but the fact is that they interact at the level of micro-body at every moment at least at the work place. A silent command of the boss gives a direction to the subordinate to work so that a defined output can be seen in the stipulated time. The exchanges are unidirectional as far as their official component is concerned; however, they could be both ways with regard to human component. In either situation the exchanges are full of prejudices and biases.

With regard to the interactions between business partners, they are not unidirectional, instead there is some sort of balance separately between official and human components of exchanges. If it is not so then the partnership breaks down.

13.3 EXAMPLES OF b-b-b INTERACTIONS

(a) Husband (b_1), wife (b_2) and the third person (b_3) interactions: In general man and woman have different body structures and different working domains and as such interact only in a limited domain. Marriage is a kind of bond between a man and woman, after which they become intimate and start interacting to the extent that their interactions (in an ideal couple) become the example of a complete b-b interaction, as mentioned before. Now, if a third person whether a man or a woman enters in their personal life then these rigid bonds of marriage become rather loose. This happens when the marriage bonds, in spite of all efforts, do not remain strong when a woman enters in the life of husband and/or a man in the life of wife as a source of attraction at a certain stage. Very often this happens because of selfish motives involved or for temporary enjoyment but the main reason is that there grows a loss of faith and confidence between the husband and wife or lack of understanding and clarification between them at the same time.

All this becomes very serious when SEP-SEP-EP type $b_1-b_2-b_3$ interaction tries to become SEP-SEP-SEP type one. Further, the nature of interaction-dynamics depends on whether b_3 is a man or a woman. If it is a man, then b_2-b_3 exchanges will increase at the cost of b_1-b_2 exchanges and again at the levels of all the three **G**, **M** and **C** domains. On the other hand, if it is a woman, then b_1-b_3 exchanges will increase at the cost of b_1-b_2 exchanges. Since b_1-b_2 interactions are supposed to start from the level of causal body, it is very difficult to find an equilibrium (may be possible in some rare cases) in the exchanges among b_1, b_2 and b_3, particularly when all the three persons are present in a given circumstance. Also, the role of $\tau_{b_1b_2b_3}$–type interactions cannot be ignored in the latter case.

(b) Mother (b_1), father (b_2) and the child (b_3) interactions: Recall that both b_1-b_3 and b_2-b_3 interactions by and large are unidirectional as the FOU of b_3 are not yet fully developed. While the interactions between b_1 and b_3 are emotion-dominated, those between b_2 and b_3 are intellect (guidance) -dominated in general. However, both these classes of interactions help in developing the FOU of b_3 but in a limited domain unless a fourth Being (b_4), i.e. a teacher comes in the life of b_3. The exchanges from b_3 side are normally B and SE dominated ones and the category of the b-b-b interaction remains of the SEP-SEP-EP type unless the child is of serious nature.

(c) The case of a trio of friends: As mentioned before, ideally the friendship between friends can continue at all the three levels, namely gross, micro and causal body and the same can be extended to third or more persons provided the latter have the same levels of development of their FOUs. For a trio to become friends, initially $\tau_{b_1 b_2 b_3}$ –type interactions start at the **G** and **M** levels and soon they convert into pair-wise b-b interactions but after keeping the remaining third person as witness or an active spectator. Only in this situation a kind of equilibrium needs to be established among various exchanges for a successful output. Once the equilibrium or understanding grows up among b_1, b_2 and b_3, then $\tau_{b_j b_k b_l}$ – type interactions again show up in addition to the $\tau_{b_j b_k}$ –type exchanges towards the success of an action performed by the trio. A true friendship of the trio continues longer, if all the variables m, i, e and σ in their mindset functions (cf. Glossary or (Kaushal, 2011, Chapter 8) are allowed to vary freely to attain the equilibrium among the exchanges.

(d) The case of a trio of business-partners: Equilibriums at different levels: Like the trio of true friends, the trio of business-partners also maintains equilibrium but at different levels, depending on the nature of business-sharing. Self-interests of each person in the trio and that too for certain material and monetary gains dominate the b-b and b-b-b exchanges and there exists a setting or equilibrium behind each material gain. Mindsets of the trio are also tuned to this kind of limited exchanges, normally they are full of biases and prejudices. This fact raises the question of continuity of business among the trio of business-partners.

(e) Some other examples of mixed category: Many examples of b-b, b-b-b, and b-b-b-b interactions can be traced in the day-to-day life, in family, at work place and in society. The same can be analyzed easily within the above framework and at times lessons can be drawn from these analyses towards an improved behavior. Some cases which could be of interest are: husband-wife and any one of the parents-in-law, mother-daughter and the son-in-law, boss-subordinate and peon, landlord-tenant and agent, etc.

When one talks of equilibriums at different levels, namely in **C**, **M** and **G** domains of the interacting members, one can as well go one step further and account for the order of dressing of EOLs of each individual (i.e., his expertise) in settling and resettling the equilibriums at every stage.

13.4 FURTHER REMARKS ON ONE-TO-MANY HUMAN BEINGS AND MANY-TO-ONE HUMAN BEING INTERACTIONS

Having learnt lessons from the methodology followed in studying the many-body systems in physics, viability of these methods was demonstrated earlier in Sect.12.5 for a variety of many-human Being systems. Using these concepts, the phenomenon of socialization and groups of different category of persons in a society was discussed there. With regard to a gathering exposed to the same human stimulant (e.g., a teacher in the class room, a politician addressing a mob, a saint delivering sermons to a gathering, etc), the fraction of beneficiaries in the gathering was investigated as a function of the collective meditation variable μ_c using the Saha-like ionization formula (cf. Fig.12.5).

When evaluated, it is found that students of different categories in the class room learn differently from the same teacher in the class, members of the public meeting gather different ideas about the politician and the theme of his speech, or devotees undergo different experiences after attending the same meditation class and so on. Thus, using the Saha's prescription it is not difficult to have a feel for the number of beneficiaries in a gathering at least for a single excitation (although it is not clear in patomic model whether the excitation is single or multiple). It may be mentioned that Saha's prescription also contains some element of statistical description (Maxwell-Boltzmann type) in it.

Now we return to many-to-one human Being interaction, i.e. when a teacher in the class, a political leader in the masses, or a spiritual leader in the meditation class, etc. is showered with questions and queries at the same time from the audience. If this conversation is one-to-one, then the life is simple for the speaker; otherwise the speaker becomes puzzled, because the quality of questions posed is not only different scale-wise (scales in the sense of different levels of development of FOUs in the audience) but also varies over a wide range for which, particularly the newly 'designated speaker' is not readily prepared to answer. At times the combined system (speaker plus audience) takes an ugly scene or becomes a chaotic one because each individual in the audience or in the gathering has different mindset and works in different circumstances to start with. Imagine the scene in the Indian context when a truck driver is caught by public after an accident on the road by his truck when some casualty occurs.

In the one-to-many human Beings case μ_c varies smoothly and systematically as it is mostly decided in advance by the speaker. However, in the present many-to-one human Being case μ_c varies randomly and at times on different scales.

13.5 HUMAN BEING INTERACTIONS IN AN ORGANIZATION

An organization is an organized body, system or a society which functions according to certain rules and regulations out of which mostly are for its internal functioning and a few for its governance from the outside. Here we discuss and analyze the behavior and interactions of an individual who enters or is working in the organization; say a school, college, office, firm, etc. Note that in an organization there is a hierarchy of status- based personalities and also are the teams and committees to look after the gains, maintenance and the future of the organization. Thus, the working of an organization, as mentioned before (cf. Chapter 9), continues on all the four fronts as far as its sustenance and the role of an individual in this respect is concerned and these fronts are, as an individual, as a team member, as the contributor to the organizational processes and as a subscriber to possible changes for its betterment in future. Regarding the individual processes we have already discussed the personality and its development in Chapter 9. Here, however, we concentrate on other aspects of the role of individual in the organization.

In fact, next comes the role of an individual in the interpersonal and team processes which regularly take place in an organization. To make his contribution effective in this domain, he should keep aside his personal gains and be loyal first to his duties (or the responsibilities assigned) and then to the organization. For this propose a serious training and practice only of some of his EOLs is necessary and the same make this aspect of his involvement in the organization a success. For example, in addition to developing communication skills, one should learn the art of working in a team (i.e., the question of co-existence in the language of patomic model). Further, if necessity arises, the art of managing the leadership of the team should also come as an important ingredient. Once you are holding the leadership of the team, certain points of difference or conflicts among the team members are naturally bound to arise. In such a situation it also becomes necessary to learn the art of pacifying the conflicting personalities through negotiation and using the method of persuasion. Very often the confrontations are of personalities and thereby of individual ego.

If one succeeds in this test of managing a team work, then authorities may assign a higher responsibility related to the running of the organization as a whole. In terms of standards, the working of the organization as a whole now has to be viewed by the individual from the state, national or international level as may be necessary. In this regard his responsibilities can be put into four broad categories, namely as a decision maker, as a realizer of the structure and design of the organization, as an explorer of links with concerned powerful and/or political personalities for betterment of the organization, particularly in the Indian context. The last but important quality that one should infuse in himself and also in other fellow workers is to maintain the values and organizational culture in whatever form the same have been prevailing there. Naturally, in order to discharge these responsibilities towards the organizational processes, one has to keep aside the limited gains at both personal and team levels.

It is only after a sufficient experience of working in an organization that one feels like suggesting some changes for its betterment. The necessity of these changes can be felt at both the internal and external levels. Further, these changes could be planned or unplanned ones. But the planned changes are normally accepted quickly by others. As a subscriber to these planned changes one has to be very clear in mind regarding their nature not only on the conceptual front but also on their practical viability. Then comes the question of following an appropriate approach to implement these planned changes keeping both economic implications and time frame in mind. Often a change is resisted by the existing staff, particularly when it is a sudden change. Therefore, the transition has to be smooth after keeping the wellness of majority, if not of all, in mind.

It is not difficult to analyze the above, rather ideal, organizational behavior of a person within the framework of patomic model. At the individual level it should be the part of his personality to have interactions with the fellow workers and these interactions have to be meaningful and a bit selective in the sense that equilibriums of human exchanges have to be restored at every stage in terms of mental peace. For this purpose he has to work with a balanced mind as a part of his personality (cf. Chapter 9). Again in the team work he has to be careful in maintaining two- and many-human Beings interactions in a rather balanced manner. At the next stage while working in the domain of organizational processes, the person has to come out from his personal gains and clearly this is not an easy task. This means he has to revisit his own way of life once again by adopting intellect- dominated ideology in actions. Finally, at the stage of suggesting and implementing the changes in the organization his experiences and foresightedness are going to pay, i.e., the role of faculty of memory appears at large at this stage. All these roles of a person are possible when the person himself is conscious enough of his actions throughout his association with the organization.

In the next section, we demonstrate the viability of concepts of Chapter 12 in analyzing certain personality attributes which have been used in recent times to rate or assess the personality of an individual.

13.6 PERSONALITY TRAITS AND SEARCH OF A PERSON WITH INTEGRATED BODY, MIND AND SOUL

Some personality attributes and their classification are discussed earlier in Chapter 9 within the framework of patomic model. Here we emphasize on some more personality traits used in recent times to assess the personality and are relevant for behavior in the organizations. Some of these traits are locus control, authoritarianism, dogmatism, Machiavellianism, risk propensity, self-esteem and self-monitoring. While their definitions are listed in the Glossary of words, their detailed applications can be found in specialized texts (see, e.g. (Singh, 2010)). In order to rate any of these features of character in a person, normally a related questionnaire is prepared in which the answer of certain queries of subjective nature is sought from the candidate in an objective manner, i.e., in a simple true/false manner. From the analysis of these answers, conclusions are drawn immediately about a particular feature in the personality of a person.

Now the question is whether these traits can help in searching persons with an integrated body, mind and soul, particularly the ones listed in (c) category of Table 9.1. Obviously, the answer is No. The reason is that such a personality belongs to spiritual zone, viz., **C**-domain working and these traits through questionnaires explore a person only to his **G** and **M** domain workings. As a matter of fact all these modern techniques of personality assessment are of objective nature, i.e., they peep only into the outer garment of the character. The subjective component of values (cf. Chapter 3) in the assessing process, however, remains at low pitch. In spite of all this, these methods are fairly accurate but not as accurate as they should be. In fact, many brilliant minds have worked behind the framing of these questionnaires which are placed before an ordinary person, with the result, the pass percentage turns out to be small. Only the enlightened persons (in terms of dressing of EOLs with consciousness) get this opportunity. The difficulty that perhaps remains with the candidate is that he has to spell out his continuous spectrum of experiences in a discrete binary (Yes/No) style. He cannot express anything that lies in-between these two extremes, i.e., nothing can be learnt about those experiences of candidates which lie 'between the lines'. Any way these methods are without doubt time-saving but may not be 100% accurate. In view of these

Table 13.1: Some Remarks on using the modern personality traits in assessing the personality of a person.

S. No.	Personality Trait	Brief Description	Remarks (observations) in the light of Vedic science
1.	Locus control	Explains the degree to which a person believes that he himself, rather than external forces, determines his own life. Here fate, luck, etc. or the role of other persons are considered as 'external' and the person himself as 'internal'.	Each individual has his own '*prārabdha*' and so are the *sancit* and *kriyamāna* actions. They are not the same for all.
2.	Authoritarianism	Explains the degree to which a person believes that status and power differences are appropriate in an organization. High authoritarian type persons arc discarded over the low authoritarian type ones.	They are appropriate but human component plays a role and a track of the same should be kept all the time while discharging the responsibilities.

continued...

3.	Dogmatism	Explains the degree of flexibility or rigidity of a person's views. Those high in dogmatism tend to be rigid and closed and those who are low are more open-minded and receptive.	Either of the extreme is not good. Views, however, be created on the basis of reasoning and scientific thinking.
4.	Machia-vellianism	This trait, named after N. Machiavelli, describes the extent to which a person manipulates others for personal gains.	This feature of personality may be good in an organization, but has no scope in the domain of spirituality, whatsoever.
5.	Risk Propensity	This refers to a person's willingness to take risks. People with a high propensity for risk make decisions faster and are willing to take chances as compared to those who are risk-aversive, but cautious and careful in taking decisions.	A balance between the two extremes is necessary for a successful output.
6.	Self-esteem	It is a judgment one makes about one's own worth. People with high self-esteem have high expectations for success and feel more confident and the like, compared to those with low self-esteem.	Gives an opportunity to a person to have a self-observation to inculcate self confidence in him— a link with spirituality.
7.	Self-monitoring	Refers to the degree to which people are sensitive to others and adapt their behavior to meet external expectations and situation needs.	These features automatically come in a person with vertical (self-created) personality and have roots directly in spirituality.

observations on the methodology used, we briefly advance some remarks on these personality traits in Table 13.1.

In an organization the power of four adds to one's own brilliance: There are four catalysts to enhance one's personality and hence the personal brilliance. They are *awareness*, *curiosity*, *focus*, and *initiative*. In fact, the awareness of the self and of environment includes being in cognizance with the real problems in hand and in deliberations. As one finds the solution to the problem, curiosity develops to think of and looks at different arenas for insights. Curiosity also helps to go deeper into obvious and for this the person remains focused so that he does not limit himself and is open to all possible solutions. The fourth catalyst, initiative, helps a person to work on this process and ultimately to implement the solution. By bringing all the four of these innate abilities into daily habit, it is not difficult for a person to enhance his personal brilliance while working in an organization.

13.7 CONCLUDING DISCUSSION

In some sense, this chapter is an extension of Chapters 9 and 12 in which the theoretical tools of analyzing two, three and many human Being interactions and also of the personality of a person were developed within the framework of patomic model. In the present chapter, some real-life applications of these theoretical concepts are demonstrated to a variety of social phenomena which involve two, three and many human Beings including an individual. Examples cover a wide range of cases starting from the family, education, work place and to the political groups and corresponding to both b-b and b-b-b interactions and exchanges. While many other examples to these theoretical concepts can be sought from the day-to-day life, only a few representative cases are analyzed here. No doubt, many of us already undergo these experiences knowingly or unknowingly but the fact is that the analysis carried out here can still offer some educative value and guidance for improving the behavior and relations of the interacting persons in the case under study. With a view to highlight that the younger generation will have some glimpses of the work culture in an organization and about the personality traits used there to assess the personality of a person, a brief discussion of these topics is given in Sects. 13.5 and 13.6 with an eye on the framework of Vedic science.

It may be mentioned that in human relations and interactions, the element of love always remains in the background in one form or the other. It is this aspect of consciousness which manifests maximum and immediately in the mother-baby interaction and in an ideal husband-wife interaction, otherwise in all other situations in which the human Being is involved, love remains a puzzle to be understood. In spite of all this, the mechanism based on the patomic model seems to offer an explanation to a variety of love-involving phenomena of daily life in conjunction with a mythological story. A brief survey to this effect is carried out right in the beginning of the chapter. As such the phenomenon of love appears to be very complicated as far as its understanding by a common man is concerned. However, a slightly conscious person can develop his FOU to visualize not only the creation, growth, and decay aspects of love but also its cosmic character, but only after undergoing a higher level meditation. To this effect, the role of creative love in giving birth to a new humanity is highlighted.

Further Reading:

The only write-up available on the enigma of love is a book by this title on the Internet by David Theodore Clayton, see (Clayton, 2011). However, there is no overlap between the contents of this book and the ideas presented in Sect. 13.1. They both cover different aspects of the phenomenon of love; also see (Osho, 2007) and (Baba, 2013). For further examples of real-life situations and details, see (Kaushal, 2011, Chapter 9).

High Skill Exercises and Projects

13.1 With regard to the meanings of the words 'greeting', 'wishing' and the phrase 'I love you' write your own experiences and understanding and compare them with those presented in the text within the framework of patomic model (cf. Sect. 13.1.1). Where do these interpretations of the last phrase stand in the light of Osho's theory and Example 13.1.1?

13.2 In order to pull on with the life partner what other possible adjustments, do you think, are necessary besides the extremes of spiritual and material adjustments? Comment.

13.3 Elaborate on the meanings of 'creative' and 'divine' love. How can they contribute to bringing new values and culture in a society?

13.4 Write a Note explaining how the husband-wife and mother-baby interactions offer examples of a perfect two human Being interactions as far as the bilateral and unilateral nature of these interactions is concerned.

13.5 With regard to a meaningful teacher-taught interaction, elaborate on the analogies borrowed from physics, namely those of 'transmitter-receiver' and 'source-sink' cases.

13.6 Explain how the SEP-SEP-EP type interaction tends to become SEP-SEP-SEP type interaction in the case of husband, wife and the third person interactions. As an example of b-b-b interaction analyze the case of husband, wife and mother-in-law interactions.

13.7 Discuss in detail the role of an individual in an organization as (i) an individual, (ii) a team member, (iii) a contributor to the organizational processes, and as (iv) a subscriber to possible changes in the organization. Comment on an ideal organizational behavior of an individual within the framework of patomic model.

13.8 In the light of patomic model what dynamics do you suggest to maintain an equilibrium among three human Being interactions by citing one example from each family, friends, workplace and societal fronts.

13.9 Use the framework of patomic model and Table 13.1 to write a Note on the search of a personality with an ideally integrated body, mind and soul. Do modern techniques used for this purpose account for the search of spirituality content in a person?

Chapter 14

SEARCH FOR AN IDEAL WAY TO LIVE IN MODERN SOCIETY

What has been covered in the preceding chapters is mainly a kind of vertical development of an individual in the society. Starting from the Science of the Self, its role in the creation of a personality, and finally the role of this personality in a family, in a group of friends, in a school or college, at a work place and ultimately in a society is highlighted.

The present chapter and the next concluding chapter will focus more on the horizontal development of the personality of an individual. In other words, we shall look for possible ways and means following which an individual can live an ideal life in a modern society. (Note that it may be an exact or approximately ideal life in the sense of physical theories since the concept of 'idealization' is a limiting case, but the fact is that the limit does exist for the yogi category of persons). The society we shall talk about is a modern one in the sense that (i) the way of life of persons is changing at a very fast pace in view of the constantly evolving newer and newer scientific technologies which in turn are leading to a comfortable and/or luxurious life-style, and (ii) the world is tending to become a global family in view of the highly contracted space and time in the present times due to scientific developments. In such circumstances the ideal way of life for an individual needs to be redefined. In some sense a balance in the personality of an individual needs to be sought due to two factors— one arises from his character corresponding to vertical component and the other out of a need from such a fast changing society corresponding to a horizontal component of the personality. In any case, our age-old traditional ways to pursue the idealization at any of the levels— family, friends, institution, work place or society, cannot be expected to work as such in the present times.

In this chapter, we plan to address such a question as to how the society or environment plays a role in shaping the new norms for an individual so that he can lead a peaceful, harmonious and an ideal life keeping the rich traditional values in mind. Although this is the problem of the sociologist to find the solution, but our aim will be to address the problem keeping the Science of the Self in mind which has been developed in the preceding chapters. For this purpose, after revisiting the role of individual in the maintenance of world-order in Sect. 14.1, we highlight possible changes which are bound to occur in both individual as well as society due to scientific advancements in Sect. 14.2. In Sect. 14.3, we briefly discuss the roles and attitudes of religious leaders and scientific researchers in framing such norms for the individual which enable him to follow an ideal way of life. It is argued in this section that this is only the element of spirituality whether on the part of religious masters or in the scientific temper of scientists that can add to such ideal norms. In Sect.14.4, it is emphasized that the integration of body, mind and soul by an individual defines a standard for the vertically developed personality and represents only one aspect of the complete personality which in turn can be used as a role model for the generations to come.

14.1 REVISITING THE ROLE OF INDIVIDUAL IN THE MAINTENANCE OF WORLD-ORDER

14.1.1 World-order and human actions

As far as the understanding of the world-order is concerned, the modern generation is living with half-truth (cf.

Sect.1.1) by way of enjoying the fruits of wonderful scientific discoveries which in turn contribute to the so-called 'man-made world'. Somehow they are least aware (or some of them may not wish to become aware) of another rather more important half- truth, i.e., the spirituality and its role prevalent in the existence and maintenance of the world-order and the latter in turn contribute to the so-called 'God-made world'. While one can gather a feeling for this human attribute at an early age, its detailed role and vitality in Nature is realized only after a vertical development of his personality and that too in totality.

In other words, in order to understand the whole-truth in Nature a certain degree of maturity in thoughts is needed which normally comes after a reasonable vertical development of personality of an individual. (Reasonable in the sense that a person also develops a habit of listening to the inner voice of the soul which is relevant to the welfare of both the world and the world-order before, during or after the performance of any action whatsoever irrespective of its relation with any of the domains **C**, **M** or **G**). This 'art' does not come through a formal education to an individual up to a desired level, instead it is attained by him over a period of time and ought to be brought in practice at all levels of action. As a matter of fact, in some persons the spirituality is an in-built characteristic. Even some philosopher-scientists, after carrying out great researches in their respective branch of objective science, realize the limitations of their own work and thinking. Once they develop a feel for the spiritual aspect of life, which generally comes in the last part of their active life, then their attitude towards the world-order changes.

In order to view the world and world-order with a 'spiritual eye' we have to go with the discussions carried out and the conclusions drawn there from in Chapters 3 and 5. In fact the terms 'world' and 'world-order' in some sense are synonym of Universe and its perpetual working in an all-pervading, fundamental cosmic consciousness field in conjunction with *paňca mahābhūtās* (five cosmic elements). Through certain mechanism these aspects are the root cause of origin of all animate and inanimate entities in the Universe. The system as a whole works in terms of certain sets of principles which are well defined and precise but at present they are beyond the reach of objective science and scientists as well. These principles work in a self-consistent manner towards the existence and maintenance first of Cosmos, then of Universe and later of the World we live in. In fact, all human actions including the scientific researches need to be performed in such a way that the equilibriums in Nature are maintained at all levels, i.e., in the Cosmos, in the Universe and in the World.

While modern scientific researches against such a 'natural call' have provided all sorts of comforts and luxuries have, however, failed in restoring these 'grand' equilibriums in Nature. As a matter of fact all the five cosmic elements in present times are polluted, which are land (earth) pollution due to the use of fertilizers, water pollution due to the use of chemicals, noise (air) pollution, air (fire) pollution and space pollution. Such hazards to environment definitely pose a question on the future of survival not only of human race but also of other species.

In summary, at this stage it is worthwhile to quote Albert Einstein (1921) regarding the maintenance of world-order through human actions and efforts thereof for this purpose.

> *'A human Being is a part of whole, called by us the Universe, a part limited in time and space. He experiences himself, his thoughts and feelings, as something separated from the rest, a kind of optical*

delusion of his consciousness. This delusion is a kind of prison for us, restricting us to our personal desires and to affection for a few persons nearest to us. Our task must be to free ourselves from this prison by widening our circles of compassion to embrace all living creatures and the whole of Nature in its beauty.'

It appears that Einstein also realized the eternal truth in Nature during his life time and in the midst of his deep scientific researches.

14.1.2 Individual in the lap of Nature and in the midst of society

With regard to the vertical development of personality of an individual, a detailed role of all the three human existences, namely gross, micro and causal bodies has been discussed in the preceding chapters in different contexts. In fact there are two more existences of the individual whose roles in his life cannot be denied and they contribute to the horizontal development of his personality. These two additional existences of a person in the environment are provided respectively by the society and the Nature as a whole. The basis for these existences comes from the fact that the individual is the part and parcel of society (i.e., of the man-made world (MMW)) and also at the same time he lives in the lap of manifest Nature (i.e., in the God-made world (GMW)).

Obviously, these two man-made and God-made worlds are governed by different but inter-dependent sets of rules. Note that GMW is the cause of survival of MMW but the converse is not true. Further MMW is temporal, transient and throws the smell of sensual pleasure, GMW, however, has its roots in eternity, and gives a feel for spirituality. In other words, sensual pleasures are the essence and end-point of actions in MMW, whereas spirituality and eternal joy are the end-point of actions in GMW. If the spirituality is added to the actions in MMW, then the corresponding norms would become the norms for ideal life. In fact on the basis of one's involvement in these worlds it becomes possible to classify the persons into four categories, viz., (i) those who are badly involved in MMW without having a feel for the GMW in the whole life time, (ii) those who are involved in MMW but also have an eye on the GMW and its role, (iii) those who are involved in GMW but also have an eye on the MMW and its role, and (iv) those who are totally involved in GMW without having a feel for MMW in the whole life time. Clearly, there could be only countable personalities of the type (iv), i.e. of the yogi-category of persons. Many of us, no doubt, fall into types (ii) and (iii), but still there is a good percentage of persons of type (i) in the modern society. Even between the types (ii) and (iii), type (ii) dominates over type (iii) as far as the percentage of persons is concerned.

For those who are totally involved in the MMW, attainment even of mental peace at times becomes a problem. On the other hand, for those who are totally involved in the GMW limiting the peace, pleasure and also eternal joy at times becomes a problem. However, for those who are living a life of type (ii) or (iii), the maintenance of equilibrium among the actions pertaining to the two worlds becomes a bigger problem. It is at this stage that the creation of the horizontal component of one's personality and its development takes place and that too in a true spirit in the sense that the spirituality remains in the background of all actions and at all space-time points. Naturally, now one needs a different type of personality creation mechanism (PCM) compared to the one discussed in Sect.9.6 for the vertical component of personality. As a matter of fact, this new mechanism (now denoted by PCM2) is nothing but defining and redefining the norms for an individual so that he can lead an ideal life in his different capacities, namely as an individual and on the fronts of family, friends, work place, society and finally nation. In some sense this idealization has to be the whole sum of its pieces which appear separately not only in the character at the individual level (vertical component of personality) but also on other fronts just mentioned (horizontal component of personality). Further the norms so framed for this idealization should originate from GMW, of course, with their applications in the MMW which also includes the various fronts. Since the changes are constantly taking place in all these fronts, therefore, the framing of norms, which can work for all times to come, is a big problem.

14.2 CHANGING FEATURE OF THE MAN-MADE AND GOD-MADE WORLDS

Change is natural. It always and constantly takes place in both GMW and MMW. While the change in GMW takes place with respect to space and time at different scales and at local, global, galactic and cosmic levels, the change in MMW, however, takes place not only with respect to space and time but also with circumstances as and when they are created and re-created in the history. Further, the changes in MMW occur at local and global levels or with respect to different cultures, societies and nations. Here, we concentrate more on the changes in MMW as the changes in GMW by and large are beyond the human control.

Note that not only the individual mind but also the collective mind of a group of persons is a function of space, time and circumstances. As history reveals, now and then in conjunction with intellect, the human mind has been searching for alternative ways and means so that the life becomes comfortable (in terms of necessary facilities but not at the cost of deterioration of GMW) and luxurious (in terms of more than necessary facilities and at times at the cost of deterioration of GMW). Thus, the luxuries at the cost of deterioration of GMW are not acceptable by any standard as it will leave the future of mankind in danger by way of disturbing the equilibrium in GMW.

There is another important factor which has been responsible for the changes in MMW in the recent history of mankind— scientific researches and inventions. In fact until a few centuries ago (and a few decades ago in the Indian context), i.e. prior to scientific inventions, the life was more or less static in the MMW. Until this time, the norms for a person to live ideally either at individual or at societal level definitely existed and were more or less static because the growth in a culture or society was also more or less static. Mainly after the scientific advancements, the changes in MMW have grown fast, rather exponentially, in recent years. As a result, the traditional norms to live ideally in a society have shaken and thus one feels necessity to redefine them in the changed (modern) society.

The change due to scientific discoveries forms a kind of vicious circle to which the line of spiritual growth passes tangentially: The change in MMW due to the scientific discoveries in fact forms a kind of vicious circle. When the results of a scientific research are thrown open to masses for their use, the media and advertising agencies impress upon the person to adopt the newly developed technology. The technology or the new item/appliance, no doubt, turns out to be useful and makes life comfortable but the excessive use of it makes life luxurious, mostly at the level of sensual pleasure. For example, eyes want to see movie on T.V. or cell phone (whether good or bad from the point of view of ethical values, it is a different thing), similarly ears run after music, tongue after taste of food (whether hygienic or not), nose after artificial scents, etc. Human body wants to remain in a car or aeroplane for its comfort irrespective of the urgency of the work. Over and above that, if a fraction of mind is left from these sensual pleasures, then that is also taken away by their desires and attachments at the mental level and also by the office projects and assignments which are focused around the working in MMW. Then, for a person where is the time for thinking of GMW or at last for the self-observation? While such a daily routine takes away the mental peace of a person, it also distracts him from the GMW. As a matter of fact, common man is least aware of these realities of modern society. Once you are accustomed to these scientific assets, then you become habitual and addicted to the extent that at times your commitments to family and relatives, to friends, to work place and to society as a whole are not fulfilled and problems crop up at the social and higher levels. With the result that earlier unheard diseases and social problems start emerging. Besides, physio-therapist and other medical experts are needed to cure these newly emerged diseases. Scientists also take up the projects and come out with newer and newer discoveries to make life luxurious and thus vicious circle becomes complete. This is how the life in a developed society or country goes but at the cost of spiritual damage of an individual or of GMW in general. Instead of living in the lap of Nature, a person now prefers to enjoy the luxuries given by science. It appears that, the day is not very far when more people will die as a result of psychic diseases than those due to natural calamities. Thus, as far as the growth of spiritual life in a society is concerned, the scientific discoveries are not of much use as they create hurdles in such an endeavor. They do help in enhancing the religiosity in a person but not the spirituality.

14.3 A SEARCH FOR IDEAL NORMS

14.3.1 Ideal norms should comply with all the five existences of a human Being

Drawing lessons from the discussions in preceding sections, note that, for a horizontal development of his personality, first a person in principle should realize his worth of living in both society (MMW) and in the lap of Nature (GMW). After that, at the next stage, he should direct all his actions including thoughts towards the maintenance of the GMW and its order while actually living in the MMW. This is possible only by keeping an eye all the time and everywhere on the grandeurs of Nature which are spread all over in one form or the other via its sentient (manifest) mode or its derivatives. (Recall that this component of Nature is spread all over through PMs and via the mind, intellect and the ego as far as the individual is concerned). The individual himself via soul is the part of the cosmic un-manifest (insentient) mode of Nature. Even scientific research is not outside the domain of this eight-fold (five cosmic elements or PMs and the mind, intellect and the ego) working mode of Nature.

Once such a working spirit in a person emerges, next comes the question of norms to be framed and followed in this working in an ideal sense. As a matter of fact these ideal norms should be such that they yield a balance among the fruits of actions performed towards the development of both vertical and horizontal components of the personality of a person. In other words, a person should be able to justify his existence ideally at all the five levels, namely causal (**C**), micro (**M**), gross (**G**), societal (*S*) and natural (**N**). Chapters 2-10 of this book already advocate the role of the first three existences of human Being, Chapters 11, 12 and 13 that of societal existence and the present and the next chapters will focus on societal and natural existences of a human Being.

Further, as we have seen, the societal existence of a person rely on its various sub-existences, namely family, friend, work-place, society and nation etc.

14.3.2 Search for ideal norms in literature and religious texts

As the history of mankind reveals, the norms to be followed in a society are framed by the prevailing intellectuals in the society and very often in cognizance of the earlier available ones. Although the quality of norms depends on the level of development of FOUs of intellectuals involved in this job, but one can always trace an element of spirituality in the earlier norms while incorporating the same in the new ones. In some sense, the spiritual aspect is ever green as it basically originates from the first and the fifth existences of a human Being, namely causal and natural. Further, these existences are the important ingredients of the GMW in the spirit of Vedic science which emphasizes the fact that "*yathā pinde tathā brahmānde*" or there is "*vyasti in samasti and samasti in vyasti'* (see, (Kaushal, 1994)).

As per English dictionary meaning, literature deals with the writings of country and period whose value lies in beauty of form or emotional effects. However, in Hindi, the word 'literature' has very wide meaning when translated as '*Sāhitya'*, i.e., the writings which maintain the welfare of all including the maintenance of world-order. Similarly, every religion in its knowledge component has certain element of spirituality. (Every religion is supposed to have three components, namely knowledge (*jňāna*), methodology (*upāsanā*) and practice (*karma*), see (Kaushal, 1994, Chapter 7). In this way, while a part of literature which deals with the philosophy of life and human behavior has spiritual component, a great deal of spirituality is also present there in all religious texts. In fact, it is only this aspect of traditional wisdom of a country that keeps the human values alive; otherwise there are plenty of ways to eliminate them from the society in which demonical personalities often come out for ruling over the society.

In the Indian context, both literature and religious texts have been helping in this endeavor all throughout the history. In fact, not only the Vedic literature but also the great epics like *Rāmāyana* and *Mahābhārata* are full of such ideal norms defined for all fronts, namely family, friends, workplace, society and nation. For example, in order to have some glimpses of idealization in the character building or in ethical norms, look at the role of characters in these great epics. In a nut-shell, as per saying, one should do what Lord Rama did on all these fronts in *Rāmāyana* and one should obey what Lord Krishna has conveyed in *Mahābhārata* with reference to horizontal and vertical development of personalities, respectively. This is possible when one takes lessons from both of them in a positive spirit. This policy, in author's opinion, works even today in the age of modern science. Only thing is that one has to accept and interpret the underlying morals according to his own circumstances.

14.3.3 An element of spirituality in norms makes them truly ideal

In order to understand spirituality and its role in human behavior and actions we have to return back to the ideas of Vedic science as presented in Chapters 5-7. It has been argued earlier that there are two thresholds which need to be crossed to understand the worlds described by the dynamics of inner EOLs at a subtle-level and these worlds are the domains of working respectively of **M** and **C**. First the controlling of mind M allows the entry to the domain of **M** from that of **G,** then at the next stage the suppression of ego E allows the entry to the domain of **C** from that of **M**. While controlling of M goes with many of us at least for the vested interests or for the survival in MMW, suppressing of E does not go with many of us to understand and survive in GMW. Once the suppression of E takes place in an individual, then not only the understanding or realization of the domain **C** or that of the role of pure soul SO becomes possible but also its cosmic connections and networking (cf. Sect.5.2.1) becomes clear. This realization of cosmic connections and networking of SO through an element of love (cf. Sect. 13.1) by an individual not only with other human Beings or in general with other living Beings but also with inanimate objects through the universality of force of attraction makes the person spiritual. Such a sustained feeling in all actions performed by an individual qualifies him to enter the spiritual zone of SO itself and thus changes his attitude towards the world-order.

Spirituality in some sense is over and above the scientific attitude and the religiosity of a person, i.e., both atheist and theist can be spiritual. It is not the monopoly only of theist or religious persons alone. No doubt the scientific understanding of many bewildering phenomena in Nature or the methodology and practice component of different religions accordingly make a person 'scientist' or 'religious priest' but the fact is that the spirituality is a game which can be played by both of them at further higher level and in a competitive manner. As a matter of fact they are playing now and have been playing in the past for several centuries, particularly in the Western world. If such an attitude (which will definitely bring a balance between the human existences in both MMW and GMW) is kept in mind by the intellectuals at the time of framing the norms for a society, then the corresponding norms will be truly ideal. To this effect, one can find many examples in mythology and in the history of mankind when the rulers of a country or a majority of their councilors happened to be spiritual in the above spirit then the corresponding nation or society has left behind a mark of idealization as the history reveals.

It may be mentioned that once a person attains the state of a sustained spirituality then he becomes capable of facing all problems whatsoever of mental (psychic) domain in the same way as a person with a controlled mind can face all problems of the external world (or of the domain of **G**) whatsoever. In other words, a person becoming a spiritual means he has realized all his five existences, namely causal, micro, gross, societal and natural in their subtlest version or has developed both vertical and horizontal components of his personality in totality.

In the above spirit, we now attempt to present a sample analysis of different types of human interactions in a rather suggestive manner and in the domains of various existences and sub-existences of a human Being. In particular, some observations are made in Table 14.1 on the view-points of an atheist (scientist), theist (religious person) and a spiritual person on the same set of interactions (of course constrained with a limited understanding of the author). In fact giving a spiritual flavor to these interactions means invoking the roles of quanta $\tau_{cc,}$ $\tau_{ccc,}$ ... ,etc. in different types of human interactions discussed in Sects. 12.2 and 12.4 and this becomes possible for a person with appropriately developed FOUs.

Table 14.1 : A comparative analysis of attitudes of an atheist (intellectual class), theist (religious class) and spiritual class of persons with reference to different existences of a person in this world. Note that the spirituality just adds a different flavor to the existing thoughts, actions and behavior of a person consistently on all the fronts and inspires him to realize his existence in GMW and hence in the cosmos.

S. No	Work front or existence of a person	Atheist (intellectual or scientist) attitude	Theist (religious person) attitude	Spiritualist attitude
1.	Basic characteristic-s achieved out of the vertical development of personality	Extrovert, with I-dominated personality. Attachment and detachment in the fruits of action performed in the MMW are very intense which often lead to extreme steps.	Introvert, with M- dominated personality. Attachment and detachment in the fruits of action in MMW are intense but are considered as God gifted or his designed acts in relation to both MMW and GMW.	A combination of both introvert and extrovert, but with both I- and M- dominated personality. Knows the Art of remaining over and above these evolutes of mental domain.
2.	Societal: (a) Family and its members	Having a family and becoming its member is considered as chance sheer out of scientific processes. Discharge of duties only in moral and ethical terms, also necessary	Existing family and its members are the result of an intelligent design of a Super Power (*prārabdha*) and considered as a gift of God. Discharge of duties takes place as with love and affection in the domain of MMW while always	While living in the family or discharging his duties towards family members in the domains of both MMW and GMW, always works in an unattached

Continued...

		towards survival in MMW; occasionally with an eye on GMW but only as a rational thinker.	keeping an eye on GMW more in a fearing than believing manner.	manner like the lotus flower in water and strong believer in GMW.
	(b) Friend's circle means company for (i) attainment of (true) knowledge (ii) family problems (iii)business problems (iv) the discarded actions (*misedha karma*) in society	Normally (iii) and (iv) dominate by suppressing (i) and (ii); thinking finally reduces to the philosophy of 'eat and be merry' in MMW.	Normally involves in (ii) and (iii) with a little benefit of (i) but by discarding (iv); belief ends-up in 'live and let live' with the grace of God and in the GMW.	Normally (i) becomes primary by keeping a balance between (ii) and (iii) and there is no question to opt for (iv) at any cost. Believes in a fine networking of human dynamics and its cosmic connections through GMW.
	(c) Work-place	Unless vested interest is there the principle of "work to rule" is strictly followed. Hardly any scope for human consideration-s towards colleagues	Unless vested interest is there the principle of "maximum facility within the rules" is followed. There is always a scope for sympathetic consideration but within the rules	The same as for theist but personal interests, if at all they are there, are always at a low priority over those of others.

Continued....

		and sub-ordinates beyond the ones defined technically and for all.		
	(d) Society	Believes in the "same for all" philosophy and hence remains active in social and community gatherings for the welfare of society, more as a rational thinker.	In addition to the attitude of an atheist, the religious dimension is added to his social involvements. Believes in Karmic theory and works more in accordance with religious scriptures and in a God-fearing manner.	A combination of both theist and atheist attitudes but always considering the society as a collection of ideal individuals with their vertically developed personalities. Always thinks of and accounts for the realms of GMW and cosmos.
3.	Natural front of existence in the domain of GMW	For him, the quality survival in the MMW remains the main goal while natural front, hinting to GMW, remains at low priority. Laws of objective sciences are believed to be	For him, no doubt, the survival in MMW becomes important, but the attainment of God, the creator of GMW, remains the main goal. For him, the laws of objective sciences show limitations and	Believes in a perfect science which accounts for both objective and subjective descriptions of Nature and its phenomena. Laws of this new science

Continued....

		complete and consistent in themselves as far as the description of Nature and its phenomena are concerned. Hardly any scope for subjective science and thinking.	thus he believes strongly in subjective science and its laws through an intelligent networking in the maintenance of world-order.	work in a self-consistent manner which enables the maintenance of the world and its order.

14.4 DEVELOPMENT OF COMPLETE PERSONALITY VIS-À-VIS INTEGRATION OF BODY, MIND AND SOUL

As far as the integration of body, mind and soul is concerned, it appears as a small subset of exercises and efforts of an individual in the present general scheme of study, particularly when one considers the above defined five existences of a human Being, namely causal, micro, gross, societal and natural. As a matter of fact, the integration of body, mind and soul is a particular aspect of vertical development of personality and confined mainly to the first three (cf. Chapter 9) existences, namely causal, micro and gross. Once a person succeeds in attaining this stage of integration (which in fact becomes a prerequisite for a spiritual life), thereafter comes the question of its applications and the same takes place during his societal and natural existences respectively in MMW and GMW. This, in turn, defines the horizontal development of his personality. If a person succeeds further in applying these 'hard earned' tools while working in the domains of societal and natural existences and that too in the spirit of Table 14.1, then he qualifies for becoming spiritual. As to how the components and sub-components of personality originate from different existences of a human Being and contribute to the complete personality of a person, are shown schematically in Fig.14.1. As a matter of fact spirituality has everything to do with our mental attitude and almost nothing to do with our life in the physical world. Further discussions on spiritual life we postpone them to the next chapter. However, a few remarks on the development of complete personality are in order here.

It can be seen from Table 14.1 that the spirituality in actions of a person can either be added to (if it is earned in this life time) or reflects (if it is God-gifted to an individual as an attribute of *prārabdha*) in any one, some or in all the domains (fronts) of his working. This, in turn, suggests a wide spectrum even of spiritual persons in the world. This means one can as well rank the spiritual Masters of the world in terms of the degree of development of their the so-called 'complete personality' (a combination of both vertical and horizontal components). Although the vertical component more or less ends-up at the level of integration of body, mind and soul (note that there can still be variations in the extent to which this integration is carried out), the horizontal component however keeps on varying from one spiritual person to another as per their deeds performed in MMW and GMW. Such an analysis of great souls is carried out in Appendix A. It is worthwhile to recall here yet another standard to measure the greatness of great persons and that is the *Asthānga* yoga of Patanjali as discussed in Sect.8.4.2. Whether it is the development of complete personality or the practice of *Asthānga* yoga by a person, both appear synonym of each other on the face value, but the fact is that there is definitely a big difference at the subtle level in these methods. We refrain ourselves from going into such details here.

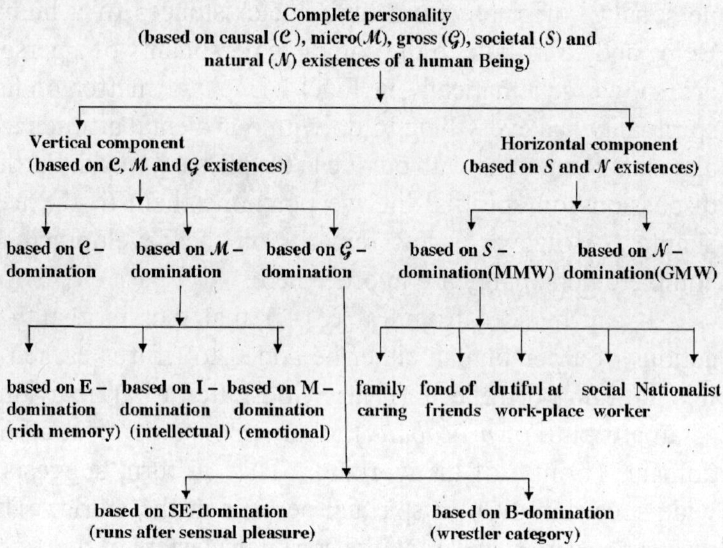

Fig.14.1: A schematic picture depicting components and sub-components of complete personality of a person. The complete personality together with **C**-dominated and **N**-dominated components defines a spiritual personality (or the 'man of perfection') in general and the same is highlighted in Table 14.1 (last column).

14.5 CONCLUDING DISCUSSION

Attempts are made in this chapter to look for ideal norms to live in a modern society. Since these norms have to work rather ideally on all the fronts of human existences towards the maintenance of world-order, naturally they have to have a common thread of spirituality all through in them. To this effect, in the process of their search several new terms and concepts have been introduced in this chapter which, in turn, help in exploring certain ways and means towards improving one's thoughts, actions and behavior and consequently in filtering out the experiences so derived. In particular, the concepts of man-made world (MMW) and God-made world (GMW) introduced in Sect. 1.1 are now generalized as the working domains of another two existences of a human Being, namely societal and natural. In fact this is a reality and these two domains of working of a person together offer a ground for the horizontal development of his personality via another personality creation mechanism (PCM2, cf. Sect. 14.1.2). Thus, the vertical development of personality of a person as described in Chapters 3-12, when combined with the horizontal development through an element of spirituality gives rise to the so-called 'complete personality' which defines none other than the 'man of perfection' of SMBG (cf. Ch.2).

As far as the growth of spiritual thinking in modern times is concerned, it is more or less static. It is argued that the scientific discoveries although responsible for a fast change in MMW, yet they have not contributed much to this growth; rather one can notice a deterioration of moral/ spiritual values in the society. If at all one frames the ideal norms to live in a modern society then they should comply with all the five existences of a human Being. Also an introduction of element of spirituality in these norms is absolutely essential in order to make them truly ideal. In the next chapter, we shall continue our discussion on a spiritual life and visualize as to how a spiritual society, if it can be made to exist, will look like.

It is argued (cf. Sect. 14.4) that a person with integrated body, mind and soul (or for that matter even with ideally integrated body, mind and soul) remains at a lower level as compared to a completely developed personality. Further, note that various ingredients which contribute to the shaping of the complete or perfect personality of a person come from his different existences, namely causal, micro, gross, societal and natural and these contributions could be in a different proportion in different spiritual persons. Before proceeding further we elaborate here on ideal aspects involved in both vertical and horizontal components of a personality. Such a limit for vertical component is already discussed in Chapter 9 (cf. Table 9.1) as an ideally integrated (*satoguni sātvik*) personality. With regard to ideal aspect in the horizontal component of a personality, note that it is the culture (as a combination of both MMW and GMW) which provides people with a set of values and assumptive beliefs including the implicit inferences about how these worlds operate. This in turn enables people to find meaning in and make sense of the events of their lives. Thus, the culture of a society or country in which a person lives in and also the local and global environment provided by Nature to him have an impact on his personality. If all these factors, when given the choice, contribute to the personality in an ideal sense, i.e., they lead to the welfare of the world as a whole and to a sustained maintenance of the world-order, then that defines an ideal aspect in the horizontal component of the personality. A categorical account of these various factors in shaping both vertical and horizontal components rather ideally and thereby the complete personality suggests a basis for classifying even the so-called spiritual persons. If we look at the history in retrospect, we find that different spiritual persons in different cultures and civilizations appear with varying specialties and super-specialties. We plan to continue such a study in Appendix A, particularly in the Indian context.

Further Reading:

For further details on spiritual thinking of an atheist see (Kulkarni, 20013); on spiritual secularism, see (Kundu, 2013; Chopra et al, 2013), and on integrating body, mind and soul, see (Bahai's, 2013), and for integrating body, mind and heart in a Gandhian way, see (Pradhan, 2014).

High Skill Exercises and Projects

14.1 Define the 'ideal way' to live in the modern world with reference to both society and environment as a whole. How does such a life style would support the statement, "positivity in thoughts, words and actions adds to order in the Universe whereas negativity in them leads to chaos"?

14.2 What do you understand by the 'man-made' and 'God-made' worlds? How does the knowledge pertaining to the former remain a half-truth about Nature? Discuss possible links between societal and natural existences of a person with the MMW and GMW, respectively.

14.3 Justify the statement, "if the spirituality is added to all actions in MMW, then the corresponding norms would become the norms of ideal life".

14.4 Explain with examples how the ideal norms to live in MMW keep on changing with scientific researches and discoveries. Further discuss how the spiritual growth of society has not been affected much by these scientific advancements.

14.5 Identify and justify all the five existences of a human Being during his life span. Explain how the ideal norms for working of a person should comply with these existences and how this will contribute to the maintenance of world-order, in general.

14.6 "While framing the ideal norms for working through all the five existences of a person, the presence of spiritual content in them is a must". Comment and write a Note on this statement.

14.7 "Spirituality in some sense is over and above the scientific attitude and the religiosity of a person", explain and comment on this statement.

14.8 Add a new column to Table 14.1 and write your own observations on the relative comparison of attitudes of atheist and theist towards the world-order against each point.

14.9 "Integration of body, mind and soul is a prerequisite for a spiritual life", comment on this statement and write a Note on it.

14.10 Explore the differences at subtle level between the two methods for assessing the greatness of great persons, namely the *Asthanga* yoga of Patanjali and the development of complete personality. Can you define the 'quotient of greatness' in the light of discussions in Appendix A, like the other quotients discussed in Sect. 1.2.

14.11 Extend the list of great (spiritual) persons given in Appendix A (cf. Table A.1) to accommodate six more cases from Indian context and six cases from other countries about whom you know well.

14.12 Analyze and discuss in detail the difference between the two ways of classifying the personalities in mathematical terms (cf. Appendix A, Eqs. (A.1) and (A.2)). How do you accommodate ideally integrated personalities of Table 9.1 in these general schemes of classification?

14.13 *Our attitude towards the life and the world-order as a mathematical riddle:* Identify the 26 letters of English language alphabets, namely A, B, C, D, ……,X, Y, Z with 26 numbers 1, 2, 3, …., 25, 26, respectively in chronological order. Then compute the sums of numbers associated with each letter in the words HARDWORK, KNOWLEDGE, LOVE, LUCK. Note that none of them make the sum 100. Also compute the corresponding sums for the words MONEY and LEADERSHIP, which also do not come out to be 100 separately. However, if you compute the sum for the letters in the word ATTITUDE, it exactly turns out to be 100. What conclusion do you draw from this riddle? Thus, write an essay to emphasize the importance of having a 'positive attitude' towards the life and the word-order keeping other factors in mind for the success. [Hint: Also see Exercise 8.17].

Chapter 15

SPIRITUAL LIFE: A CONTINUOUS CONSCIOUS EFFORT

In the preceding chapter (cf. Sect. 14.3), it is emphasized that the spirituality is over and above the scientific attitude and the religiosity of a person, i.e., both atheist and theist can be spiritual person. Moreover, spirituality guides a person towards the actions in the mental domain whereas the ethics and morality guide him in setting up the norms for actions in the society, although not in an independent manner. In fact, the ideality of norms in society further demands a spiritual component in them. Most of the religions of the world end-up at the level of ethics and morality, only very few of them go deep into their roots which lie in spirituality or in the realm of soul. Vedic wisdom and related scriptures are one such a source. The latter are full of the theories of spirituality. To this effect, some glimpses are already given in Chapters 2-10.

As a matter of fact for a common man it is not an easy task to follow a spiritual life all the time, everywhere and in all the circumstances. Only yogi-category of persons can lead such an ideal life, other categories of persons, however, have to maintain continuous and conscious efforts for this purpose. Conscious efforts in the sense that even if a person has taken *sankalpa* to follow such a life at the E-level, he has to live in this mundane world for his physical survival and here comes the roles of mind (M), SE and B. For the performance of his actions in this physical world, rather successfully, his intellect, I, plays a crucial role at every step in fixing the mindset in the spiritual zone, i.e. in the realm of soul. The present chapter while elaborates on some aspects of such a life, also outlines a vision to attain such a life in society by way of just moulding the thinking appropriately.

In some sense we try to justify here the words of the French philosopher Teilhard de Chardin, namely "we are not human Beings having a spiritual experience. We are spiritual Beings having a human experience". After emphasizing the co-existence of material and divine civilization as it is prevailing since the time memorial, we highlight close connections between the spirituality and the unconditional love in Sect. 15.2. It is argued here that pure form of bound love when combined with the unbound cosmic love gives birth to spirituality in a person. In Sect. 15.3, we emphasize on another connection which the spiritual thinking of a person can maintain with the cosmos. As a part of it, the role of love and spirituality in human relations and interactions thereon is discussed here. A fact that the spiritual experiences are universal and are realized by persons of all castes, colors, creeds and countries and at all the times, is emphasized in Sect. 15.4 in the light of some analogies drawn from physical theories. Further, a direct link of these experiences to what one calls as 'perpetual joy'–an ultimate aim of human life, is also discussed here. In Sect. 15.5, we make some concluding remarks on the Art and Science of integrating body, mind and soul–a central theme of this book. Finally, summary remarks on the content of the book are made in Sect. 15.6.

15.1 MATERIAL AND DIVINE CIVILIZATIONS: THE ROLE OF SPIRITUALITY

Like other idealized situations, there might have been pure divine civilization in imagination on this planet earth; otherwise in reality the divine and the demonic civilizations have been going on together since time immemorial. Also, there is no doubt about it if these two classes of civilizations or the corresponding cultures have originated with the origin of human race itself. And, why should it not be? The Vedic science has an answer to such queries. After all, all Beings including human Being originate from the same all-pervading cosmic consciousness field out of its second quantization by certain mechanism as per Vedic science (cf. Chapter 5). The extent to which this pure quantum (soul) remains pure while evolving through the fields of five cosmic elements and dwelling in the cosmic fields of mind, intellect and ego (insentient mode of Nature), defines the divine or demonic nature of an individual. Such a picture of evolution of soul in fact finds a justification in the second half of Teilhard de Chardin philosophy, i.e., "we are spiritual Beings having a human experience". The collections of such individuals finally constitute the so-called divine and demonic societies and later cultures and civilizations.

Material goals of development of a society and hence of culture while defining the material civilization (such goals in fact begin and end mostly in MMW itself in terms of sensual pleasure and temporal mental peace), divine goals of development of a society and hence of corresponding culture, on the other hand, define the divine civilization. (Such goals begin and end jointly in both MMW and GMW via stable mental peace and eternal joy). When one thinks deeper into these two phases of human race, there appears a common thread of spirituality between them as a measure of purity of soul. While both the extremes, i.e. the purest version and the most impure version of the quantized souls may be present in a society at a given time, each individual himself can also have a varying proportion of pure and impure components of the same soul. When the majority of persons in a society are with a good percentage of purity of souls, then this defines a divine society and contrary to this when the majority of persons are with a good percentage of polluted souls, this corresponds to a demonical society. History of human race reveals a perpetual conflict between these two ideologies at all the times. In the Indian context, the themes of the great epics like *Rāmāyana* and *Mahābhārata* are the well known examples of such conflicts of ideologies.

In spite of all this, there have always been certain personalities in the society who may have conscious and constant awareness of the purity not only of his own soul but also that of others. This, in fact makes the person a spiritual one. Once the person becomes spiritual his inner eye (i.e. the subtle intellect) becomes capable of seeing the world and its order over and above the prevailing duality that is there in an individual as well as in the society or cultures. Through his actions, words and thinking, such a person is ever devoted to the welfare of society and to a positive contribution to the maintenance of world-order in general. For further details on divine and demonical properties in the nature of a human Being and their roles in human actions in the spirit of SPP and SNP we refer to (SMBG, Chapter 16). With a view to having some glimpses of these individual based virtues one can note that non-violence in thought, word and action, truthfulness and geniality in speech, absence of anger even on provocation, renunciation of idea of doer-ship in action, tranquility of mind, kindness to all creatures, detachment from sensual pleasure, sublimity, forgiveness, fortitude, purity (external as well internal), absence of malice, absence of feeling of self-importance, etc. are the few examples of divine virtues. Contrary to them hypocrisy, arrogance, pride, anger, harshness, greed, desire for sensual pleasure, etc. are some examples of demonical virtues.

It may be mentioned that while spirituality prevails at the highest strata of human EOLs (i.e. in the domain of soul), at the lower strata (i.e. in the domains of micro and gross bodies) each of these two cultures is found to follow distinct but well defined rules with reference to the ethical and moral values in the corresponding societies. Further, the goodness or badness of these values at lower strata appears only in relative terms in the respective societies. In the spiritual zone, however, such values could be good or bad in absolute terms, particularly when the question of their following-up in society arises with reference to the maintenance of world-order in general.

15.2 DO SPIRITUALITY AND UNCONDITIONAL LOVE GO TOGETHER?

From the earlier discussions it has become clear that our spiritual identity is defined by soul. On the other hand, the unconditional love to someone whether animate or inanimate, also originates from the level of soul in the patomic model. It is only at the lower strata of EOLs where the unconditional (unbound or infinite) love becomes conditional (bound or finite) and thereby manifests in a variety of ways (cf. Sect.13.1.1). In some sense, unconditional love and spirituality are synonym of each other and this gives the answer to the question posed in the title in affirmative. In what follows, we plan to analyze this assertion with reference to the societal existence of a human Being.

15.2.1 Bound and unbound love: Different phases and expressions

At the level of soul, the originated love in conjunction with cosmic consciousness is unbound. As soon as it crosses the barrier of ego a fraction of it converts into a variety of bounded forms at lower strata. In fact, at this stage, it starts manifesting through different heads and by various names (cf. Sect. 13.1.1), i.e. while flowing through intellect, the love for knowledge of animate and inanimate entities, through mind, the love and respect for feelings of other living Beings, through senses of knowledge, the love for perceiving the external world, through sense organs responsible for external actions, the love for performing actions, and through biological body, the love for its maintenance, automatically evolves. In this process the person showering the bounded love accordingly gets pleasure, peace or joy or any combination of them, depending upon the state of his mindset and on the external entity on which the love is showered.

There are several factors which decide as to what fraction of the original love goes into a bound form at various levels of EOLs and what remains in the unbound form. The fraction of love that takes the bound form, although depends on the individual but it normally attains a polluted flavor. In this regard, beside the roles played by the *prârabdha, sancit* and *kriyamâna* category of actions related to the individual, the level of development of his FOUs also matters for which a feedback comes from the external world and its order. The nature of *sankalpâs* taken by the individual and enveloped with either or all the three *gunâs*, namely *sâtvik*, *râjasik and tâmasik*, also helps in defining three categories of bound love, namely 'divine love', 'human love' and 'demonic love', respectively. A fraction of pure love left in the bound form in conjunction with the unbound love derived from the cosmos further defines the domain of the so called 'perfect spirituality ' of a person. It may be noted that while MMW contributes to this faction of pure bound love, GMW totally contributes to the unbound (which is always pure) love. Schematically, this kind of partition of cosmic love is shown in Fig. 15.1.

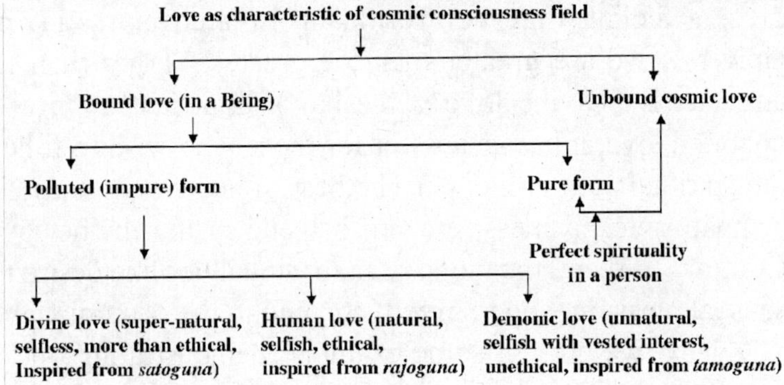

Fig. 15.1: A schematic display of different manifestations of cosmic love, that also defines the 'perfect' spirituality in a person.

If love means possessing someone or something, then that is not the real (pure) love; rather this is the case of polluted or impure love. Pure love or for that matter the divine love means giving and becoming one with everything, with humanity and divinity. Where there is oneness, it is all pure love. At every moment we have to be very cautious and conscious whether the showered love is a divine, human or demonic love. In any case it should not be the demonic love which is never taken in good taste as far as the maintenance of world-order is concerned. In divine love we give something for the sake of giving and do not expect anything in return. This is unconditional love. In human love we also expect something in return, whereas there is a kind of tug of war between the persons who are giving and taking in the demonic love. Following Sri Chinmoy (2013) some other features of the divine love can be listed in nut-shell as follows: (i) Divine love makes no demand. It is spontaneous and constant. It is unlimited in every way like that of a mother on her children, or that of God on His devotees. (ii) In divine love there is no possession–only a feeling of oneness. This oneness can enter into an animal, flower, tree, or even a wall. (iii) Divine love gives a feeling that we are not an isolated entity in this Universe; we are greater than the greatest, larger than the largest. (iv) Divine love while has a limit in the pure or unbound love, it has an answer for those who wish to follow the spiritual path in life. (v) The best of human qualities like sympathy, forgiveness, etc. in fact end in the divine love. Contrary to them, the worst of human qualities like desire for sensual pleasure, anger, greed, etc. end in the demonic love.

Next we present some examples demonstrating one of the divine qualities, namely, forgiveness quality of human Being, which constitutes the spiritual thinking.

Example 15.2.1: Forgiveness in different religions: Jesus asked God to forgive those who crucified him. "Father forgive them, for they know not what they do". The Hadiths show Prophet Mohammad forgiving those who abused him. In Judaism it is said, "who bears a grudge acts like one who, having cut one hand while handling a knife, avenges himself by stabbing the other hand". In SMBG while Lord Krishna defines forgiveness as the characteristic of a divine nature, in Buddhism the forgiveness is seen as a practice to prevent harmful thoughts from causing havoc in one's mental peace. Swami *Mahavira* said "By practicing repentance (*prāyacita*), a soul gets rid of sins, and commits no transgressions".

Example 15.2.2: Forgiveness with regard to another person: There was a saintly old person in a village who was once going to another far away village on his horse for some work. On the way he saw a person along the bushes who appeared to be sick and was mourning out of some pain. The old man stopped and enquired the well-being of that person. In response the fellow pretended to be sick and sought a ride on the horse to reach the nearby village. The old man extended the help and took him also on the back of his horse. After traversing some distance, the person who was posing to be sick kicked the old man down on the ground and started running away with the horse. When all this happened, the old person who was helpless now, called the person who cheated him and only told him not to narrate this episode to anyone else in the village, otherwise people will stop helping the sick and needy. After reaching home the cheat (thief) could not sleep the whole night as he could not devour the last words of the old man. He lost his mental peace to the extent that a great transformation took place in him and he decided to return the horse to the old man in his distant village. He realized the greatness of the old person and this inspired him to return the horse back to him and not only this, he also transformed himself into a gentle man for the rest of his life.

Example 15.2.3: Forgiveness with regard to another person: Once a saintly person has taken a vow to bathe daily in a holy river and this fact was made known to all in the town. A man in the town doubted about the genuineness of the vow of the saint. So he thought, why not test the saint? One day when the saint was returning to his hut from a bath in the river, the *skeptic* spat at him. Without uttering a word, the saint went back to the river to bathe once again. Once again the *skeptic* spat at him and saint again returned to the river to cleanse himself and this happened several times that day. Ultimately, after seeing the unexpected and unprovocated behavior of the saint the *skeptic* fell to his feet and started crying, seeking the pardon for his misbehavior. With the same calmness the saint said, "do not feel ashamed. Rather, I am grateful to you, that because of you I could have the opportunity to bathe so many times in the span of single day in this sacred river. Thank you, my son, and God bless you". This is the magical power of forgiveness.

Example 15.2.4: Forgiveness with regard to other living Beings: A saint was taking bath in a river and he saw a scorpion swimming on the surface of water near him. He picked up the scorpion and tried to place it on a safer place at the bank. In the meantime scorpion stung the saint in his hand. As a result the scorpion fallen back in water. The saint tried again to save scorpion from the water flow, but it stung again. The saint tried to save scorpion several times, but every time the scorpion stung in the hand of the saint. A person on the bank was watching this act of saint carefully and he asked the saint as to why he was trying to save this dangerous creature. The saint replied, "while the creature like scorpion cannot leave his habit of biting, then why should I leave my habit of saving the life of others, as a human Being".

15.2.2 The question of loving negativities in a person or thing

Negativities in a person (like lust, anger, greed, etc.) which finally end-up in the demonical nature, are normally defined with reference to his character or with regard to his actions in the maintenance of world-order. Also note that love is normally showered on a person (or a thing) to whomsoever one likes. (Further note that this liking, in some sense, can also be of three degrees, namely most, more and normal and accordingly becomes the fraction of love that is showered by you). Sometimes one has to shower his love on a person or thing to whomsoever he may not like. This happens when there is a question of adjustment or survival. Loving negativities of a person or thing in such a situation could be for vested interest also. There is another possibility when a few habits of someone are not liked but still loved by the person. We shall return to this case later.

In fact the nature of the love you wish to shower on the other person could be divine, human or demonic depending upon the circumstances and the nature of your own *sankalpās*. If your love is divine, then you will not only ignore all negatives in the other person but also interpret the existing negatives in him in a positive spirit; if the love is human, then you will make the other person to feel of your love as conditional and also remind the person of all his negatives. However, if your love is demonic, then you will exploit the negatives of other person and that too for your vested interest.

Example 15.2.5: Mother's love for her children most of time is divine and the same could be the case of other relatives like sister, brother, father, etc. but only in an ideal situation and occasionally. The love in the latter case for the most of time is not divine but it is human or at times it could be demonical in exceptional situations.

15.2.3: Love can cure negatives in a person

In case of human category of love, the lover can cure a few negative of his beloved provided he likes all other habits of the latter. In order to do so, one has to make some extra efforts, namely (i) come out with a *satoguni sankalpa* which will first convert the human form of love to a divine form, and (ii) prepare yourself to do some sacrifices for this purpose. These sacrifices may be required with reference to all the three fronts, namely (a) at the mental level by discarding mental peace at least for some time, (b) at the gross-body level by way of performing some extra outward actions and (c) by making available worldly objects particularly the money to the beloved. It might take some time but the person (beloved) on whom you shower your divine love will soon return to your expectation. If you continue with a human or demonic love, then there is a possibility of deteriorating the case.

It might be a bit difficult but one can as well try to cure the beloved who is living with many more negatives at the same time. Only thing is that in this case some priorities need to be fixed and certain degree of logic is needed. In fact a balance between the two, i.e., love and logic, need to be kept at all the time. As a matter of fact, even in a person with lot of negativities there always exist some aspects of pure love, which can be achieved by destroying the polluted form of love (cf. Fig. 15.1) inside him.

15.2.4 Divine love needs a balance between love and logic

In the common man's language the love in general is considered as the subject of heart or that of the EOL mind alone. But the fact is that the divine form of love at its subtle level has a direct link with spirituality. This happens by suppressing the *rajoguni* and *tamoguni sankalpās* to their maximum. In fact, the love when springs out on an outer object it is influenced by both intellect and mind. The turbulent nature of the mind, in fact, adds to the polluted version of love. As a matter of fact there is always a fraction of love, however small it may be, that remains in the bound form but connects to the infinite (ocean of) love. At times, this conversion of *sankalpās* from *satoguni* to *rajoguni*, either from *satoguni* to *rajoguni* and then to *tamoguni*, or directly from *satoguni* to *tamoguni*, respectively leads to human, mixed or demonic forms of love. Further, this conversion takes place at such a fast pace that it often goes unnoticed to an individual since his intellect and mind in this case play a passive (or silent) role.

Again, in the common man's language, it is said that the 'love is blind' and the 'love is mad'. In fact both the phrases make sense in their own right. In the first case the mind plays the dominant role by suppressing intellect whereas in the second case it is intellect that plays the dominant role by controlling mind. In either case the role of *sankalpās* is there in making love but regarding the decision or choice of the nature of its flavor, the level of development of one's FOUs again comes on the way through the so-called *sanskārās* in Vedic science. Thus, there are varieties of ways by which the pure bound love becomes the polluted one during its spraying out in the outer world. At times a lover has to play multiple roles while expressing the divine form of his love. In fact at the higher strata of EOLs there exists the divine version of love but when the question comes to its expression in the outer world through lower strata of EOLs, namely SEK, SEA and B, it appears as human, demonic or a combination of both. For example, a mother uses several flavors of her love at the same time while feeding her child; or a doctor also in the same way carries multiple flavors of love while injecting his patient or doing surgery. A good teacher at times has to adopt different ways to express his love to his student.

What we have tried to analyze in this section is a possible fundamental process of spraying out the love in the outer world. But in reality the love is spontaneous and the concerned phenomenon is more complex than it is outlined above. As a matter of fact love is nothing if it is not spontaneous. It cannot be the conclusion of reasoning precisely. It is not fruit of the spirit of bargain. If one wants to be certain about the object of love, it is only a form of calculated selfishness. Moreover, with regard to living objects making love is a two way process and accordingly plays a crucial role in two, three and many human (or non-human)- Being interactions. In the next section, we shall briefly remark on this aspect of love.

15.3 SPIRITUAL THINKING AND COSMIC CONNECTIONS

15.3.1 Spirituality in action and its role in the maintenance of world-order

Love only offers a kind of lubricating oil in the working of EOLs of a Being in general and of the human Being in particular. It makes EOLs to function efficiently. While the oil of love in conjunction with consciousness is necessary for EOLs to work efficiently, its intensity as the lubricity of the oil further matters in defining the efficiency of a particular EOL expressing the love. No doubt the system can work with impure or polluted oil (hatred), but the efficiency enhances at a fast rate only with pure oil. For becoming a spiritual person, a cosmic form of love is an important ingredient. It is the combination of the two, namely unbound cosmic love and the fraction of the pure bound love (cf. Fig.

15.1) that inculcates the perfect spirituality in a person. Further, the uneven contribution of the constituents in this combination is the basis for different categories of spiritual persons in this world. As a matter of fact the cosmic form of love or the 'spiritual love' when sprayed on an object has altogether a different or at times an extraordinary effect on the object compared to other forms of love. Note that a person with such a perfect spiritual love develops a habit of seeing *'one in all and all in one'* as far as the living creations of God are concerned. With regard to nonliving creations of the Supreme the spiritual person notices a kind of orderliness in nature and tries to maintain the same at all its levels, namely at micro, macro, mega and gigantic scales and also through all his existences, namely causal, micro, gross, societal and natural. Here we suggest some tips for a person to become spiritual and list a variety of examples of spiritual taste.

Some possible tips to inculcate spirituality in one's personality: Besides living and spending time in the company of spiritual and elderly persons some other ways to inculcate spirituality in one's personality are: (i) to develop a habit of enquiring into or to look for cosmic connections of every event that occurs suddenly in life or in the daily routine, (ii) to develop a habit of self-enquiry and self-observation and to scrutinize all his own deeds (good or bad) performed throughout the day, (iii) to develop a habit of reading value-based religious literature, (iv) to search unity in diversity while enjoying beautiful man-made and God-made worlds, i.e. try to become cosmozen from citizen, and (v) try to be rootless to reach infinity, i.e., lift the FOUs above the mundane living. In what follows, we present some examples carrying certain content of spiritual experiences:

Example 15.3.1: When *Adi Shankaracharya* was hardly eight years old, *Sri Govindpada* asked him, "who are you?". The little boy answered in Sanskrit verses which translate as "I am not mind, nor intellect, nor ego, /nor the reflections of inner-self, /I am not the five senses, beyond that I am. I am not the five (cosmic) elements– neither ether/nor earth, water, wind or fire. /I am indeed that eternal knowing and bliss, /eternal love, pure consciousness .... ".

Example 15.3.2: By serving others one creates heaven and by getting lost in self, the person creates hell: A person was on his deathbed. In his dream an angel took him on a tour of hell and heaven. First he visited hell. There each one's hands were tied with a spoon in one hand and a fork in the other. Most delicious food was ready in front of them. They were struggling to eat because the spoon and fork were tied to each person's hand with a one foot long stick. They were in fact starving. Then the person was taken to heaven where again the scene was the same as in hell, but here people were enjoying and laughing, as each one was serving and feeding the other even with the tied hands. Thus, the moment you serve others, you connect with infinite and the Nature helps those who serve others.

Example 15.3.3: Restoring the energy of the Self (cosmic connections): Take a vessel with nine holes and put it under the water tap. Note that whatever quantity of water comes in from the tap, the same flows out of the holes. Now place this vessel in a bigger bucket which is already filled with water. Pour the water in the vessel from the tap again as before, but now the water does not flow out of holes of the vessel anymore. Similar is the case with a person when the spiritual energy is stored in his Self. It is constantly (knowingly or unknowingly) flowing out through the nine holes (two eyes, two ears, nostrils, mouth, skin, copulatory organ and anus) in the human body. The best way to check or control this flow of energy is to remain in constant contact with the cosmic source of consciousness.

Example 15.3.4: Enjoy the present with full awakening: Many of us, as per saying, spend 50% of time in thinking over the past, 25% of time in thinking of future and only 25% of time in enjoying the present. Contrary to this, the present example suggests to enjoy the present in totality: Two army men were penalized for disobeying certain command of the officer concerned. As a result, they were granted the same punishment. According to this punishment, both these persons were supposed to climb the hill in sight with a 5kg weight on their body. One of the persons collected 5kg stones and pebbles in a bag and started climbing on the hill in a lamenting and sad mood. All the time he was repenting for the mistake he committed. The other person, however, used his best of intellect and filled the bag with 5-10kg of eatables, drinks, fruits, etc. and started climbing on the hill in a jolly mood, naturally with a regular consumption of eatables without bothering much about the past. Thus, the second person made his present rather more enjoyable than the first one but only after using his intellect.

Example 15.3.5: Actions in the mental domain are more subtle than those in the gross-body domain: Two friends with their turbulent mindsets, decided to pass the evening time for a change. One of them decided to go to a bar whereas the other decides to go to a temple. However, after reaching their respective destinations and involving themselves in the respective activities, the mind of the bar-friend while sipping the bear, was always fixed on the activity of his 'temple-friend', i.e. on the worship of God. On the other hand, the mind of the temple-friend while performing worship and other rituals, was always fixed on the glass of bear and the enjoyment thereof. In relative terms, the actions of bar-friend were more positive than those of temple-friend as far as values are concerned.

Example 15.3.6: Spiritual experience enhances the level of development of one's FOUs: Two persons decided to view a religious procession from a distance. They went to a nearby tower to enjoy the best view. One person who already had some taste for the religiosity climbs to the tower to view the scene whereas the other person decides to stay at ground and viewed the scene only partially. Clearly, the person who is at higher platform will enjoy viewing for a longer time and in a better way as compared to the person who stayed at the ground and who could only view when the event just occurs in front of him. Naturally the person on the ground cannot have a distant view of the procession. Thus, the level of development of one's FOUs also matters in the quality performance of actions.

As per SMBG one out of millions of persons who born on this planet is truly spiritual. Again one out of millions of such true spiritual persons, is the perfect spiritual person who rarely descends on this earth. If one goes with the theory of rebirth then becoming a perfect spiritual person is a continuous and conscious effort of an individual soul. Spiritual experiences and practices are carried forward from one birth to another with possible additions and subtractions. In some sense we all are born with certain degree of spirituality and love but as far as the 'gold standard' is concerned the spirituality varies from person to person. There is full freedom to an individual to reduce or enhance this God gifted fraction of spirituality in him by way of performing the so-called 'good deeds' at each space-time point and in all the circumstances. Further, the spirituality need to be practised at the level of all the five existences of a human Being, namely causal, micro, gross, societal and natural (cf. Chapter 14) and again through thoughts, words and deeds . Here also comes the role of *prārabdha*, *sanci*t and *kriyamāna* category of actions. In spite of the fact that we all want to be spiritual or rather perfect spiritual, we cannot become the same as per the theory of *karma*. In what follows, we briefly highlight the role of spirituality and love in societal existence of a person.

15.3.2 Role of love and spirituality in human relations and interactions

Spiritual life is essentially based on love, and our love depends on the vertical development of the personality, i.e. the character and the nature of our relationships. Relationships are great fabric of life. They not only make the life enjoyable but also suggest an art of living. In fact the spiritual life and the art of living are the two ways which are synonym of each other. Generally, the spiritual life is associated with a belief system but that is not the case. Basically, it is a purpose of living. When we refer to spiritual life, we need to remember that no one's life is autonomous or isolated rather it is inter-dependent on other living Beings as well as on other human Beings.

As a matter of fact the interactions among human Beings in the spirit of Chapter 12 are necessary and formal for survival whereas the net-working of relationships in an ideal sense is necessary and sufficient and also informal. Whether these are the interactions or relationships, both are God gifted in a broad sense and are necessary for the survival in a society.

There is nothing wrong in saying that the love is an extra dimension of consciousness. Recall that the consciousness plays an important role in human interactions by way of dressing various EOLs with it. On the other hand, spirituality also contains a considerable fraction of love, particularly that of unbound love. Jointly or separately when these two manifest in human relations and interactions, then they take an altogether new shape and this brings in some kind of lubricity or smoothness in them. Further, in the process of dressing of EOLs with consciousness in the spirit of Chapter 12, particularly in higher orders, the concerned EOL gathers this extra dimension of love and spirituality. Once this extra dimension is achieved by the interacting EOLs of the participating persons, then the outcome of the corresponding interaction/relationship turns out to be the best possible as far as the social norms and the maintenance of world-order are concerned.

Although the love (may not be the spirituality in a broad sense) manifests in all well- maintained relations in a family or society in varying proportions but after the yogi category of person (i.e., the man with perfect spirituality) the next category is the motherhood in females that sprays maximum of it in both MMW and GMW. In a lighter mood, the following joke elaborates the role and meaning of love in human relations:

Example 15.3.7: Role of love in family relations is defined as follows: love +full-fledged care = mother; love +fear = father, love +company = sister; love +quarrel = brother; love +lively life = girl friend; love +enjoyment = friend, but love +full-fledged care +fear +company +quarrel +lively life+ enjoyment = wife. This is how the husband-wife interactions offer an ideal and perfect example of love between the two human Being interactions (cf. Sect.13.2).

As a concluding example, we cite here certain phenomena in Nature which can also inspire a person to develop a kind of spiritual love.

Example 15.3.8: Spiritual experiences out of the GMW: natural benefits are the same for all: (i) The sun never differentiates while showering its light on objects. Even if one abuses sun for intense heat during summer or praises sun for enjoying morning rays during winter, gets equal share and the sun remains unaffected; (ii) trees never eat their own fruits rather give them to others to enjoy, and (iii) rivers never drink or use their own water rather supply it to all others for their use. A conscious person watches such phenomena in Nature and tries to come out from his bound form of love to its unbound form that needs to be sprayed on others which in turn converts into the spiritual love.

15.3.3 Love brings order and hate adds to chaos in the Universe

A connection between love (hate) and the creation (destruction) of Universe has been described recently by Jug Suraiya (2014) in an interesting manner when discussing the natural and unnatural love. An essence of these arguments lies in the fact that love brings order and its opposite hate adds to the chaos in the Universe. In fact the maintenance of love and order has been the aim not only of all the existences of a human Being but also of all actions performed and efforts made by the individual to this effect during these existences. Arguments in fact take us one step further and elaborate on the source of creation of the cosmic unbound love (cf. Fig.15.1). According to Jug Suraiya, the 'love' that creator has for that which is created is the source of all the many forms of love, which is perhaps the most overworked word (or its synonym) in all languages. All these very different 'loves' derive from the original love: the love of the Creator (*Purusa*) for Creation (*Prikriti*). Creation is nothing less, and nothing more, than love made manifest. As argued earlier, love forms the basis not only for all sorts of religiosities but also embedded in the realm of spirituality whether perfect or partial (cf. Appendix A) that is immaterial.

As far as the objective sciences are concerned, theoretical scientists always look for the underlying systematics, symmetries, equilibriums, stabilities, order, etc. in the system rather than for their opposites. Clearly, the study of such features of a system (whether micro, macro, terrestrial, galactic) describe and lead to the order may be at different scales in the Universe rather than the chaos. As a matter of fact the chaos becomes exception in the studies; neither the Nature nor the human Being likes it. Moreover, it is the universality of the force of attraction (i.e. love) (cf. Sect. 8.1) in Nature which manifest more than that of repulsion (i.e. hate). In nut-shell, the love and order contribute to creation and maintenance of the Universe whereas chaos to its destruction.

15.4 SPIRITUAL EXPERIENCES AND THEIR UNIVERSALITY

15.4.1 Spiritual experiences and the five existences of human Being

Basically an experience is the storage of information and knowledge in E that one gathers as a result of certain observations on an object in the seer-seen chain (cf. Example 2.4.1). Depending on the object in the seer-seen chain, the quality of experience also varies from the domain of one existence to the domain of another existence. This happens in the four existences, namely **N**, **S**, **G** and **M** (cf. Chapter 14). In the domain of causal existence it all becomes directly the spiritual experience. For example, the experiences gained through SE and B in the field of WO corresponds to the gross-body existence of a person. Similarly, for the outcome of actions performed by SE and B in terms of attachment and detachment with their fruits at the mental level is the experience gained through M, I and E and the same belongs to the micro existence of the human Being. However, for the experiences in the domains of societal and natural existences, the human Being as a whole offers as the device of gaining experience from MMW and GMW. In order to call an experience as the spiritual one, the same has to appeal to the soul either directly or through various stages of analysis in which the intellect in conjunction with the ego plays a dominant role at every stage. The faculty of decision, intellect, while offering a discriminating instrument, the faculty of memory, ego, however offers past experiences for the comparison so that only a best resultant (after the test) passes to the soul. For those who have not developed their FOUs sufficiently but are eager to become spiritual, the above process knowingly or unknowingly proceeds constantly with reference to every action performed by them and the experience gained thereof. However, to connect an experience directly with the soul there is a short-cut for some who have sufficiently developed their FOUs, controlled their mind M and suppressed the ego E. In fact mind and ego are the two main obstacles in connecting an experience to the soul directly and the same in turn enables the experience to become spiritual. An example of direct link between an experience and the soul is the one experienced by the Yogi category of persons (cf. Chapter 1).

Besides the *prârabdha*, there are several other causes and stimulants in one's life which inspire him to become spiritual. For example, by noticing the intricately interwoven net-working of Nature through various phenomena and events, one at times is forced to think spiritually. These phenomena or events no doubt occur in the outer world but sometimes they shatter the inner world of EOLs including SO and the person accordingly gains an spiritual experience of certain category.

While the experiences in the domain of causal existence of a human Being are always ideally spiritual, the experiences corresponding to the domains of other existences can also be spiritual but of a lower category. From this point of view we analyze the examples listed in the previous sections. For example, the cases listed in Example 15.3.8 and the one listed in Example 15.2.4 are of spiritual experience in the domain of natural existence of a person and those in Example 15.3.7 are in the domain of societal existence. The case listed in Example 15.2.3 is the spiritual experience at the level of gross-body existence. The cases in examples 15.2.2 and 15.3.2 are of spiritual experience in the domain of micro existence of a person. One can as well analyze the cases discussed in other examples of this and of previous chapters with reference to the observer of the event. For a similar way to understand the quality of an experience, we refer to the discussions in Sect.8.5. Next we discuss the Universality of these spiritual experiences after having some lessons from physical theories.

15.4.2 Lessons from physical theories V: The concept of Universality

Since physical laws are expected to work at all space-time points in the history of evolution of the Universe, the concept of universality is very common in physical sciences. At times this concept not only extends the viability of laws but also becomes the testing ground for their foundation in physical theories. The universality of various concepts, quantities and laws in physics is normally established by studying their invariance with respect to time, space or both in mathematical terms. As one deals mostly with closed systems in physics, the significance of invariance with respect to space becomes less as compared to that with respect to time. For example, the conservation of energy, momentum and angular momentum for a system in classical mechanics is the outcome of isotropy of time, translational invariance and isotropy of space, respectively. To this effect, one normally attempts to find space time symmetries in the system and accordingly associates with it a conserved quantity (cf. Noether's theorem).

There are three types of physical quantities which can account for the concept of universality or invariance and these are, (i) true constants like velocity of light, Planck's constant, charge and mass of electron, etc., (ii) physical (dynamical) variables themselves like energy , momentum, etc., as mentioned above, and (iii) the functions of dynamical variables, like the Hamiltonian function, etc. In the present context, while analyzing the quality of human experiences it is worthwhile to make use of these concepts of physics, after all the Science of the Self and the laws of human interactions in it are as perpetual as the laws of physics. In this regard we have already discussed the universality of certain behavioral facts in Chapter 8.

15.4.3 The question of Universality of spiritual experiences

Except for the experiences gained in the domain of causal existence note that all other experiences gained in the domains of other existences are temporal and/or circumstantial. They are not only qualitatively different among themselves but also leave distinct impact on different individuals and accordingly play the varying roles in their corresponding manifestation. In spite of all these variations, most of these experiences, though may not be spiritual, but are universal in the sense that they do not depend on the age, caste, color, creed or country of the experiencer and to some extent also not on the space and time in the historical sense. Further, an experience could be of just a single event, of a sequence of events or of the phenomenon as a whole. Also, an experience by the experiencer in general is a function of the level of development of his FOUs and to be more specific, it depends on the efficiency of his different EOLs. In this regard the inner EOLs of the experiencer play a dominant role and always leave the impact somewhat deeper and longer than that of outer ones.

In view of this analysis of the experiencing process that goes on inside the experiencer, it is not difficult to define an 'experience function' in analogy with the above concepts of physical theories. As a matter of fact the 'experience function' itself now becomes the function of mindset function in addition to other variables associated with various inner and outer EOLs, namely m, i ,e ,q, t (see, (Kaushal, 2011, Chapter 8)). To extend the analogy further, note that the variables like m, i, e, ... as the attributes respectively of M, I, E, ... here play the roles of dynamical variables of physical theories in the same way as they have been used in the mindset function (Kaushal, 2011). From this point of view certain experiences will disappear in the **N** domain itself, some in the **S** domain, and some in the **G** and **M** domains. Only a few experiences will be left which will pass to the **C** domain and that too after overcoming the barrier of E. Truly speaking these are the experiences which are Universal as well as spiritual; otherwise Universal experiences can as well occur at the lower strata of existences. Only thing is that their ways and means of expressions by an individual keep on changing with space, time, circumstances and cultures (cf. Chapter 8). Although the analysis of experiences in the present framework can be extended further but we restrict ourselves here from going into such details.

15.4.4 Spiritual experiences and the concept of perpetual joy

It has become clear by now from the preceding chapters of the book that sensual pleasure, mental peace and joy are the main goals and outcome of human actions performed respectively in the domains of three existences, namely **G**, **M** and **C** of the human Being. As far as the role of material cause in the origin of these goals is concerned, it is more for sensual pleasure, somewhat less, for the mental peace and not at all for the joy. In fact joy is something that originates without material cause. The greatest wonder is that it can be achieved in the mortal world with our mortal body. Another wonder is that only the rarest of rare of us achieves it in its eternal or perpetual version. The main hurdles which prevent from attaining eternal joy are greed, jealousy, meanness, praise (fame), desire of respect, etc. These hurdles, no doubt, can be overcome at the threshold of mind in the process of experiencing the outer world, but it is really difficult to overcome them at the next threshold of ego. Note that it is only after this second threshold that the experience becomes spiritual and contributes to attaining joy which later in turn can become eternal or perpetual. As a matter of fact in this regard a stage comes when the mind itself becomes our guide and eternal joy becomes a part of our existence. Our choice or priorities determine its accessibility and once it is tapped, it gives unique feeling. Even in the midst of worldly miseries the overflow of such a joy can be seen.

In the preceding chapters, efforts have been made to give some glimpses of the Science of the Self and the same is exploited first to develop the complete personality of a person and then to offer a guide for leading a spiritual life. As far as the purpose of this science in Vedic scriptures is concerned it is all focused around the so-called '*moksha*' at the end-point, i.e. towards the liberation of soul or towards the convergence of finite (soul) into infinite (cosmic consciousness field) but with its purest form. Whole of the karmic theory in Vedic scriptures in fact works towards this purification of soul of an individual. These are the spiritual experiences of a person which become asset towards this processes of purification of soul, Further, when a person is in the state of perpetual joy, he is able to see the Self as separate from the non-self or knows the art as to how to detach the roots in the finite to reach the infinity. Such a person, in fact, can enjoy the experience of a kind of eternal or perpetual joy which are synonym of each other.

15.5 THE ART AND SCIENCE OF INTEGRATING BODY, MIND AND SOUL: CONCLUDING REMARKS

The answer to the question addressed in this book and in Sect. 1.5 has been sought in preceding chapters at various stages of development of the Science of the Self, more by following the methodology of objective science and often by having lessons from physical theories. Such a development of the subject of psychology in conjunction with modern physical theories has given an altogether new flavor to the discipline of psychophysics initiated by G.T. Fechner about 150 years ago. The mechanism of integrating body, mind, and soul (towards the success of an action) as elaborated in the preceding chapters can be viewed as an Art by the persons who specialize in soft disciplines and as a full-fledged science, though with poor predictions, by those who specialize in hard disciplines. In any case the subject matter covered here appropriately fills the gap of missing value education in the curriculum that is needed most in modern times, particularly for scientifically trained minds.

After briefing the goals of actions performed in the domains of body, mind, and soul, namely as pleasure, peace and joy in Sect. 2.5, a connection between the Science of the Self and the art of integrating the body, mind and soul is demonstrated in Sect. 5.4 in the Indian perspective. Further, the proposed personality creation mechanism in Chapter 9, in the context of vertical development of personality, is found to have some links with this Art of integrating the body, mind and soul. To this effect some new traits and dimensions for classifying the personalities are suggested in Sect.9.5 mostly on the basis of Vedic science (cf. Table 9.1). These discussions are further elaborated upon in Sect. 13.6 with regard to many human Being interactions. It is argued here that a person with integrated body, mind and soul can serve an organization better. Finally, it is argued in Sect.14.4 that a person who has developed both vertical as well as horizontal components of his personality is an example of ideally integrated body, mind and soul in the real sense. From this point of view, the life and work of several great persons and prophets are analyzed in the Indian context (cf. Table A.1).

15.6 SUMMARY AND DISCUSSIONS: FINAL REMARKS

It can be seen that the subject matter of the whole book is focused around the development of the sovereign science of the Self as per Vedic wisdom and in modern scientific perspective. Its subsequent applications (cf. Parts B and C) provide tips for a spiritual evolution of a person but again in a scientific spirit. The present chapter in this survey is the end-product and in some sense presents in nut-shell the purpose of the entire training intended to be given to an individual trainee. As a matter of fact the Art and mechanism of integrating body, mind and soul with reference to an individual is explored at various stages of development of the subject matter, particularly in the context of all the five existences of a human Being, namely causal, micro, gross, societal and natural. This mechanism, defined basically in the domain of micro existence of a human Being, however, uses ingredients from the domains of causal and gross existences. Further, it turns out to be the part of the character building and hence of the vertical development of one's personality. As far as the applications of this vertical development are concerned, they are very much there as the part of horizontal development of one's personality in the domains of societal and natural existences, i.e., in the MMW and GMW. Further note that the Parts A and B of the book have dealt with the development of the first aspect of the personality and Part C is devoted to the development of the second aspect and finally demonstrating the end-product of these studies in the present chapter.

It may be mentioned that developing a formal theory of the psycho-analysis of various underlying fundamental processes and phenomena that take place inside the human Being prior to and after his performance of an action, is a

Herculean task because of the involvement of subjectivity of highest order. Also, the philosophy and belief system of an individual come on the way in this endeavor. But in order to understand these subtle and intrigue processes in modern scientific age, one has to start from somewhere. In author's opinion, the Vedic wisdom, once encouraged Erwin Schrodinger (1964) for postulating the probabilistic interpretation of quantum mechanics, again seems to come for rescue. This is how the author is inspired to use this wisdom, perhaps for another noble cause. For this purpose, following the earlier work (Kaushal, 2011), the tools of the game are developed in Part A. The viability of patomic model of human Being (cf. Sect.6.3) to this effect is revisited in the present context on various fronts of working domains of a person. The role of these tools in motivating and improving one's behavior in the outer world is further emphasized in Part B. As to how these tools, namely the inner EOLs, actually work in unison in the personality creation mechanism is demonstrated in this part of the book by pin-pointing various roles a person can play on different fronts, namely in the family, society or life in general.

Real life applications of a vertically developed personality of a person began in Chapter 11. Having lessons from physical theories on several fronts, the nature of possible interactions of such a person with other persons, in a family and society is explored in Chapter 12 onward. To this effect, many examples from the real life situations pertaining to human relations and interactions (with other persons) are discussed in Chapter 13. Also, the role of love in these relations and interaction is highlighted here. Once the role of love in human relations is defined, then comes the question of existence of an ideal society in modern times which, in principle, should be full of the best of human relations, love and affection. Such possibilities are explored in Chapter 14 and in the maintenance of such a society once again the roles of deities, prophets and spiritual persons are highlighted. The dynamics of human interactions developed and analysed up to this stage is mainly suggestive and inspiring in practical terms as far as the complete development of one's personality is concerned. However, a maximum share to inspiration comes in its invisible form and the same one draws from the outer world and absorbs it by understanding the role of spirituality in life. In fact both theist and atheist can be the spiritual persons; since the spiritual persons are considered to be much above the concept of caste, color, creed and country. Depending upon the development of one's FOUs vis-a-vis his domain of actions in any one or some out of the five existences, one finds gradation even among the spiritual persons. A criterion to this effect is suggested in mathematical terms in Appendix A.

What one needs are the continuous and conscious efforts to pass a truly spiritual life. A justification to this phrase has been the theme of the present chapter. As a matter of fact the doors of spirituality are open to both the categories of persons, namely of divine and demonical nature but somehow the former can approach faster to the limit of truly spiritual person. In fact it is the love, as an attribute of consciousness, which plays the important role in transforming a person to become spiritual. It is argued that an inculcation of the divine form of love and/or the pure bound love in one's personality is a prerequisite for becoming spiritual. Similarly, an inculcation of unbound love is a prerequisite to become truly spiritual. Thus, besides the unbound love another prerequisite suggested in this work is the spiritual thinking which in turn will enable the person to seek cosmic connections in the chain of cause and effect related to his performance of every action.

Having a spiritual experience is a grand experience in itself. Keeping the examples of physical theories in mind the Universality of these spiritual experiences is discussed in Sect. 15.4. It is argued that these are the spiritual experiences of universal nature which in turn can provide a flavor of eternal or perpetual joy. Because spiritual reality is omnipresent, omnipotent and benevolent, it is always ready to guide and merge us back in the source. We have to do a bit and the divine grace takes care of the rest. All we need to do is to develop a sense of right intention and purpose and live life accordingly. Let us not forget that life is an opportunity for us to become spiritually evolved, and thereby discover the divine within and around us. If our intentions and goals are in consonance with cosmic harmony, this will be an asset to our fast spiritual progress. In conclusion, we once again recall the words of Teilhard de Chadrin that we basically are the spiritual Beings having a human experience.

Further Reading:

For further reading on the subject of love we refer to recent writings (Clayton, 2011), (Baba, 2013), (Chinmoy, 2013) and (Suraiya, 2014) and for further details on various other topics in this chapter see (Mitra, 2013), (Parthasarathy, 1992), (Jain, 2013), (Row, 2013) and (Deshmukh, 2012). For understanding spiritual living in Indian way, see (Sood, 2010).

High Skill Exercises and Projects

15.1 Compare and explain with examples the differences between pseudo-love as discussed in Sect. 8.1 and human and demonic love as defined in Sect. 15.2.

15.2 "While material goals of development of a society define material civilization, the divine goals of development however define divine civilization and hence culture". Comment and justify this statement.

15.3 Explain how the unbound love and spirituality are synonym of each other. Following the flow chart of Fig.15.1, define 'perfect' spirituality in a person.

15.4 Keeping Examples 15.2.1-15.2.4 in mind write an essay on the divine quality of 'forgiveness' in a person by adding a few more examples for this purpose.

15.5 In view of Example 15.3.3 explain how a person, who has tuned his EOLs with cosmos, can not only restore his limited (spiritual) energy but can enhance it to its maximum.

15.6 "Spirituality takes us to the highest top whereas science looks at the foundation". Elaborate on the meaning of this statement.

15.7 Explain as under what conditions a person loves negativities in another person and how these negativities can be cured by showering his/her love.

15.8 "Divine love needs a balance between love and logic", justify this statement with some examples from (a) family life, and (b) friend circle.

15.9 Explain the analogy, "love is lubricating oil and its intensity is the lubricity of oil" with examples from (a) family, and (b) friends circle.

15.10 What moral do you draw from each of the examples listed in Sect.15.3.1? Collect five more similar examples of spiritual taste.

15.11 Write an essay on the role of love and spirituality in human relations and interactions.

15.12 Differentiate and explain human love, divine love and spiritual love. How do you connect them with the platonic love?

15.13 "Love (and spirituality) contributes to order (and maintenance) in the Universe whereas hate (and demonical acts) contributes to chaos in the Universe", comment and advance your arguments in support of this statement.

15.14 Keeping the universality of physical quantities and laws in mind, discuss the Universality of spiritual experiences with reference to space and time.

15.15 From the point of view of an analytical development of the subject elaborate on the notion of 'experience function' as introduced in Sect.15.4.3.

15.16 The case of '*all in one and one in all*' as a mathematical riddle: Unification of religions: In continuation of Exercise 14.13, now compute the sums corresponding to letters in the words SHREEKRISHNA (Hindu), MOHAMMED (Muslim), MAHAVIR (Jain), GURUNANAK (Sikh), ZARATHUSTRA (Parasi), GAUTAM (Budhist), ESAMESSIAH (Christian). You will find that each one ends with number 9, either at the first stage sum of numbers, or at the second stage sum of digits in the resultant sum. What moral does one draw from this puzzle regarding unification of religions? In this spirit write an essay on '*all in one and one in all*'.

Appendix A:
CLASSIFICATION OF SPIRITUALLY DEVELOPED PERSONALITIES AND EXAMPLES

This is in continuation of Sect. 14.4 where the components and sub-components of the complete personality are discussed. In this regard we briefly re-emphasize here the criterion for classifying the spiritual personalities. No doubt, the criterion is applicable to all spiritual persons of the world but here we list and analyze the cases mostly in the Indian context and that too within the limitations of the author. What is important here is the criterion or the method and not the examples since a lot of subjectivity or personal bias may be involved in the analysis of the cases.

A.1 A POSSIBLE CRITERION FOR CLASSIFICATION OF SPIRITUAL PERSONALITIES

As argued in Chapter 14, the complete personality is the combination of the following two components: (i) vertically developed component which is a collective attribute of causal (**C**), micro (**M**) and gross (**G**) existences of a human Being. This attribute along with other characteristics, reflects to the extent to which the integration of body, mind and soul is achieved by an individual while performing an action, and (ii) horizontally developed component which is a collective attribute of societal (**S**) and Natural (**N**) existences of a human Being. This attribute reflects to the extent to which the 'hard earned' tools created during the vertical development of the personality of an individual are successfully applied while performing actions in the domains of MMW and GMW through human interactions. Corresponding to these five existences (cf. Fig. 14.1) of a human Being, namely **C, M, G, S** and **N**, one can assign five parameters a,b,c,d and f as the measure of relative contributions of these existences to the complete personality. Further, one can account for the sub-classification of existences in accordance with three adjective degrees (or in accordance with three *gunās* of Vedic science, namely *sātvik*, *rājasik*, *tāmsik*) in descending order as 'best' 'better' and 'good' respectively by lebelling these parameters with the numerals 1,2 and 3. For example, $\mathbf{M}_1$, $\mathbf{M}_2$, $\mathbf{M}_3$ identifies the ranking of mentally developed persons in the order— most, more and normal, and likewise one can have interpretation for the other variables **C, G, S** and **N**.

In general the complete personality is a complicated function of all the five existences, viz., (CP)=F(**C**, **M**, **G**, **S**, **N**), since one is not sure as to what extent which spiritual person develops what types of existences more out of all the five. This is mainly because of the fact that, it is a highly subjective matter. For a common man, however, if one starts with a linear superposition of the existence variables that are introduced above, then the complete personality CP can be expressed as

$$(CP)_{ijklm} = a_i \mathbf{C}_i + b_j \mathbf{M}_j + c_k \mathbf{G}_k + d_l \mathbf{S}_l + f_m \mathbf{N}_m \qquad (A.1)$$

where i, j, k, l, m = 1, 2, 3 (or s, r, t) corresponding to the best (*sātvik*), better (*rājasik*) and good (*tāmasik*) category of persons as discussed in Chapter 9. Here the coefficients a_i, b_j, c_k, d_l *and* f_m are the measures of relative contributions of the correspondingly ranked existences in (A.1) to a given complete personality. To elaborate further the meaning of the notation $(CP)_{ijklm}$, consider for example the case corresponding to $(CP)_{13212}$. This means that the personality is the best for his actions in the causal and societal domains, good in the mental domain and only better in the gross and natural domains. Note that the superposition law (A.1) is justified for a common man, otherwise for philosopher, scientist or for yogi-category of persons, the definition (A.1) may involve nonlinear superposition in some terms as well. We shall avoid further details of such a law even though it is desirable for certain category of spiritual persons.

Alternatively, by considering **C**, **M**, **G**, **S** and **N** as vectors in the three dimensional space spanned by s, r, t (i.e., of *satoguni*, *rajoguni*, *tamoguni* as in Sect. 9.6), it is more transparent in mathematical terms to define complete personality as a tensor of rank five, namely with the components,

$$(CP)_{ijklm} = P\ \mathbf{C}_i \mathbf{M}_j \mathbf{G}_k \mathbf{S}_l \mathbf{N}_m , \qquad \text{(A.2)}$$

where again i, j, k, l, m = 1, 2, 3 and P is some constant. Thus, CP-tensor has 3^5=243 components and one can accommodate these many varieties of personalities in the present criterion out of which $(CP)_{11111}$ and $(CP)_{33333}$ are the two extremes— best and worst cases, respectively in the spirit of Vedic science. As far as the spirituality factor in the complete personality is concerned, it is decided by the presence of $\mathbf{C}_i$ and $\mathbf{N}_m$ in (A.2). Note that both these existences and so their components are interconnected not only at the local and global levels but also at the cosmic level. Further for these features only certain souls on this planet leave their imprints on the sand of time. Next we analyse certain personalities within this frame work.

A.2 EXAMPLES

While the description of the development of vertical component of complete personality is highly subjective and focused around the individual and his efforts for this purpose, the development of the horizontal component can easily be noticed by an observer in the societal domain of his working

(MMW) and in the natural environment (GMW). In fact all this makes a mini vicious circle in the sense that when a person becomes conscious of the world around him after the birth, then he is bewildered as well as puzzled by certain phenomena prevailing in MMW and/or in GMW. Inspired and motivated by the amazing nature of such problems of the outer world, the person, as a truth seeker, looks for the solution to these problems as a challenge. A kind of churning of thoughts goes through inside him for a period of time and in the process he also seeks help from elderly persons (Spiritual Masters) or from religious texts. After continuous and conscious efforts, a stage comes when the person finds a solution to these problems according to his own conviction and understanding. While this adds to the vertical development of his personality on the one hand, it also makes him capable of setting ideal norms in the society through his actions and thus toward the development of horizontal component of his complete personality on the other. It is at this stage the person returns to the society as a spiritual master or social reformer with his new convictions and experiences and thereby completes the vicious circle.

For the spiritual person, while the natural environment defines only the working boundaries in terms of language and culture, the society, however, offers him different fronts to work such as political reform, religious reform by way of reviving of moral and spiritual values or for that matter any other social reform like that of upliftment of downtrodden, women, farmers, etc. depending upon the requirements of the society. In Table A.1 we present some examples of spiritual persons who have served the society for its welfare on different fronts or have started a new religion on similar grounds at different points of time. In fact there could be thousands of such examples all over world but we limit our observations here only to a few representative cases essentially in the Indian context. In this regard, recall the three categories of great persons discussed before. In the first category are those who are born great; in the second are those who achieved greatness during this life itself, and in the third are those who become great by having greatness thrust upon them. We, however, restrict ourselves to the first two categories and the only example listed in Table A.1 of the second category is that of Mahatma Gandhi.

Table A.1: Examples of some spiritual persons who accepted the challenges of society and were inspired to work for the welfare of MMW and GMW. Attempts are made here to highlight separately the growth of the vertical and horizontal components of their complete personalities which in turn is the root cause of success in their great deeds.

S. No.	Spiritual person (period)	Challenge(s) accepted (or inspiration sought) from MMW and /or GMW	Vertical development of personality (character building)	Horizontal development of personality (service to society)	Remarks (moral/ message conveyed to masses)
1.	M. K. Gandhi (1869-1948)	Aristocracy of British rulers in India and prevailing social evils	Practiced only a few sub-components of *Asthānga* yoga, namely truth, non-violence and celibacy in real sense, i.e., in thoughts, words and actions, not only on his self but also saw them to work on masses. Practiced several aspects of Vedic traditions again in a real sense.	Spiritual powers so developed had not only eradicated British rulers from India, but also helped in the up-liftment of women and downtrodden in India.	Personality grew from society to national level and later as an international figure.

Continued.....

2.	Gautam Buddha (563 BCE-483 BCE)	Inspired from the pain, sorrow and unrest that existed among the people in the society	Underwent constant meditation and tough training of his Self, leading to the vertical development of his personality to the highest order.	After enlightenment returned back to society to deliver goods to masses towards their mental peace at any cost following a process of self-observation, introspection and self-enquiry; also suggested to follow a middle path in life.	Buddha advised to develop cosmic awareness leading to empathetic compassion from awareness of objects to awareness of subject, and then to awareness of awareness itself. Propounded a kind of non-Brahmanical Hinduism.
3.	MahavirSwami (599 BCE-527 BCE)	One of the prophets in the series and the reviver of values from their further deterioration due to contamination of soul that had led to violence in the society.	Personality developed vertically on the principle of not causing harm to others, i.e., non-violence— a basic tenet in Jainism based on all-pervading character of soul, i.e., one in all and all in one.	Most of the principles are individual based and are connected with the five events in the life of each prophet in the series (Tirthānkers), namely descent into the mother's womb, birth, renunciation, attainment of omniscience, and emancipation of Jina.	The way to liberation is through three jewels, namely right faith, right knowledge and right conduct. Right conduct presupposes the attainment of right faith and knowledge and is thus a spontaneous quality. It represents the rules of moral discipline and constitutes the right activities of body, mind and speech.
4.	Guru Nanak Dev (1469-1539)	Prevailing conflicts among various cults	In the vertical development, the tenets of	The same tenets when transmitted to common	A practical religion cannot remain static, it has to

Continued.....

		of Hinduism forced him to come out with a progressive approach to Hinduism, which was later propagated by Guru Gobind Singh as a new religion.	Vedic science and scriptures were practiced to the highest order.	people in a simple language, i.e. in *Guru Bani,* highly touched their hearts.	progress with space, time and circumstances. In some sense, Sikhism is a progressive component of Hinduism.
5.	Sufi Saints (a particular class of spiritual persons, who live at all times)	Normally inspired from conflicts among various cults and cultures in MMW while remaining highly conscious of GMW.	They try to develop vertical component to highest order but within the limits of their FOUs and according to the need of time. Prevailing religions do not hinder their spiritual progress. Love for humanity is the greatest religion for them.	Whatever little they have learnt and experienced towards the vertical development, try to propagate the same to masses more by way of roaming here and there but with a personal feel of people. They see God in a common man.	For them spirituality has no boundaries, forgiveness and compassion has no caste, no creed, no sects and no divisions. Love is the spiritual quality of every religion. It is not any attribute of God but it is God itself. Examples: Saint Kabir, Sai of Shirdhi, etc.
6.	Ram Krishan Paramahans (1836-1886)	Real search of oneness in all religions of the world.	Personality developed vertically to the extent that he internalized the experiences of all religions of the world—a unique case in itself.	Arrived at the conclusion (mainly by remaining as a true practitioner and actor) that Ram and Rahim, Krishna and Christ are the same Devine light of the infinite one.	There is enough reason to say no to religion and yes to spirituality. We have unnecessary imprisoned God and drawn boundaries around the Devine, and in the process created bloodshed.

From Table A.1 it can be noticed that all spiritual persons, although develop their complete personality in a varying manner, but definitely leave an impact not only on an individual but also on the society they lived in and that too on more than one front. Further, the messages given by them to masses or the morals provided by their life and teachings also affect the thinking of masses and thereby change the society as a whole. Also note that while some spiritual persons have very little vertical component in the personality, somehow do wonders in the domain of horizontal component. Similarly, some have huge vertical component but do not succeed in the horizontal domain unless the followers pursue their teachings at a later date. Quotient of greatness of all great persons of the world can be analyzed in the same way as above. Further, the type of analysis presented in Table A.1 can also help an individual in picking up a suitable role model out of the huge spectrum available in this world, whichever the individual wishes to follow in life.

With regard to attaining the greatness by or grading the greatness of a person, while above prescriptions will work, for practical purposes however one finally has to resort to the moral that one draws from the conversations of Yaksha and Yudhishthira in the epic *Mahābhārata*, namely,

Vedā vibhinnā Smritiyo vibhinnā,
nāsau munirasya matam na bhinnam ;
Dharmasya taṭtvam nihitam guhāyām,
mahājano yena gatah sa panthāh.

Meaning thereby, "Vedas speak differently, *Smritis* too speak differently, there is no saint on this planet who does not advise differently on a particular issue. The fact that needs to be followed, however, remains in the murky depth of ideas. The best path to be followed in life is the one recommended by the greatest of great persons."

GLOSSARY OF WORDS, TERMS AND PHRASES USED IN THE TEXT

Here we present detailed meanings of certain words, terms and phrases used in the text for their ready reference in alphabetic order.

1. Analogy: A concept which generally helps in understanding the unknown in terms of known. In some sense it is the generalized version of the concepts like simile, metaphor, parallelism, etc. used frequently not only in literature but also in other disciplines of knowledge depending upon the phenomenon under study. Further, the analogies can be of different orders or categories, for details, see (Kaushal, 2003).

2. Authoritarianism: It is the degree to which a person believes that status and power differences are appropriate in an organization. Such a belief develops particularly when the individual is passing through the phases of organizational and change processes in an organization.

3. Basis of actions performed: As per Vedic science, there is a basis of all actions performed by an individual and of the fruits obtained thereof. On this basis, three categories of actions are *prārabdha*, *sancit* and *kriyamāna*. Destined due to previous (past) birth(s) are the *Prārabdha*, accumulated in this birth itself are *sancita* and the ones performed in present are the *kriyamâna* actions.

4. Biological body (B): Biological body of a human Being including both inner and outer organs.

5. Broad classification of actions (need to be performed): These are of four categories: *Nitya* (daily routine), *Neimitik* (social obligation), *kāmya* (by choice or desire), and *nisedha* (prohibited or immoral). Man is free to perform karma (actions), particularly in *kāmya* category. In fact, a person must perform *nitya karma* but he must not perform *nisedha* karma. Other karmas are social and moral obligations.

6. Causal body ($\mathcal{C}$): It consist of the EOL, SO, alone or $\mathcal{C} = \{SO\}$.

7. Cosmic consciousness field (of which the soul is a part thereof): In analogy with the physical fields, it is the all-pervading subtlest possible field in which not only the cosmic elements (*panca mahabhūtās*) in their primordial form but also the cosmic versions of mind, intellect and ego are embedded. The space and time and their mediated four physical fields are the later offshoots of this field. A kind of second quantization process in this cosmic consciousness field gives rise to its discrete version, i.e., the quantum like soul which in turn carry all the features of this most fundamental field.

8. Cosmic elements (*panca mahābhūtās* of Vedic Science): In Vedic science they are believed to be five in number and according to their increasing fineness they are arranged as earth (E_a), water (W), air (A), fire (F), and ether (E_t). Again there are concepts of perceived (*pancikrit* according to the *panci karan* rule or the dressed one with consciousness) and the physical or nascent (*apancikrit*) cosmic elements in Vedic science, used heavily in the text.

9. Definitions of Yoga as per SMBG: According to SMBG, controlling the flow of consciousness towards worldly objects through mind, body and senses and reversing the flow towards SO, is called 'meditation'— a basis for 'yoga'. With reference to other definitions note that relinquishing attachment, and becoming indifferent to success and failure or equanimity is called yoga. In fact skill in action lies in the practice of this equanimity, which suggests another definition of yoga. (Also see definition 58).

10. Dogmatism: It is the personality trait which refers to the degree of flexibility or rigidity of views of a person.

11. Dressing of EOLs with Consciousness: The concept of *paňci karan* rule for creating the perceived *mahābhūtās* from the nascent (physical) ones was known in Vedic science. The same is now generalized for other entities like M, I, E as '*tri-karan rule*' or for SE and B as '*dvi-karan rule*' and that too in higher orders (see, (Kaushal, 2011)). In fact, the infinitely dressed versions of these entities with consciousness become the part of cosmos and embedded in the cosmic consciousness field.

12. Dressing of objects: the word 'dressing', coined by the author in the present context, is basically a discrete method to account for the evolution with consciousness. In Vedic science, it appeared only in a 'crude' form as '*panci karan* rule' for *panca mahābhūtās* and only in lowest order. But here the author has generalized the concept for other entities and that too in higher orders as well(see, (Kaushal, 2011) and (Kaushal, 2013)).

13. Ego (E): Faculty of memory or the self- conscience.

14. Essentials for life (EFL): The items needed for the survival of human Being are termed as essentials for life. In Vedic science such essentials for life are earth, water, air, fire and ether and they are termed as *pañca mahābhūtas* (PM) or five cosmic elements.

15. Essences of life (EOL): Human Being is said to be the perfect creation of God. The items needed for the existence of a conscious human Being (b) in functional form, are termed as the essences of life in this work, and in their decreasing order of fineness they are the soul (SO), ego (E), intellect (I), mind (M), senses of knowledge (SEK), motor organs responsible for action (SEA), and the biological body (B). The composite of all of them, i.e. the human Being b works in the field of worldly objects (WO), which basically are the dressed version of *panca mahābhūtas* with consciousness.

16. Faculty of understanding (FOU): The Mind, intellect and ego in the presence of consciousness collectively work in perceiving a physical object with the help of senses of knowledge and action. These inner essences of life working to this effect in a coherent manner constitute the so-called faculty of understanding and the development of the same becomes an asset in the process of realization. In some sense it is an elevated version of faculty of memory.

17. Five existences of human Being: Vedic science clearly emphasizes on the three existences, namely causal, micro and gross existences of a human Being. In the present work, however, two more, namely societal and natural existences of a person are also postulated to define the complete personality of a person. First three existences in fact define the vertical component of the personality whereas the other two define the horizontal component of the personality (cf. Chapter 14 and Appendix A). Note that corresponding to the domains of working of these five existences of a person the quality of experience gathered from the MMW and GMW is also affected.

18. Forces in nature: Physical theories deal with two types of forces— contact force and action-at-a-distance type force. Former comes in existence when the objects are in physical contact, like the railway engine dragging the bogies or the horse dragging the cart. At finer level there is still a difference between these cases. In the latter case, however, the horse being an alive object, can use his free will in generating necessary self- organizing forces, of course, on the initiative of the cart driver. On the other hand, engine cannot generate self-organizing forces, if at all it can, then it cannot go beyond the defined efficiency for which it is manufactured. Action-at-a-distance type forces come into existence even if the objects are not in contact with each other but are at a distance, like the gravitation force between two masses, Coulomb force between two charges or magnets etc. In these cases, objects are assumed not to possess memory and this is possible only with inanimate objects. For animate objects, however, not only memory, but emotion and/or decision making contents are there in the object. As a result, other types of forces like action-at-a-time or action-at-a-distance time are bound to come in the dynamics of living object. For this reason the physical laws as such do not work on living objects. If at all they are made to work, then such effects are tactfully avoided at the cost of certain postulates/approximations in the theory.

19. Four Category of persons: On the basis of development of one's faculty of understanding (FOU), the people in this world can be classified broadly into four categories, namely common man, scientist, philosopher and yogi. The development of FOU in the first case is limited only to day-to-day life, in the second case (extrovert persons) the perception of the outer world is developed more than inner, in the third case (introvert persons) the perception of the inner world is developed more than the outer one and in the case of yogi the perception of both inner and outer worlds is developed to its maximum possible extent. The existence of these categories of persons in a society can be seen at all times and in all cultures. It is only the degree of development of their FOUs that may differ.

20. Four known fundamental physical forces: They are gravitational force, working through masses of objects all over the Universe; electromagnetic force working through charges and magnetism of objects all over the Universe; weak and strong forces, work inside the nucleus and also through the phenomenon of radioactivity in some elements. These four interactions differ in strength and range. Gravitational and electromagnetic forces are of infinite range whereas weak and strong forces are of very short finite range. Regarding strength, there is orders of magnitude difference between their strengths; weakest is gravitational, next to it is "weak" force and then electromagnetic and finally the strongest one is the 'strong' force.

21. Glossary of some interesting abbreviations (Courtesy late Mr. Balram Krishna Arora, Private communication): [ABCD: Awareness, Bliss, Contentment, Detachment, (Ways to have a feel for Brahmna); CYBER: Conscious You (are), Brahmna (is) Everywhere, Realise (it), (A way to seek cosmic connections); DIP: Disposition In Possessiveness, (An art of attaining peace); GOD: Generator, Organizer, Destroyer, (Three characteristics of God); ICS: Imperishable, Changeless, Stable, (A definition of Supreme Self); IEC: Infinite, Eternal, Changeless, (A definition of Supreme Self); ITDC: Inference, Tradition, Direct, Comparison,

(Ways to acquire wisdom); PET: Perception, Emotion, Thought, (Role of senses, mind and intellect in human behavior); SELF: Supreme Everywhere Living Force, (A definition of Brahmna); SKILL: Scientific Knowledge (for) Inspirable Lovable Life, (A symptom of developed FOUs); TENSE: Tongue, Eyes, Nose, Skin, Ears, (Five senses of knowledge); VEDANTA: Very Effective Dispensation Against Negative Thoughts Arrival, (A definition of *Sanātana* Dharma)].

21a. God: In addition to several other characteristics, Generator (G), Organizer (O) and Destroyer (D) of five cosmic elements (namely, earth, water, air, fire and ether), which in some sense are essentials for the existence of life in this Universe, is defined as 'God'. In fact, the *Sanskrit* word '*Bhagavāna*' for God also carries the spirit of all five cosmic elements when its letters are interpreted as '*Bha*' for '*Bhumi*' (earth), '*ga*' for '*gagan*' (ākāsh or ether), '*va*' for '*vāyu*' (air), '*ā*' for '*anala*' (fire) and '*na*' for '*neer*' (water).

22. Gross body ($\mathcal{G}$): It consists of outer EOLs SE, B and WO or $\mathcal{G}$={B,SE,WO}.

23. Gross and sub-conscious part of micro body: In fact each of the inner EOL mind, intellect and ego has two components–gross and subtle. The gross components of all the three combined together constitute the gross part of $\mathcal{M}$, whereas the subtle components of all the three combined together form the sub-conscious part of $\mathcal{M}$. It is the gross part that manifest more in the actions of $\mathcal{G}$-domain whereas sub-conscious part play more active role in the actions of $\mathcal{C}$-domain. In fact a cut off in the order of dressing of inner EOL with consciousness (which varies from person to person) can define such a bifurcation of M, I and E (cf. Fig. 7.1).

24. Human Being (b): Life principle or the seed of life (Sanskrit word is Jiva), the 'self' of the 'myself'.

25. 'Inside out' and 'outside out' pictures: For the meaning of these phrases, the attention is drawn to the patomic model of human

Being (cf. Fig. 6.1). The inner contents of the model while control the outward actions, the outer contents of the model however control the inward actions of the Being which again give command for an improved version of outward actions. In atomic model these are the electrons in the outermost orbits which participate in chemical reactions, i.e. an 'outside out' picture, whereas in patomic model it is B and then SE which are first to participate in interactions with the outer world, i.e. an 'inside out' picture.

26. Intellect (I): Faculty of decision also includes subtle intellect.

27. Interaction: The resultant effect (normally the force) that comes into existence when two or more than two living or nonliving objects come in vicinity or close proximity which otherwise is absent. Here, the word 'existence' means it should be detectable or measurable in physical theories, particularly for the inanimate objects and it should be perceptible or realizable in philosophical terms, particularly for living (animate) objects. Similarly, the word 'closeness' has different meanings for physical, epi-physical and special epi-physical entities. For physical entities it should be understood in terms of space-time whereas for the other two categories of entities, the meditation parameter should also be included in defining it.

28. Locus of control: It is a dimension of personality that explains the degree to which people believe that they themselves determine their own-lives rather than external forces.

29. Machiavallianism: It is a personality attribute that describes the extent to which a person manipulates others for personal gains, chances of developing such a dimension of personality in a person are there when he is working in an organization.

30. Meditation: The process is already elaborated under the heading 'meditation variable'. Meditation basically is a method of diffusing the mind-body interaction to achieve a channelized and focused consciousness.

31. Meditation variables (μ): When a conscious person sits in meditation the depth or the degree of achieving a focused or directed consciousness is characterized by this variable. In some sense, μ is a collective representation of the parameters responsible for the roles of inner EOLs M, I and E in a decision towards the success of a task. It can never be zero for an alive person but can become infinite for a yogi sitting in *Samādhi*. Note that the same focused attention, when directed towards WO via SE and B, is termed as 'concentration' (of mind).

32. Micro body ($\mathcal{M}$): It consists of inner EOLs, M, I, and E or $\mathcal{M}$={M,I,E}.

33. Mind (M): Faculty of emotion also includes subconscious mind.

34. Mindset function: The state of mind at any stage of meditation is characterized by the so-called 'mindset' function $\mathcal{M}$. At a gross level $\mathcal{M}$ is considered as the function of meditation variable μ and at finer level, however, it is a complicated function of several variables, representing respectively the roles of inner EOLs mind, intellect and ego and that of space, time and circumstances in the dynamics of the system. (For further details see the definition 55 and (Kaushal, 2011, Chapter 8).

35. Model: As such it is not possible to express the ultimate reality in nature through conceptual expression then what to say of verbal expression. A model is conceptual expression of reality that prevails in a phenomenon. While the ultimate realty remains the matter of realization only, the glimpses of the same one can have through models to a fair degree of accuracy. Note that a model, in fact, is a particular case of analogy, for details, see (Kaushal, 2003).

36. *Panci karan* rule: In Vedic science this rule differentiates between the perceived (dressed with consciousness) and unperceived (physical, nascent or not dressed with consciousness) *mahābhūtās*. According to this rule the perceived *mahābhūta* consists of 50% of its physical version and 12.5% of physical versions of each of the remaining four *mahābhūtās*. For example, the perceived earth consists of 50% of physical earth and 12.5%

physical version of each of other four, namely water, air, fire and ether; and the same is the case with other perceived *mahābhūtās.*

37. Patomic model: An arrangement of essences of life for a human Being in analogy with the atomic model for the structure of matter, is termed as 'patomic' (philosophical atom type) model. The word patomic can also be derived from the word 'patois' which means "differing materially from the literary language". Further an elaborative meaning of the ingredients of patomic model, i.e. essences of life, namely worldly objects, biological body, senses of knowledge and action mind, intellect, ego and soul including the Being, can be traced in this Glossary.

38. Physical (P), epi-physical (EP) and special epi-physical (SEP) matter: Physical matter (P) for which the laws of physical or chemical sciences work successfully, is basically an object of instrument; otherwise as and when this matter is watched (or thought of) by a Being, an element of consciousness is added to it. Such a matter is termed as epi-physical (EP) (which has a ground on physical) matter. If the source of consciousness is also contained in the epi-physical matter (as is the body of a conscious person) then such a matter is termed as special epi-physical (SEP) matter. Sometimes EP and/or SEP matter is termed as non-physical matter.

39. Pleasure, Peace and Joy: The same eternal joy (*ānand*)— a characteristic of soul comes in three colors at three distinct levels, namely (sensual) pleasure at the level of $\mathcal{G}$ which one draws by engaging senses in their respective sense-objects; the peace which one draws at the level of $\mathcal{M}$ by employing M, I and E to their maximum efficiency (i.e., to their subtlest capacity) towards the success of an action performed in the outer world. The joy is something which one draws at the level of soul in the causal domain ($\mathcal{C}$) by way of withdrawing the Self from the fruits of all actions performed in the domains of $\mathcal{G}$ and $\mathcal{M}$ and by way of suppressing the subtlest form of ego E. In general, all the three pleasure, peace and joy are spatio-temporal. There eternity however gives a feel for the *ānand*— the eternal joy. Alternatively, a state of satisfaction is achieved by an individual from a successful performance of his actions. If this happens in the domain of $\mathcal{G}$, it defines pleasure, in the domain of $\mathcal{M}$, it defines peace and in the domain of $\mathcal{C}$ it defines joy.

40. Risk Propensity: This is a personality attribute which refers to a person's willingness to take risks in life.

41. *Sankalpa*: A hard-core decision taken by subtle intellect (or highly dressed trio of M, I and E at supra-conscious level) but with a dominating role of E and ready for implementation in the domains of $\mathcal{M}$ and $\mathcal{G}$. Such decisions are normally taken by highly dressed (with consciousness) versions of EOLs, M, I, and E, accordingly *sankalpās* could be emotion, intelligence or memory dominated ones at their very root itself.

42. *Sanskāra* : In some sense the level of development of one's FOUs defines his *sanskārās*.

43. Second quantization: It is purely a mathematical concept of theoretical physics related with the discretization of continuous medium having infinite degrees of freedom, (the so-called 'field').

44. Self-esteem: An important personality trait which basically is the judgment one makes about one's own worth.

45. Self-monitoring: This refers to the degree to which the people are sensitive to others and adapt their behaviour to meet external expectations and situation needs.

46. Sense objects: Corresponding to each of five senses of perception there are five sense-objects or stimuli. For example, ears run after nice words, eyes go for a pleasant view, nose goes for pleasant smell, tongue for a tasty food and skin for a pleasant touch.

47. Senses of knowledge and action (SE): In all there are ten senses—five senses of knowledge (SEK) and five motor organs responsible for action (SEA). Senses of action are hands, feet, power of speech, copulatory organs and anus; and the five senses of knowledge are ear, eye, skin, tongue and nose, whose corresponding sense objects are sound, shape, touch, taste and smell. These five sense objects respectively have an intimate connection with and are sensitive to the five cosmic elements (*pañca mahābhūtās*) ether, fire, air, water and earth through five *tanmātrās* (quanta of interaction).

48. *Sristi/Brahmna*: An all-pervading fundamental cosmic consciousness field.

49. Soul (SO): The inner-most existence, the pure Self characterized by consciousness and bliss and which is beyond the concept of space and time.

50. Systematic of negative pursuits: The sequence of human characteristics that one is forced to follow towards his downfall when he departs from his higher goal in life. As per SMBG such a sequence is attachment to sense objects which brings in desire, from unfulfilled desires comes anger, from anger arises infatuation, from infatuation originates the confusion of memory which in turn leads to loss of reason and there from one suffers from ruination.

51. Systematic of positive pursuits: The sequence of human characteristic that encourages one in achieving his higher goal. This is possible for a self-controlled practitioner who enjoys the sense objects through his senses in an un-attached manner (not a easy task but the practice makes a man perfect), which are disciplined and free from likes and dislikes resulting into the placidity of mind. All sorrows come to an end after attaining this placidity of mind and the intellect soon withdrawing itself from all sides and becomes established firmly in the higher goal (materialistic or spiritual).

52. Three types of yoga: In Vedic science we have three possible types of yoga, one is *karma yoga (yoga of action)* —connecting $\mathcal{G}$ with the Self in all actions or the performance of actions in a self-less or an unattached manner, is called *karma yoga*, *Bhakti yoga* (yoga of devotion)— connecting $\mathcal{G}$ and emotion-dominated $\mathcal{M}$ with the Self is called *Bhakti yoga*; and finally, connecting the Self with the Self through knowledge, called *jňana yoga* (yoga of knowledge).

53. Tips of life (magic of three repetitive letters abbreviations) (Courtesy late Mr. Balram Krishna Arora, Private communication): [AAA=Aim, Attitude, Action (ladder of success); BBB = Braveness, Boldness, Bliss (Supreme qualities); CCC = Character, Commitment, Confidence (A person's ornaments); DDD = Desire, Demand, Dependency (Lead to slavery); EEE = Energetic, Egoless, Efficient (One should be); FFF = Faithfulness, Firmness, Fearlessness (Add to vertical development of personality); GGG = Governance, Guardian, Grief (Always welcome); HHH = Hand, Heart, Head (Coordination of the three leads to noble actions); III = Importance, Intention, Integrity (A noble action contains all the three); JJJ = Job, Judge, Jurisdiction (Always respect); KKK = Knowledge, Knower, Known (Constitute an action); LLL = Love, Liberty, Liberation (Thrust of life); MMM = Mind, Meanness, Much-ness (To be controlled); NNN = Noble, Natural, Notorious (A person's nature); OOO = Oneness, Otherness, Openness (Kinds of relation); PPP = Purity, Patience, Politeness (Winning Qualities); QQQ = Qualification, Quickness, Quietness (A server should have); RRR = Receipt, Reaction, Response (Execution of an action); SSS = Stability, Sincerity, Smile (Merits of an action); TTT = Truthful, Trustful, Tasteful (Words should be); UUU = Understanding, Unity, Upliftment (Scales of friendship); VVV = Vision, Value, Victory (An action should contain); WWW= Woman, Wine, Wealth (Be careful from); XYZ = Xenialness, Yieldingness, Zealness (Qualities of a preacher)].

54. Trinity of *gunās*: With a view to categorizing each of, the human actions, qualities, feelings and experiences, the concepts of three *gunās* (temperaments) is frequently discussed in Vedic science. The concept of trinity of *gunās,* namely, *Tamas* (inactive), *Rajas* (active) and *Sattva* (trans-active), in the spirit of three adjective degrees (positive, comparative, superlative) i.e. good, better and best, basically, are the three modes of working of non-

Self (*Prakriti*) and the same provide a fine thread in weaving the human dynamics of Vedic science. In fact, *tamas* is the state of inaction, ignorance and inertia. *Rajas* is the state of desire-ridden passionate action full of mental agitations. *Sattva* is the trans-active state, one of poise and contemplation. The purpose of human existence is to move from *tamas* (state of inertia) to *rajas* (state of activity) and to *sattva* (quality of goodness).

55. Variables of Mindset function: Mindset is a representation of the micro-body $\mathcal{M}$ or of its dressed version $\mathcal{M}^{(n)}$ as a whole, i.e. for all n. When it characterizes the mental state undergoing through its three constituents M, I and E (which, in fact, keep on cooking a 'pudding' during the process of performing an action of priority), it is quantified through a 'mindset function' $\mathcal{M}$ as $\mathcal{M} \equiv \mathcal{M}^{(\mu,q,t,\sigma)} = \mathcal{M}$ (m, i, e, q, t, σ), where m, i, e, q, t, σ are the parameters/ variables responsible for the roles of mind, intellect, ego, space, time and circumstances, respectively. (For further details see the definition 34).

56. Vedic science and Vedic Literature: Starting with four *Vedās* namely *Rik*, *Yajur*, *Atharva* and *Sām*, the Vedic knowledge later appeared through *Brāhmanās* and *brahma Sutra* and then through *Upanisads*. *Rik* deals with the question of eternal truth and processes in the Universe. While *Yajur* deals with the description of rituals, *Atharva* is full of the descriptions of technology and *Ayurveda*. It is the *Sām* that deals with music and the philosophy of life which later transcended to *Upanisads* and other scriptures. The great epics like *Rāmāyana* and *Mahābhārata* written at a later period are full of this Vedic wisdom in the form of conversation among various characters.

57. Worldly objects or the outer world of objects (WO): Worldly objects which act as stimulants, namely kith and kin, money, prosperity, lust, pleasure, fame, honour, etc. Dressed *pañca mahābhūtas* or the parts thereof also act as worldly objects.

58. Yoga: Connecting the Self with the non-Self is termed as yoga derived from the *Sanskrit* word '*yuj*' meaning the connection.

For example, the domains of $\mathcal{M}$ and $\mathcal{G}$ together and separately as well, constitute the domain of non-Self and each concept and action pertaining to these domains have two meanings or parts— one pertaining to non-Self, i.e. gross, verbal, literary or visible and the second pertaining to Self, i.e., micro, subtle, inherent or invisible, connecting directly or indirectly with the domain of soul. Yoga in terms of physical postures is not of much use unless it brings in oneself an element of spirituality by way of directing the consciousness towards higher goals like attaining the Supreme or any other goal of similar nature in the domain of spirituality. (Also see the definitions in 9).

REFERENCES AND BIBLIOGRAPHY

Acharya, Sriram Sharma (1995), "***Sanskriti-Sanjivani Srimad Bhagavada and Gita***" (Hindi), Akhanda Jyoti Sansthan, Mathura.

Adi Sankaracharyn Krit, "***Vivek Chudamani***" , Hindi Translation by Muni Lal, Gita Press, Gorakhpur.

Baba, Avtaar Meher (2013), "New Humanity and Creative Love", The Speaking Tree Column, ***Times of India***, 16 October.

A Baha'i Perspective (2013), " Relationship of Body, Mind and Soul", The Speaking Tree Column, ***Times of India***, 27 May..

Chalmers, D. J. (1996), "***The Conscious Mind: In Search of a Fundamental Theory***", Oxford University Press, Oxford.

Chinmoy, Sri (2013), "Love, the Secret Key of Life", The Speaking Tree Column, ***Times of India***, 13 April.

Chinmayanand, Swami (1998), "***Atma Bodha***", Sri Adi Sankaracharya Krit (commentary), Central Chinmaya Mission Trust, Mumbai.

Chopra, Deepak, et al. (2013), "Lower-Case Truth and Absolute Truth", The Speaking Tree Column, ***Times of India***, 9 December.

Clayton, David Theodore (2011), "***The Enigma of Love***", First published by Author House, U.K. Ltd., 500 Avebury Bouleward, Central Milton Keynes, MK92BE, (Available in part on Internet).

Deshmukh, Pratap B., Ayer, Radha K. and Kaushik, Deepak K. (2012), "***Value Education for Consciousness Development***", (Gyan Books Pvt. Ltd., New Delhi, 2nd ed.); The variety of concepts and topics covered in this book can find roots in the present text, particularly when they are analyzed in philosophical terms.

Ellis, G.F.R. (2005), "Physics and the Real World", Physics Today, July issue, **11**, 49 54, (The World Year of Physics).

Fisher, Ian and Dean, Correlia (2006), " Darwin vs. Design: Evolution Still Rules", The Speaking Tree Column, ***Times of India***, 20 January.

Goendka, Hari Krishna Das, An elaborated commentary on Brahm Sutra, "***Vedanta Darshan***" (Hindi), Geeta Press, Gorakhpur.

Goendka, Hari Krishna Das, An Elaborated Commentary on "***Isadi Nau Upanisads***" (Hindi), Gita Press, Gorakhpur.

Goldstein, H. (1981), "***Classical Mechanics***", Addison-Wesley Publishing Co., Reading,, 2nd ed.

Goswami, Amit (1990), "Consciousness in Quantum Physics and the Mind –Body Problem", Journal of Mind and Behaviour **11,** 75.

Goswami, Amit (1992), "***Quantum Mechanics***", Wm. C. Brown Publishers.

Jain, Anupama (2013), " Heal with Heartfelt Forgiveness", The Speaking Tree Column, ***Times of India***, 20 September.

Jhunjhunuwala, Bharat (2005), "Intelligent Design and Darwin go together" The Speaking Tree Column, ***Times of India***, 21 December.

Kant, Immanuel (1883), "***Metaphysical Foundation of Natural Sciences***" Bell Publishers, London.

Kaushal, Radhey Shyam (1994), "***The Philosophy of the Vedanta: A Modern Scientific Perspective***", Garib Dass Oriental Series No. 179, Indian Book Centre, Delhi.

—— (1998), "***Classical and Quantum Mechanics of Noncentral Potentials: A Survey of Two-Dimensional Systems***", Narosa Publishing House, New Delhi, Springer-Verlag, Heidelberg.

—— (2000), "Patomic Model of Human Being in the Context of Modern Science", Ph.D. Thesis (unpublished), University of Delhi.

—— (2003), "***Structural Analogies in Understanding Nature***", Anamaya Publishers, New Delhi.

—— (2008), "A Model of Quark-Gluon Plasma with Pentaquark Baryons and Tetraquark Mesons", Indian Journal of Physics **82,** 891-906.

—— (2011), "***The Science of Philosophy: Theory of Fundamental Processes in Human Behaviour and Experiences***", D.K. Print World, New Delhi.

—— (2011a), "Paòca Mahâbhûtâs and Natural Remedies of Diseases", Light on Ayurveda Journal (USA) **10,** 21-29.

—— (2012), "A Possible Mathematization of the Philosophy of Srimad Bhagvad-Gita", Presented in WAVES-2012, held at Univ. of Massachusetts, Dartmouth, July 13-15, (To appear in Proc.).

—— (2013), "Cosmic Consciousness Field of Vedic Science and the Concepts of Many Universes and Higher Dimensions in Physical Theories", accepted for presentation in the first International Conference on " Ancient, Indian Wisdom and Modern World" Organized by Indian Society for Indic Studies at Delhi during March 29-31, 2013.

Kulkarni, Kishor (2013), "You Could be Spiritual Atheist", The Speaking Tree Column, ***Times of India***, 22 October.

Kundu, M. N. (2013), "The Culture of Spiritual Secularism", The Speaking Tree Column, ***Times of India***, 18 February.

Laughlin, R. B. (2005), "***A Different Universe: Re-inventing Physics from the Bottom Down***", Basic Books, New York.

Lindsay, A. D., "***The Philosophy of Immanuel Kant",*** T.C & E.C. Jack, 67 Long Acre, W.C. and Dodge Publishing Co. Edinburgh and New York, Rare collection.

Mitra, Arup (2013), "Is it Possible to Attain Perpetual Joy?", The Speaking Tree Column, ***Times of India***, 18 March.

Mlodinov, Leonard (2012), "***Subliminal: How Your Subconscious Mind Rules Your Behaviour***" , Pantheon Books, New York.

Osho (2007), "Transfer Heat to Light with Inner Alchemy", The Speaking Tree Column, ***Times of India***, 3 March, and the reference cited therein.

Parthasarathy, A. (1992), "***Vedanta Treatise***", Vedanta Life Institute, Bombay, 4th ed..

Penrose, Roser (1994), " ***Shadows of Mind: A Search for Missing Science of Consciousness***", Oxford University Press, Oxford.

Pradhan, Ram Chandra (2014), "***Integrating Body, Mind and Heart***: ***The Gandhian Way***", Trinity Press, New Delhi.

Richards, Jay (1999), "Intelligent Design Theory: Why it Matters", (Article), Discovery Institute's Centre for the Renewal of Science and Culture, Seattle, USA, Feb.25, 1999, (Available at Google and Speak.out.com).

Row, Jaya (2013), "The Divine and the Demonic", The Speaking Tree Column, ***Times of India***, 9 November.

Saha, M. N. and Srivastava, B. N. (1931), "***A Treatise on Heat***", The Indian Press Pvt. Ltd., Reprint ed. (1972) and First ed. (1931).

Saraswati, Swami Dayanand , "***Satyârth Prakash***", Arya Sahitya Prachar Trust, Arya Offset Press, Delhi.

Schrodinger, Erwin (1964), "***My View of the World***", Translated from German by C. Hestings, Cambridge University Press; Also see, "***What is Life?",*** Cambridge University Press, 1944.

Singh, Kavita (2010), "***Organizational Behaviour: Text and Cases***", Pearson Education, Dorling Kindersley (India), Pvt. Ltd., Delhi.

Singh, Bal Ram (2012), in Proceedings WAVES-2012, held at Univ. of Massachusetts, Dartmouth, USA, during July 13-15, 2012.

Singh, Jitendra K. , Mishra, Girishwar and De Raad, Boele (2012), "Personality Structure in the Trait Laxicon of Hindi: Major

Language Spoken in India", Preprint, November 2012, (to appear in European Journal of Personality).

Sood, Mohan K. (2010),"***Spiritual Living: Eastern Wisdom for Today***", get copies from "Xlibris corporation" ph.1-888-795-4274, San Marcos, California.

"Srimad Bhagavad-Gita", Geeta Press, Gorakhpur, Abbreviated in the text as SMBG and citations are made in the form SMBG: Chapter No.Verse No.

Stapp, H.P. (2009) : ***Mind, Matter and Quantum Mechanics***, Springer-Verlag, Heidelberg, 2nd ed.

Suraiya, Jug (2014), "No Love can be 'Unnatural'", The Speaking Tree Column, ***Times of India,*** 30 January, 2014.

Townes, C.H. (2015), "A Physicist's Faith in Science and God", The Speaking Tree column, ***Times of India***, 31 January, 2015 (Excerpts from the Interview of Noble Laureate Charles H. Townes by Narayani Ganesh when he visited India in 2003).

Weisskopf, Victor F. (1977), "Frontiers and Limits of Science", American Scientists **65** , 405.

INDEX